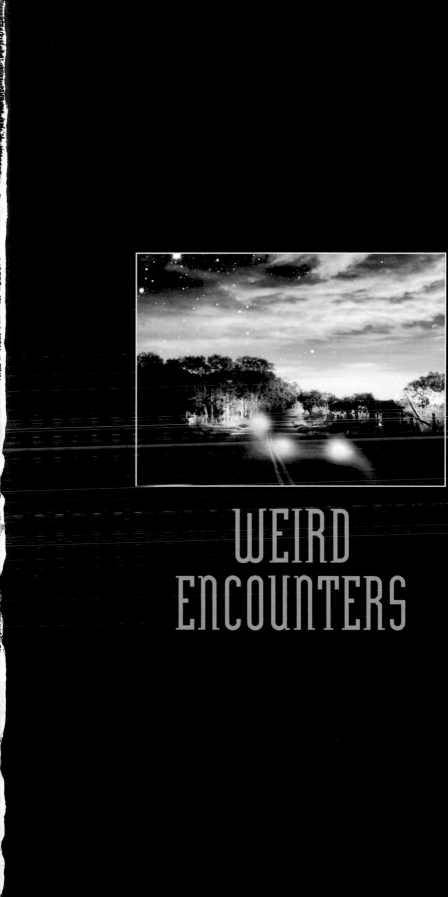

WEIRD
ENCOUNTERS

MARK MORAN AND MARK SCEURMAN,

authors of

present

WEIRD
ENCOUNTERS

TRUE TALES OF HAUNTED PLACES

Compiled by
JOANNE M. AUSTIN
Illustrated by RYAN DOAN

STERLING

New York / London

WEIRD ENCOUNTERS

STERLING and the distinctive Sterling logo are registered
trademarks of Sterling Publishing Co., Inc.

Published by Sterling Publishing Co., Inc.
387 Park Avenue South, New York, NY 10016

Distributed in Canada by Sterling Publishing
c/o Canadian Manda Group, 165 Dufferin Street
Toronto, Ontario, Canada M6K 3H6
Distributed in the United Kingdom by GMC Distribution Services,
Castle Place, 166 High Street, Lewes, East Sussex, England BN7 1XU
Distributed in Australia by Capricorn Link (Australia) Pty. Ltd.
P.O. Box 704, Windsor, NSW 2756, Australia

10 9 8 7 6 5 4 3 2

Manufactured in China.

Photography and illustration credits are found on page 320
and constitute an extension of this copyright page.

Sterling ISBN: 978-1-4027-5461-6

For information about custom editions, special sales, premium
and corporate purchases, please contact Sterling Special Sales
Department at 800-805-5489 or specialsales@sterlingpub.com.

Weird Encounters is intended as entertainment. Be advised
that many of the sites described in *Weird Encounters* are
located on private property and should not be visited, or
you may face prosecution for trespassing.
    Some stories herein have been edited from their
original versions.

To Jim

—Joanne M. Austin

CONTENTS

INTRODUCTION

IN SHAKESPEARE'S MACBETH, three witches stand around a bubbling cauldron and speak in ominous tones of toil and trouble, eye of newt and lizard's leg. Ancient and powerful, they are modeled on the Fates—three mythological women who divvy up the jobs of spinning the string of a life, measuring it out, and cutting it off at the end—and are known by many names in different cultures: Norns, Parcae, Moriae and, most important to us here, the Weird Sisters.

The Weird Sisters cryptically tell Macbeth of his fate not once but twice in the play, and in plucking them from myth, Shakespeare planted the seed for the popular usage of the word *weird*. Back then, the word had more to do with fate or destiny and only later picked up the eerie connotations that today frighten some people more than ghosts do.

It's funny how weird brought me to Weird. In my formative years, I would have been a little disturbed if the Weird Sisters showed up and said that one day I'd be pulling scary stories from my own little editorial cauldron to compile both this book and its predecessor, *Weird Hauntings: True Tales of Ghostly Places*. But that's what happened and, to be honest, being a junior-level Fate (anthology division) is kind of fun.

And it's fate that brings you to hold *Weird Encounters: True Tales of Haunted Places* in your hands. Full of creepy new stories, we'll take you on a tour of our favorite Historic Haunts and Hostel Environments, and introduce you to a new class of Educated Entities, Workplace Wraiths, and Fresh Air Phantasms. Some of your favorite authors from *Weird Hauntings* and many of the Weird state books have returned with nightmarishly new tales, and we're excited to include new writers you might not be as familiar with . . . for now. It's another beautifully designed and illustrated book, too, with even more ghost photos presented for your inspection.

The result: ghost stories that I believe readers will find to be more fun than a cauldron full of newt eyes, dog tongues, bat wool, and maybe a few dead Scottish kings thrown in for good measure. So ends the haunted thread of this introduction. Snip!

—Joanne M. Austin

9

Thanks to my dad's tireless tomfoolery, I have a healthy appetite for the paranormal. A childhood full of encounters with the unknown, would-be ghosts and sinister shapes—conjured by my dad—helped me learn to face my fears and eventually led me to the career I now enjoy. Our encounters, however trivial and fleeting, make us who we are. In this book you will come across many true (at least to those who experienced them) and often frightful tales of some of America's haunted hot spots. Perhaps they will help form you, affect you in some way, even if it is only by interfering with your good night's sleep. Much as the following encounter helped shape me . . .

When I was just a big-headed five-year-old, *Cheers* was a staple of prime-time television and the show's theme song signaled my bedtime. I slept with the door open so I could hear the song, which became a sort of lullaby for me. (I was usually sound asleep by the time Norm came barging into the bar.) On this particular night Mom tucked me in, leaving the bedroom door open. I had the flickering light of the downstairs television and my border of stuffed animals to protect me from whatever might come calling, so I went ahead with my mandatory check under the bed (readers of *Weird Hauntings* may recall my prankster father would often hide there). The coast was clear. I slipped into the bed as if it were a sleeping bag, with the warm covers pulled tight over me like a second skin.

After a kiss, I watched my mom's head descend the stairs and disappear just as the *Cheers* theme song floated up into my open room. I was just drifting off . . . "where everybody knows your name" . . . when a violent tug of my blanket forced my eyes open in alarm. I felt the covers being pulled again and again, and although I tried desperately, I couldn't hold on to them. Was my father up to no good? Had he somehow gotten past my wary guard? I was contemplating dipping my head over the edge to check when, suddenly, the tugging stopped. Then even more abruptly, the covers were ripped from the bed and went sailing across the room. I let out a blood-curdling scream, leapt from the bed, and ran frantically downstairs. My fear was assured; both of my parents were sitting cozy as could be on the couch.

A good while later they calmed me down. They half convinced me that I must have dozed off, and that by rolling over in the tightly packed bed, the covers were made to feel like they were being pulled from me. They had no explanation for the blanket flying across the room. My mom put me back to bed, leaving the door open wider and the hall light on, at my request. From my bed I watched the top part of the stairs, the horizon and dividing line between

10

my room and safety. Then movement. Rising like a dark sun against the top stair was a shape coming toward my room. A limb rolled over the shape pulling itself toward me, then another limb. The thing was like a giant humanoid crab awkwardly breaking the light of the hall as it crawled in the direction of my room. It wasn't some demon or pit-beast—it was my father contorting himself in some awful shape like Linda Blair on the stairs in *The Exorcist*. He couldn't let the moment of my jilted nerves go without taking advantage with his own brand of troublemaking. He untwisted himself and took a more human, familiar shape and we both erupted in laughter. So much so that I forgot what really did happen moments before. I knew something had been lurking in my room—it wasn't in my head—but whatever that unknown thing was, it couldn't be scarier than my own parents. Still, it was the first night I heard the music of *Cheers* during the ending credits.

—Ryan Doan

11

12

HAUNTED HOUSES

"If your mama ever comes back to my place in the basement again, I'll do more than just knock her in the head. . . ."
—An angry ghost

GHOSTS AREN'T *ALL* BAD. Sure, there are angry spirits—like the Georgia ghost that dumped one man headfirst into a garbage can—and volatile entities that inflict mysterious illnesses on unsuspecting families, as was the case with a father and son in Texas. And other ghosts *just miss* winging a basketball (in New Jersey) or wok lid (in Washington) at people's heads, or appear menacingly over another person's Pennsylvania bed like a sick wake-up call. Some like to touch the sleeping, including a ghost in Florida that tickles noses. Of course, some ghosts are just plain mean-spirited: In Michigan, the Man in the Black Hat tripped a woman on the stairs and then threatened her two small children.

Okay, so there's a whole spooky spectrum of colorful spirits out there, but in addition to the devilish and destructive, there are altruistic entities that seem to watch out for the living, comforting people and pets or stopping angrier ghosts from doing harm. But let's not forget the tricksters: poltergeists appear in many of these stories—moving furniture; locking, opening, or banging on doors in the middle of the night; ripping home decor from walls, and shattering wineglasses. Such are ghostly antics that confound rather than hurt, but still they hold a disturbing thrall over many.

Maybe you've experienced similar events in your own home and can relate to the stories told here. Or maybe you haven't, preferring an armchair relationship to the paranormal. Regardless, please make yourself welcome . . . if you dare . . . in the ghostly homes within.

THE MAN IN THE BLACK HAT
by Linda S. Godfrey

THE HOUSE NO LONGER STANDS. Its destruction was unexpected and mysterious to many of its neighbors, but Terri and Ed, a young couple who lived in the place for a year, think they know why the new owners chose to dismantle the historic home.

The old red farmhouse was not without its charm. Terri and Ed loved its rural location outside of Onsted, a small town southeast of Jackson in southern Michigan. It stood on ten rolling forested acres cut through by a ribbon of stream, with a windowed gable facing the road and a side porch to soften the entryway. When the previous owners warned the couple it was haunted, Terri and Ed chose not to let it bother them.

"I thought they either had an active imagination, or if they were okay with the haunting, then we should be also, so we bought it," said Terri. Her optimism would prove unfounded, to say the least. The couple made their purchase in May 1996, and one of the first things Terri did was phone her bank to change her address. The teller was pleasant, asking Terri the required questions, but when Terri told the woman her new address, the voice on the other end of the line seemed to freeze.

"I wouldn't move there if I were you," the teller finally replied in a solemn tone. "I've been in that place. I know it's haunted. I was there alone for a few minutes one time while I was visiting the last owner's daughter, a friend of mine, and she had to run to the store for something. I'm sitting there minding my own business, when I hear this *thump, thump, thump* like someone's running across the floor upstairs. I knew nobody else was home, and the hair just stood up on my neck. I ran out the door, I didn't even wait for my friend, and I never went back in that place again. You're not gonna like living there." Again, Terri managed to laugh the warning off. She and her husband rather liked the idea of sharing their house with a spook. "I thought it might be neat," she said.

At first, Terri and Ed thought the former occupant and the teller must have been exaggerating. It seemed like the perfect country home for their young family, with nothing out of the ordinary going on. The farmhouse was, however, around a hundred years old and had become a bit run-down, so Terri and Ed began remodeling the place before moving in with their two-year-old, Alex.

15

An Unwelcome Visitor

It's well known among those who study haunted houses that remodeling can "stir up" spirits lurking in the home. Terri and Ed had no idea they were roiling a wraith's cauldron as they hammered away, polished the hardwood floors, and painted the old plaster walls. But one night, while Ed was working by himself, they got a glimpse of what lay in store. He hadn't meant to spend the night—his car battery had accidentally drained and he didn't have a ride back to town. There weren't any beds in the house yet, so he settled down on the floor to try for a little shut-eye. As he was drifting off, there was a knock at the front door. Ed's first reaction was relief; someone must have realized he was stranded and driven out to take him home. But when he opened the door, he found nothing except the wind whistling over the dark fields. Disappointed and puzzled, he returned to his makeshift bed and lay down, only to be roused again by insistent pounding on the front door. Again, only darkness met him.

Ed slept very little that night.

16   Still, he and Terri moved in on schedule, and everything was fine for a few months until autumn began to creep in, bringing shorter days and colder nights. The family had been sleeping with the windows open, but Terri decided it was time to shut them and walked around one cool evening buttoning the house up for the night. She tucked her now two-and-a-half-year-old son in bed and then turned in herself. That evening Terri and Ed awoke to the sound of their son's terrified screams. They found him cowering under his covers, shivering with fear and yelling, "No more! No more!"

Terri instinctively whipped the blanket off, and Alex jumped, looking shocked. He stared as if to make sure it was really his parents there in the room with him. After that, nothing could induce him to sleep in his room again.

Is That Daddy?

As the crisp autumn turned to a brisk winter, Terri and Ed decided to move their bedroom to a downstairs area to help save on the heating bill. They transformed the dining room into a family sleeping room, and for a while all was calm.

"One morning my son woke me up, asking, 'Is that Daddy?' " said Terri. She sleepily told him his daddy was at work—Ed plowed snow for a local landscaping firm, sometimes tiptoeing out of the house at three or four in the morning after a big snowfall. Alex was staring out the window, gazing at what appeared to be a human figure. "I don't like that man, he scares me," said Alex. "Can I get in bed with you?" Terri lifted up the covers for him, by then feeling frightened herself.

At breakfast, she asked Alex to tell her what the scary man looked like. The little boy described a man wearing a black hat—something like a cowboy's—and blue jeans. It seemed an unlikely costume for a ghost, but a few weeks after the incident, Terri ran into the previous owners. She told them what Alex had seen and described the ghost's attire—they weren't surprised. They had seen two different ghosts while living at the house and the man in the black hat was one of them. Apparently he had owned the farmhouse before them and had died after falling off the roof. They believed Alex saw the man's ghost. "You don't want to have him around," they warned Terri. "He's bad news. But the lady ghost, she's okay. She's nicer."

Somehow, Terri found that little comfort.

Strange things began to happen. The creaky basement door was latched with an old-fashioned hook and eye, and Terri regularly found it unlocked and open. The basement appliances and utilities started to behave erratically, suddenly failing to run for no apparent reason. "I would never go down there since the dirt-floor basement gave me the creeps," said Terri. In fact, the basement scared her so much that she would just do without water or electricity until her husband got home, rather than venture downstairs alone to attempt repairs. Alex began to talk about seeing a lady around the house. He called her "the angel."

One time, said Terri, Alex solemnly informed her, "Great Grandpa was touched by an angel." Terri didn't think too much of the statement, but the next day Alex repeated his assertion to "Grandma" Ruth, his babysitter. Grandma

Ruth gasped, and told Terri that her father had died on the previous day, at about the time Alex had made his pronouncement. The angel had told him, explained Alex.

Another time, a friend who claimed to be sensitive to spirits offered to have a walk through the house to see if he could sense any presences there. He walked upstairs, said Terri, and after a few minutes came tearing back down, declaring he would never go up there again. "He didn't see anything, but something completely freaked him out," said Terri. Other friends told her they just plain didn't want to visit her in that house.

A photo Ed and Terri took of the home's exterior showed a mysterious face in the upstairs bedroom window, although no one was in the house at the time. The photo later mysteriously disappeared from their picture collection.

GHOST IN THE CELLAR

Somehow, Terri and Ed managed to get through the long winter, and once warm weather returned, they moved back upstairs to their regular bedrooms. By summer, their little family had grown with the arrival of baby Matthew. Alex still didn't want to sleep in his former bedroom, but was finally persuaded since his baby brother was now in the room with him.

One morning, Ed had left for work when a loud noise startled Terri awake. It sounded almost like a tornado, she thought. She glanced out the window and saw the sky had taken an eerie green cast. It *was* a tornado! She leaped out of bed, scooped up the baby, and grabbed three-year-old Alex's hand, running with them toward the basement. Yanking open the door to the cellar, she held the boys tightly and picked her way down the worn, narrow treads. Halfway down she stumbled and fell. The three bumped their way to the bottom of the stairs and Terri landed on the edge of the furnace, gashing her head. She felt warm blood trickle from the cut. Miraculously, Matthew and Alex were both unscathed. Shaking, Terri huddled in the dirt-floored cellar with her children and tried to keep them calm until the storm abated. She dared not even think about her fear of the cellar.

When the roaring ceased, Terri ran up the stairs to see if the storm had passed, leaving Alex with his baby brother alone in the cellar for just a minute. Everything was calm and quiet upstairs, so she hustled back down and carried the little ones to the car and drove to her mother's house a few miles away. Alex had been strangely silent since the ordeal, but piped up once in the safety of his

grandmother's house. He said the man with the black hat came to visit him in the basement while Terri was upstairs checking the house. The man leered as he spoke to Alex: "If your mama ever comes back to my place in the basement again, I'll do more than just knock her in the head next time."

Terri, shocked, asked her son why he didn't call for her.

"The angel came," Alex said. "She told the man to leave me alone, so he went away."

Alex's encounter with the man in the black hat was the last straw—Terri and Ed put the house up for sale. By the end of summer the place had new owners who opted to tear down the red farmhouse, despite all the remodeling Terri and Ed had done. Terri never had a chance to ask them why. In a way, she admitted, it seemed better not to know. Once they moved, Alex never saw another ghost. And whether the man in the black hat still haunts the ground that once harbored his basement "place," no one has been able to say.

PHANTOM PAINS
by Boyd E. Harris

IN THE SUMMER OF 2006, a longtime friend and college roommate from Venezuela called and told me that he and his son were on the road to recovery. Both Ricardo and Michael had been in bad shape; and over time he revealed what really happened.

Ricardo, his wife, and their two sons rented a relatively modern house in Spring, Texas. Within days of moving in, odd things began to occur. Sixteen-year-old Michael was unhappy with his room, and on some mornings Ricardo found him sleeping downstairs on the living room sofa. When Ricardo pressed the issue with his son, Michael revealed to his parents that his bedroom felt strange, and he sometimes saw things when he dozed. What kinds of things? Ricardo wanted to know. Michael never could explain what they were to his parents' satisfaction.

Not long after moving into their new house, Michael spoke to his father about a sensation he felt while sitting at his bedroom desk. He said it was like a rush of cold air running through his body and that it happened a number of times.

A few months later Michael became ill. At first he missed a day of school here and there, but it quickly turned into something more serious. The family doctor was stumped by the mysterious illness; and when the case was referred to medical specialists, his condition eluded diagnosis. By then he had severe pain running through his abdomen, and as months passed the illness grew worse, and Michael grew weaker. He was incapable of any physical activity—a teenage boy who was a star athlete in his early high school career was forced to spend his days in bed or on the sofa.

Spending more time at home, odd things happened around him. One afternoon, while sitting up in his bed reading, he heard one of the heavy mahogany dining-room chairs scoot away from the table. It wasn't Astro, his white boxer, who was dutifully at the foot of Michael's bed and growling as he faced the doorway. Michael carried his baseball bat downstairs, scanned the living and dining rooms, and found nothing out of place, except for one chair that was sitting awkwardly apart from the dining table.

Michael's condition continued to worsen as the weeks passed and his parents became desperate. Some worried that Michael had been cursed with the "evil eye," and Ricardo's sister-in-law brought in a spiritual specialist. The woman broke an egg under the bed and performed a ritual to no avail. Michael's parents took him for further medical exams, which once again revealed only that he was perfectly healthy. The various specialists consulted were completely baffled, each explaining that Michael simply was not sick.

And yet, no medicine, no diet, and no amount of rest could make him feel better.

A QUIET DEATH

One Sunday afternoon, a girl of about eleven years rolled up the driveway on her bicycle and stopped in front of Michael's mother, Theresa, who was carrying groceries from the family van.

The girl said, "I used to live there. There is a ghost in the house. Our shoes and clothes were always getting moved around while we slept, and one time two pillows flew off of the couch. When my daddy found out about the man who killed himself there, we moved."

School had started that week, and classmates teased Michael and his brother, Christopher, about the haunted house. Apparently everyone in the neighborhood, apart from Ricardo's family, knew about the house's harrowing history. Their leasing agent had been less than forthcoming about this information, so Ricardo began investigating. When he spoke with the agent and pressed her for the truth, she admitted that someone had died there years before. He then learned from several neighbors that one of the first owners of the house had committed suicide after losing his wife and kids to divorce. Apparently the forlorn man had planned a quiet departure, lying perpendicular to the fireplace, with his head propped up on pillows inside of it. He turned the gas on and, within a matter of minutes, died.

Although Ricardo himself is not superstitious, he made plans to move his family out of the house shortly after learning about the demise of its former owner.

A PERFECTLY HEALTHY KNEE

Late one night, a couple of weeks before the move, Ricardo got up from bed to pour himself a glass of water. Walking to the kitchen, he felt a little spasm in

his knee. "A tweak," he called it, that ached for a few seconds until he stretched it out. He drank his water and went back to bed. When he sat up the following morning, his knee had nearly doubled in size, swollen from an apparent injury—one he knew he had not suffered.

That morning, Ricardo's wife took him to an orthopedic surgeon. The stress tests and X-rays showed no signs of injury to his knee. Within a few days, despite ice packs and rest, it had grown still worse, so he sought a second opinion from a well-known arthroscopic surgeon. After reviewing the results of the MRI scan, the doctor could find nothing wrong with the knee. He drained the accumulated fluid and sent Ricardo home. A few days later, the knee had refilled with fluid and the swelling grew even worse. The doctor performed exploratory surgery and found nothing—no damage of any kind. The doctor was baffled. According to the tests and surgery, Ricardo's knee was perfectly healthy.

A few days after the surgery, the family moved to their new home. Two weeks later, Ricardo called me to tell me that his knee was recovering remarkably well—almost 100 percent—and that Michael was back in school full time. His and Michael's ailments had disappeared as quickly and mysteriously as they had come.

I believe this family endured a true haunting—and a nasty one, at that. Whether the activities that took place in that house were the ill will of an angry spirit, or just a confused and disturbed soul recklessly groping for help, moving out was the best decision Ricardo ever made for his family.

Michael remains skeptical about his experiences in the house. He believes the events that transpired were nothing more than a series of odd coincidences, and his parents are perfectly happy to agree with him.

But I know that they know better.

NEW HOUSE, OLD HAUNTS
by Charlie Carlson

THERESA AND STUART PETERSON never thought much about ghosts until they bought a piece of land in the hilly terrain of Columbia County in North Florida. The property was down a one-vehicle road that snaked through a thick canopy and across a creek to a large, flattop hill. Here the Petersons built a small house with the intention of renting it. Theresa admitted feeling guilty for building on the spot because it had always been a favorite resting place for deer.

The house was finished about the time their daughter, Nichole, returned from boarding school and just prior to her starting community college. They allowed Nichole and some of her girlfriends to temporarily live in the house to save on renting elsewhere. That's when strange things began to happen. First, it was sounds of pots and pans moving about in the kitchen, even though no one was in there. Next, the back door that led to an outdoor deck kept opening. Nichole always made sure the deadbolt was securely locked, yet the door would open by itself. It was enough to send the other girls packing, leaving Nichole alone in the house.

After a few weeks of putting up with the strangeness, Nichole told her mother that the place was haunted. "What, a brand new house?" laughed Theresa, who was a bit skeptical, thinking only old, weatherworn houses could harbor ghosts—if there were such things.

"Well, if it isn't haunted then there are some really, really strange things going on," insisted Nichole, who went on to describe how at night when she was asleep, something unseen was tickling her nose. It happened so frequently that she began sleeping with the covers over her head. Nichole described in detail how something unseen was sitting on her bed late at night, touching her abdomen. "I can feel a presence in that house," she said, now frightened enough to move out of the house and in with her parents.

Although a little concerned for her daughter, Theresa was still not convinced any of it had to do with the paranormal. However, subsequent personal experiences soon changed her mind.

Ghostly Interference

After Nichole moved out, Theresa and Stuart decided to put the house up for sale. While alone at the house painting on the porch, Theresa had her first encounter with the unknown entity. "The front door was open so I could hear the TV in the living room," she said. "All of a sudden the TV turned itself off. After about fifteen minutes it turned itself back on. Then it started flipping channels by itself, not fast but in a slow, deliberate manner."

Theresa kept painting, but the TV continued changing channels, so she put her paintbrush down. "I checked the remote to make sure something wasn't lying on it," she explained. "There was no reason for the TV to act that way."

She then checked the electrical system. "The lights never went out . . . no power surge or anything to cause the TV to act like that." She thought about what Nichole had told her about the house. "When you see it for yourself, it's different than hearing it from someone else," said Theresa, her skepticism quickly diminishing. "Things just didn't feel right in that house. It was like sensing something invisible in there, with no way to explain it."

25

After the house was put on the market, Theresa and Stuart would visit to mow the lawn and tend to things. "Each time we visited the house the air conditioner would be set at about sixty degrees," said Theresa. "It would be freezing inside. But we always left the AC set on seventy-eight degrees." It happened so often that Stuart was now blaming the ghost in their rental house.

Later, during a discussion about the house, Theresa mentioned the strange occurrences to her mother and brother. "Do you think it could be haunted?" she asked, wondering if it was built on an old grave. According to them, in the early 1990s a close friend of Theresa's brother was killed while deer hunting in the woods where the house was built. He was shot by another hunter who mistook him for a deer.

Theresa and Stuart finally sold the house in 2007 but will always wonder about the strange events they witnessed there. "If it was the ghost of that young man, then we never felt threatened," said Theresa. "It just felt like someone wanted attention."

Spirited House for Sale
by Linda J. Adams

As a real estate agent, I've seen, shown, and sold more homes than I can count. I've also witnessed a handful of paranormal experiences, including two incidents that happened in 2005. The first was a rather whimsical and nonthreatening event: A skeleton key hanging on a hook by a stone fireplace started swinging back and forth on its own as my clients and I watched. We weren't scared—just curious. My second experience, however, wasn't as benign.

Good Bones, Bad Vibrations

It was spring, and I was showing homes to a single mom and her family. We were looking at a two-story bungalow on a small treed lot near an old family amusement park (in New Jersey) called Clementon Lake Park. The park was still in operation and open late during summer evenings, but other than that, the neighborhood was quiet, suburban, and peaceful. The home had curb appeal and my buyers immediately liked it just from the look of the exterior.

I walked up to the front door of the house to get the key from the security box hanging from the doorknob. Strangely, I could feel the box vibrating as I pulled it away from the door. I couldn't make sense of what was causing the vibration—the key box wasn't electrified and I knew the utilities had been turned off, so there was no electricity there at all. The sensation hasn't happened before or since, and at the time I quickly dismissed it and went inside with my clients.

From the front door we walked onto the enclosed front porch, and then into the living room where we stopped to take in the space. That's when I heard a vibrating noise, like an electric humming. I asked if anyone else could hear it, but only I could. I then asked if anyone had a cell phone on vibrate, and we all checked, but nobody did. I continued to hear this vibrating noise as we toured the rest of the house.

Apart from the incessant vibrating sound, I was pleasantly surprised by the condition of the house—vacant homes with no utilities are often in a state of disrepair. Here, the rooms were free of debris and the kitchen had even been remodeled. The home had character and "good bones," a real estate buzzword that means the house is well built. I could tell my buyers were getting excited about this prospect.

27

After going upstairs to see the bedrooms, we went down into the dark cool basement. Right away, the buyers noticed a variation of their last name spray-painted on one of the basement walls. They found it odd, but were nonetheless thrilled and took it as a good omen—this was the home they were meant to buy. I was delighted to hear this; after weeks of searching, we had finally found a home in which they might be happy.

Then suddenly, out of nowhere, a basketball came hurtling through the air at us. It wasn't as though the basketball had been tucked under a rafter and just fell from it; it came at us horizontally and at high speed from the other side of the basement, as if deliberately thrown. We stood and watched as it landed on the floor, bounced, and then slowly lost momentum. It finally rolled the rest of the way across the floor and stopped against a box by our feet. It had certainly startled me, and I could tell everyone else had gotten a good scare.

One of the family members and I walked over to where the basketball had come from, to see if we could figure out how it happened. We came up empty-handed. There was no one there, and nothing that would explain how the basketball was thrown through the air like that. My buyers started to go on about how the house was haunted and that there was no way they'd want to buy it now. Still curious and a little nervous, we hurried back upstairs and inspected the home's doors and windows, which all seemed to be securely closed. There were no other signs of a break-in. With no rational explanation for what happened, we left the house.

My clients and I had driven separately to the home, so once inside my car, I immediately phoned the listing agent and asked if she was aware of anything strange about the house. I told her about the vibrating key box, the electric humming in the air, and the hurtling basketball, but she laughed and said she wasn't aware of anything like that. When I asked why the previous owner moved out before the house was sold, the agent explained that the woman had lived there for five months before deciding she could no longer afford the house and put it on the market hoping for a quick sale.

Something didn't make sense. If the owner was facing foreclosure, she would have had at least eighteen months—if not longer—before the bank would make her vacate the premises. Typically, homeowners remain in the house until the last possible second, and she definitely could have stayed there longer. It's possible that she left early because she got a job offer in another state, or was able to move in with family. Perhaps something tragic had happened to a family member and bad memories in the home became too much for her to bear. Or, considering the odd electrical sensations and the flying basketball I had just experienced, maybe she fled out of fear, from tormenting spirits.

Unsalable Spirit

Two years later the house was still for sale. I arranged a showing with prospective buyers for whom I thought the house was a perfect match. At that point, I hadn't yet disclosed the story of my eerie experience from the first time I had been in the house. I decided that if they were indeed interested in the property after the showing, I would fill them in on what had happened.

When we entered the house, it felt oddly quiet and devoid of life. We spent a good deal of time inside, and although nothing out of the ordinary happened, the family decided they didn't want the home. Once the buyers left, I hesitantly went back inside to see if I might experience any activity such as I had two years earlier, but nothing happened. I took some photographs, but nothing showed up on the developed prints.

After I left the house, I spoke with neighbors who were outside doing yard work. I asked if they knew of anything odd or unexplained that had happened there. Apparently, apart from the occasional Realtor going in and emerging hurriedly several minutes later, there was nothing overtly unusual about the place. All I know is that despite the great condition of the house, its quiet little neighborhood, and its reasonable price during what was initially a housing boom, it took nearly three years to finally sell it.

29

THE SUFFOLK COUNTY CRITTER
by Robert E. Ettl

AH, COUNTRY LIFE. It was our family's dream to leave the chaos of the metropolitan area for a safer, quieter existence surrounded by nature. When I was eight years old, my parents took the first step toward realizing this dream and moved our family from New York City to a rural ocean community in Suffolk County, New York.

The house we moved to was built as a shell with just enough structure to get a certificate of occupancy from the town. It was our intent to add onto the house, as we had the time and the resources, and eventually we built a patio on the back of the house. Several years later, we enclosed it, making it a screened porch. Finally, we converted the porch into a den.

Life was good in our rural home. But then shortly after the den was completed, things got a whole lot weirder. Lights spontaneously turned on and off in rooms throughout the house. Furniture moved. We were regularly locked out of the house—when there was nobody home to do the locking!

Our mischievous entity—we affectionately called it "the Critter"—went so far as to throw things around the house. One evening we were sitting in the den when we heard a loud crash from the bedroom. After rushing to the room, we found my mom's turkey-shaped tureen smashed against the far wall. On another occasion, my dad was enjoying a pre-dinner cocktail when a wineglass rose from the table and shattered in front of him and three startled eyewitnesses. These eerie—and yet oddly entertaining—events continued for years, but despite all the activity, we never caught a glimpse of the Critter. Most of the time, our family had the sense that the Critter was a benign entity that liked playing games.

That all changed one night when we were awakened from our sleep by a horrible racket. It sounded as if someone was banging on our front door with a large, heavy object. The loud thudding continued until we reached the door— and then the noise stopped. We opened the door but found no marks on it, and the storm door that hung just a few inches away was still locked. It seemed to us then that the Critter was asserting its power and showing us what it could do.

CRITTER IN A CAGE
When I was in college, I did my dissertation on the history of our town, from its founding in the seventeenth century to the present. I dedicated a chapter to the

local Shinnecock Indians and discovered that, according to local historians, our house had been built on an Indian burial ground. Although there isn't evidence of any such graves, the property is located a few miles from an Indian reservation and our town was considered Indian territory during the Colonial period.

I described our Critter's playful and, at times, destructive behavior to an Indian historian. According to him, our family had coexisted peacefully with the resident entity until we inadvertently put it in a cage. By converting the screened porch at the back of our house into a den, we had confined the critter to a room in our house. And that's when the haunting hijinks began.

WRECK MASTER

In the eighteenth century, there were rumors that Shinnecock Indians would periodically "assist" commercial vessels in running aground. In stormy, dark, or foggy weather, they would light a bonfire on shore. Mariners traveling east on the ocean would mistake the bonfire for the Montauk Point Lighthouse and turn to port. Forty-odd miles short of the lighthouse, the ships hit the beach. The Indians then "salvaged" the wreckages, procuring whatever supplies and

31

cargo were onboard. Meanwhile, one of them watched the ship and the storm to determine when it was time to abandon the task, before the ship broke up from the pounding waves. He was referred to as "wreck master." On one occasion, the wreck master was late in making his call, and many men lost their lives as the ship broke up. This wreck master supposedly wanders the dunes for eternity, searching for the bodies of the lost Indians.

Some people believe my family's Critter is the long-lost wreck master.

CRITTER COMFORTS

At one point in my youth, my dad spoke with some paranormal specialists, who suggested we make an accommodation for the Critter, so it could come and go with ease. We took his advice and kept one of the windows in the den open, just a few inches from the top. To our surprise, it worked. With this one small concession, the mischievous activity ceased. Of course, the Critter did act up occasionally, just to remind us that it was still around.

32   I live in the house alone now, and the Critter and I still share the same den. It stops by once in a while and plays little games—just enough to annoy me sometimes, but as in the past, nothing dangerous. My kids, who are grown, love to tell their friends these stories and literally scare some people into believing they hear all kinds of strange goings-on at night when they visit. I just smile, listen, and say nothing.

A COMPLEX HAUNTING
by Joanne M. Austin

JOHN AND HOLLY QUINN moved to McDonough, Georgia, in 1999, thinking the quiet city would offer a nice change of pace after living in Atlanta. When the couple bought a mobile home in a complex not far from Route 75, they didn't realize it was located in the heart of Ghost Central. According to John, just two weeks after moving in the couple started hearing "footsteps in the home, and disembodied voices," and seeing "all kinds of unusual lights out in the yard and in the home."

Supernatural encounters involving Civil War soldiers are common fare at the Quinns' home. Although John hasn't really "seen" the soldiers, except in some photographs a psychic took, Holly, who is clairvoyant, has. She was in the kitchen one day before heading off to work when she sensed someone coming into the room from the hallway. She thought it was John, but as she turned around, John says, she saw "a full-fledged soldier in the hallway here, in full uniform." Even more, she felt "he wanted to be seen by her." Another soldier told Holly his name was Silas Adams and that he was one of the entities responsible for the unusual events occurring in her home.

Many people doubt these "soldier" ghost stories. The county historian told John that there were no battles where the complex is situated today, and thus no scenes of mass carnage that might have spawned a few ghosts. John, however, remains steadfast: "There were skirmishes through here. There had to be. Troop movement and everything."

Psychics have confirmed that two Civil War ghosts "are staying in the home." They've told the Quinns that it's a gateway entry where they've seen "hundreds and hundreds of troops, north and south, coming through." These could be troops involved in a battle—possibly the Battle of Walnut Creek—that occurred in the area in September 1864 as part of Gen. William T. Sherman's massive Atlanta Campaign.

PARANORMAL ENERGY
Like any good reporter looking for a seasonal ghost angle for the news, Josh Clark, editor of Georgia's *Henry County Times*, visited the Quinns' home in October 2004. In the story that ran later that month, Josh described his initial

33

impression of the house: "When one enters their home . . . there is a dismal quality to be felt. It lies not in the decor of the house, nor any state of disarray, rather it seems to emanate from the home itself, or perhaps the ground on which the home is situated."

Neighbors have also seen odd things. John recalls that one Sunday morning, when he was heading out to the store, a neighbor yelled to him: "Turn around quick! Look!" John did, and saw a little girl in a Victorian-era dress behind him.

The Henry County

Times

"Celebrating Henry County"

Volume 3, No. 43   Wednesday, October 27, 2004

Happy Halloween

Proudly celebrating two years of faithfully serving our readers, the people of Henry County.

Haunting in our town

John and Holly Quinn have a big problem on their hands...

By Joshua Clark
Editor

John Quinn has good reason to believe his house is haunted. In addition to the numerous encounters with the ethereal, like sounds, sightings, and physical attacks, the investigations by professional paranormal researchers, and video and audio of inexplicable phenomena, his house is likely located atop a former gravesite.

Quinn and his wife, Holly, have lived in their home since 1999, and from the day they moved in strange things have befallen the couple. Indeed when one enters their home, located just east of I-75 off Hwy. 20, there is a dismal quality to be felt. It lies not in the decor of the house, nor any state of disarray, rather it seems to eminate from the home itself, or perhaps the gound on which the home is situated. This reporter can attest that during the interview with John and Holly Quinn at their home, I suffered

Since they moved into their home in McDonough in 1999, John and Holly Quinn (above) have experienced a host of strange phenomena, including seeing entities, hearing sounds and voices and being physically assaulted.

Photo by Josh Clark

see Feature, page 6

The little girl disappeared as fast as she had appeared. Another time, a neighbor wanted to take a picture of the street because a ghost had just been seen there. John left his car running to go help his neighbor. The next thing he knew, "My car's going in reverse and getting ready to hit a house. And I had to go running after it. . . ."

It's often thought that ghosts can't cause physical harm to the living. John feels differently, and with good cause. On one occasion, John was thrown headfirst into a trash can in their backyard. "Something had physically picked me up," he says, and put him in the trash. "I had sores on my side for a couple of weeks after that incident. My sister-in-law loves that story, though!"

John says there is still paranormal activity, even though his minister and a local priest have blessed the home several times. Burning sage helps keep the spirits at bay, at least temporarily: "When I start hearing the tapping and rapping going on, I get the sage stick out and I'll say, 'I'm going to fix you.' And as soon as I bless the home and say the 'Our Father' throughout the home, the tapping and all stops. It'll calm it down for maybe a month and it'll start all back over." John also recently learned that a friend's mother, who lives in the same complex, has had otherworldly encounters in her home. He hopes to get permission to investigate the scene and gather additional information on the resident hauntings.

What's causing the eerie events at the Quinns' home? Could it be the nearby train wreck from the 1900s, the unmarked graves on the property, or the Indian burial ground? Or maybe the previously mentioned Civil War battle is the source of the spirit brigade. And if that's not enough, within eighteen feet of the Quinns' home is a power transformer—often thought to be a conduit for paranormal energy—and a network of underground streams have been detected, and they too have otherworldly associations. Still, others believe that the city of McDonough is in a vortex—or at least a site—of negative energy and that the hauntings are just by happenstance.

Award-winning Ghost Man
John, who is in his early fifties, has been interested in ghostly phenomena since the age of twelve. But it wasn't until he and Holly moved to McDonough that he found an outlet for his longstanding interests and he founded the McDonough Ghost Hunters Society in 1999. His group has investigated many locations in McDonough, and as result, he started spending a good amount of his time doing research at the local historical society: "You've got to put reasoning with the hauntings, too. You've got to have a history with that."

A natural offshoot of his research has been the ghost tours he conducts in conjunction with the McDonough Welcome Center. October is to ghost tours what April is to accountants, and John recalls one Halloween when he started doing walking tours at three in the afternoon and didn't finish until well after

35

midnight. But the hard work has benefits: John's been nicknamed the Ghost Man of Henry County, and he has also received an award. He says, "To me, just doing stuff like that is an accomplishment—any way I can help others with this kind of stuff."

BEWARE THE BOOGEYMAN
by Jeffrey A. Wargo

"Good night. Sleep tight. Don't let the bedbugs bite." Parents utter these familiar words to their children as they tuck the covers in tightly and wish them pleasant dreams. Of course, the phrase recalls times when actual bedbug infestations were rampant and the bloodsuckers scurried out of mattresses at night feasting on sleeping innocents. When I was a child, however, I often thought the phrase was a metaphor or ritualistic incantation to prevent me from being attacked by that horrific boogeyman of youthful imagination. Today, hearing these words leaves me ill at ease, and not just about the creepy crawlies!

PHANTOM FOOTSTEPS

I moved into an eighteen-room Victorian-era mansion in July 1996. It had been built as the parsonage for St. John United Church of Christ in 1887 and has housed pastors' families in the Delaware River Valley town of Riegelsville, Pennsylvania, for more than one hundred years. I felt a spiritual connection with the building from the moment I interviewed with the church, as if I needed to be there.

On my first night there, I arrived home after nine P.M. I did a little unpacking before showering and retiring to one of the upstairs bedrooms for a much-needed night's sleep. I was a little on edge about being in a big house by myself and left the door to my bedroom open, but the sound of traffic outside soon lulled me into a deep slumber.

At around one thirty A.M. I heard a rhythmic noise coming from somewhere above me. In that nebulous state between sleep and wakefulness, I couldn't quite identify the sound. And then, suddenly, I realized what it was—footsteps on the hardwood floor in the vacant room above me! I sat bolt upright and listened to what sounded like somebody pacing back and forth on the floor above me. The ominous footsteps continued for a few minutes and then the temperature in the room dropped drastically. I was scared. As I sat stiffly on my bed listening, I realized I had no way to defend myself against whoever, or whatever, was up there, and no phone with which to call for help. I heard the footsteps move in the direction of the staircase and the reverberating thuds grew louder, one at a time, as the stairs caught the footfalls of the intruder descending them.

Not knowing what else to do, I began to pray in earnest: "Our Father, who art in heaven . . ." I heard the footfalls getting closer to the bottom of the stairs. And then there was quiet. A loud silence. I shivered under the covers, wondering who was in my home. The night passed slowly as I drifted in and out of light sleep. When morning came, I rose quickly and opened the attic door. Nothing was there.

The days that followed were filled with strange encounters—shadowy figures, moving objects, disembodied voices and footsteps. Then things took an even more chilling twist. One night I settled in to read and watch television before going to sleep. My cat was curled up beside me on the bed as I drifted off to sleep.

"Jeffrey!" A gruff, unnerving voice yelled into the room. My eyes snapped open, and I looked in the direction where the sound had originated—the door to the hall. I could feel electric, negative energy pouring into the room, and it grew bitterly cold. I glanced at the cat. Her hair was on end and she was staring wide-eyed into the hall and hissing. I remember saying a prayer under my breath before getting out of bed and moving quickly to the door to examine the hallway. It was empty.

After composing myself, I walked around the upstairs and found nothing disturbed. Soon after I returned to bed, turned off the television, and turned on the radio. That night I slept with the light on and the door closed until sunlight poured through the window.

I Still Remember . . .

Seven years after I first heard the phantom footsteps, I was married and living in the house with my wife, Stephanie, who over time had grown accustomed to the haunted happenings in our home. One evening, we returned home exhausted after an outing. We went to bed with our two dogs, Jaxon and Sofie, curled up on the covers beside us. Sleep came easily.

At about three A.M., I awoke to the sound of Stephanie screaming. She jumped out of bed and ran through the open bedroom door into the hallway. I asked her what was wrong. "Someone was whispering in my ear," she said. She explained that she had been in a deep sleep when she sensed a presence leaning over her. She felt a cold breeze drifting by her head, followed by a hoarse, cold unnerving voice that said to her, "I still remember. . . ."

Sleep was sporadic for us the rest of that night, and the meaning of the words Stephanie heard remain unclear to this day. Also unnerving, the voice she described sounded eerily like the voice I had heard years before while alone in my bedroom.

Something in the Shadows

On a hot summer night several years later, we had settled into bed again, this time with the hum of the air conditioner in the background. While drifting off to sleep, we heard the closet door beside the bed click open, making a slow, creaking sound. Stephanie turned on the light, and sure enough, the door was wide open. Nothing else strange happened, so I got out of bed and closed the door, giving it a quick tug to make sure it had latched securely. I returned to bed and slept through the night without further incident.

Apart from an encounter a few nights later, when Stephanie and I spotted a peculiar shadow in the room while we were watching TV and reading, the ghostly happenings waned until late autumn. One evening in November, I was startled to hear a child's voice demanding that I wake up. I opened my eyes and looked around, but no one was there. About a week later, I once again awoke to the sound of Stephanie's screams. She explained that someone had lightly touched her leg while she slept and that an unseen hand had slid up her leg and onto

her thigh. Eventually we fell back asleep and remained undisturbed through the night.

On yet another night, Stephanie caught a fleeting glimpse of the spirit who kept opening our closet door. We had settled into our usual habit of reading before falling asleep when we heard the familiar sound of the closet door creaking open. I remember looking at the closet but not seeing anything. Stephanie did not look up and tried to ignore the paranormal presence.

Later, she explained that while focused on her book, in her peripheral vision she saw a woman step toward the bed from the direction of the closet. She wore a black Victorian-era dress that had tight-fitting sleeves and held her hands in front of her abdomen. The spirit didn't return to the bedroom after that night, though the closet door continued to open regularly over the following weeks.

Then the nature of our encounters shifted in an unsettling way. On several occasions, Stephanie described waking up in the middle of the night to see a black cloudy shape standing at the bottom of the bed. It moved up along my side of the mattress and seemed to hover over me, then passed through the headboard and the closed door behind it. I slept through these incidents until one night, when something woke me up. Darkness swirled around me as my mind began to register the sights in the room. Hovering beside my bed, within an arm's reach, was a man's face looking down at me with dark eyes. I pulled the covers over my head and tried to calm down. When I peeked out from under the blanket, the face was gone.

40   Later that fall, some friends took a picture of our home during the haunted walking tours in our town. A chilling portrait appeared in one of the pictures— the face of the man I had seen in our house, by our bed!

I read an article recently that said bedbugs were making a comeback in the United States because of imports from third world countries. If this is the case, I hope they will bypass Riegelsville. We already have enough chilling nocturnal activity in our home as it is.

KNOCK IT OFF, RALPH
by Mary Trotter Kion

THE FIRST TIME I entered my house in Kennewick, Washington, I felt welcome, despite its rundown and dirty condition. I was there only two weeks when I first heard the faint sounds of a baby crying. It seemed to be coming from the other end of the house, but I was paying more attention to my several cats, including Cookie, a particularly chatty feline. I heard this faint wailing several different times, always from the opposite end of the house. I had already assured myself that my neighbors had no small children or babies; and each time it happened, Cookie wasn't in sight, so I assumed she was meowing up a storm on the other side of the house.

Mystery solved. I continued unpacking boxes and making the place my own. If anything else unusual happened, I was far too busy to notice. Then one day, I again heard a baby's faint cry coming from the other end of the house. This time, however, Cookie was sitting beside me. As the cries continued I stared down at Cookie, who was quieter than I had ever remembered. That was the last time I heard the crying, and I still have no idea what caused it.

I soon forgot this and continued to transform my house into a livable space. Its residents initially consisted of the squeaky, four-legged, and long-tailed variety, but I had soon eliminated those unwelcome boarders. One afternoon, however, I discovered evidence of another uninvited guest lurking inside my house.

THE FLYING WOK

As a housewarming gift, a coworker gave me a heavy wind chime made from an inverted clay flowerpot that hung by a leather thong. It was winter, so I hung the chime from a hook in the ceiling over the dining room table. It would take a big wind to activate the clapper, and inside with all the doors and windows tightly closed, there was no breeze to move it.

One day I entered the dining area and was startled to see the wind chime swinging back and forth a good eight to ten inches in either direction. I stood there in disbelief as the chime swayed before my eyes. Then suddenly it came to a dead stop. At first I thought one of the cats had swatted the chime and then scurried away before I got into the room. But after doing some measuring, I ruled that theory out—even my largest cat wouldn't be able to jump that high. The chime swayed one other time shortly after that, then never again.

I had lived in the house for nearly three years, and although unusual things happened from time to time—pictures falling off the wall, objects tumbling off of the top of the refrigerator—I was never harmed. One time, the large electric wok I kept on top of the fridge attacked me! Out of nowhere, the wok's lid flew off and I had to duck quickly to keep it from hitting my head. As the lid clattered to the floor, I yelled, "Ok, Ralph, knock it off!" My invisible housemate had a name. I don't know why I called him Ralph. I don't even like the name. Since then, however, I've yelled at Ralph on many occasions.

A few years later, I began to babysit my three-year-old granddaughter at the house, and I don't think Ralph cared much for her being there. I had some small, plastic decorations on one wall that were extremely difficult to put up and take down. Several times when my granddaughter was within a few feet of where the decorations hung, one or the other would fly off the wall straight at her. They always just missed hitting her, and thankfully they wouldn't have hurt her if they had.

A year or so went by with no indication that Ralph was lurking about. Then suddenly he pulled one of his pranks: locking me out of the house. Early one morning, I stepped out with the dogs and closed the door behind me. When I tried to go back into the house, it was locked, even though I know I didn't lock it. It was no fun having to climb back into the house through a window.

At the time I didn't even consider that Ralph might have locked the door, but it happened once again while my sister was visiting. We stepped outside together and I closed the door, only to find we had been locked out. If Ralph did it, however, he goofed. My brother-in-law was inside and let us back in. Many times now after coming inside, I have found the turn button turned to the locked position. Telling Ralph to knock it off doesn't always work.

Mind Games

When Ralph's games eventually do seem to end, I'm always certain that, with time, something new will happen. This was exactly the case when a necklace chain I thought I had lost for good suddenly reappeared.

The chain and the silver crucifix that hung from it had particular meaning for me. They had been purchased years earlier, after I had suffered from tremendous headaches. Doctors weren't able to identify the cause of the headaches and none of the medications they prescribed did any good. The headaches didn't stop until after I first burned a piece of "blessed" tissue a friend had given me shortly before my painful ordeal had started, then put on the crucifix. The pain went away overnight.

I continued to wear the crucifix for many years and went through several chains. In 1993 or 1994 I had used string for a quick repair job on the newest chain, and after it broke, I couldn't find the chain or the crucifix anywhere in the house. I thought it was lost forever.

In November 1996 I made a number of Christmas gifts, including a large cloth doll for my granddaughter. Late one night, after sitting at my sewing machine for a while making the doll's dress, I went into the kitchen to refill my teacup. What I discovered when I returned to the sewing machine astounded me: The chain, with the string still tied on it, was draped across the machine's footfeed. At first I thought the chain dropped out of something I was using, but I had bought my sewing supplies just a week before. Besides, it was obvious the chain had been gently draped—not dropped—across the footfeed. It must have been Ralph, though I wondered why he hadn't returned the crucifix as well. That is a little too scary for me to consider.

43

Now and then the scent of male cologne would waft through the house, with no logical source. Other times, there was a distinctive scent of a woman's perfume that was not my own—was Ralph entertaining female guests? And on a few occasions, the aroma of brewing coffee would suddenly permeate the house. Not only do I not drink coffee, but I don't even own a coffeepot or stash coffee anywhere in my home.

The Cowboy in the Rocker

By the time Cookie was fourteen, she had survived a mild stroke that left her less agile than before, and she began resting in the living room rocking chair. My cats had always avoided the chair because the lightest touch set it into erratic motion. But it became Cookie's spot, and while she was in it, the chair ceased its erratic rocking, until after her death. She occupied the chair most hours of the day, though on one occasion I caught someone else sitting in it—someone who quickly dissolved into nothing.

44

I came through the front door one afternoon clutching overfilled grocery bags in both hands. Out of habit, I looked down to ensure I didn't step on a cat, since a couple of them hadn't yet learned to not be underfoot. If not for this precaution, I might have missed seeing the lower legs of a man in well-worn jeans and cowboy boots, sitting in Cookie's rocking chair. Was this Ralph? In my astonishment and fright, I failed to glance upward to his torso and face before he disappeared. Since this strange occurrence, I often wonder if Cookie was attracted to Ralph's lap rather than the rocker itself. If so, I thank him.

Ralph's antics have settled down, but I'm certain he is still here. Lately he seems to cause my computer screen to scroll and other strange things. At first, I assumed it was a problem with the computer, but when I say, "Ralph, *please* knock it off," it mysteriously stops.

When I first wrote this account a couple of years ago, Ralph's antics greatly increased. Now, as I edit the story, he's up to his old tricks again. All in one day, the handles of my two favorite combs suddenly snapped off as I was using them, and my toothbrush broke in half with a loud pop, as if it had been forcefully snapped, again while I was using it. Does Ralph disapprove of this account? On one hand, I hope Ralph still haunts the rooms of my little house, but a kinder instinct in me hopes he has moved on to that better place in the clouds.

THE ELBERON HOUSE
by Ryan Doan

NOT EVERYONE IS BORN WITH the chemical disposition to get his or her jollies from being scared. Such is my friend Ray, which made it all the more amusing when my friends and I decided to ambush him on Thanksgiving night in 1997. We intended on stumbling across something frightening and dragging Ray into it with us. The joke, however, would be on me.

My friends and I weren't content with just burning our turkey off at home. Ray was the only one of the group not privy to our true agenda, because we knew he would be a conscientious objector. Dave, Ashley, Holly, and I told him we were going to get some coffee at The Inkwell in Long Branch, New Jersey.

When we pulled up to the dark property, Ray—knowing he'd been had—conceded he wouldn't run if we agreed to a few terms. He was probably succumbing to an "if I can't beat them, I'll join them" mentality, but it's also a testament to the allure of the mansion. He didn't want to get out of the car and asked us to stay in there with him. But we ignored Ray and exited the car shortly after arriving at the house. Then he made us promise not to go too close, and again we ignored him. At that point he simply gave up and agreed to join us, as long as he had control of the flashlight, which he grasped like a vial of antidote in a snake pit.

The Elberon House was a grand sight. It stood two stories high, excluding an amply sized basement and attic. The wings of the enormous, whitewashed building folded out on each side from a center entrance like arms stretching to pull us in.

We made several attempts to get past the broken white picket fence that surrounded it—not because we had difficulty getting around the fence but because of the sheer terror that the deserted mansion inspired in us. Every time we got close, our imaginations would make the darkness congeal into some horrific shape that would send us running back to the car. Finally we huddled together and walked around the side of the building to the back porch, which was faintly lit by the moon. Retro school desks stood there, cast in a dim blue and looking out of place. Beyond them a heavy door was slightly ajar, daring us to enter. We took the dare.

We must have looked pathetic the way we held so tightly to each other, appearing as a single organism inching our way through the building. With

45

every bit of progress made, Ray's lone flashlight illuminated some aspect of the place we would have been better off not seeing. Its light nervously danced over old iron stoves and floral patterns on the rotting walls.

Eventually we were farther in than out, at our point of no return. There was no visible end to the hallways we crawled through. We began to feel suffocated in the darkness, and the girls started to tear up, but the tension broke when we came to the center of the mansion. The hallways opened into a huge, twisted ballroom with a huge staircase and a fireplace.

We shuffled up to the second floor, the tension returning when we saw the rotten bathrooms and what we perceived as secret passageways through the broken walls. These were the kind of spaces just large enough for a killer to hide in. I led the group, Ray's flashlight shaking over my shoulder as everyone pressed up against one another. An evil grin played across my face as I realized the opportunity I had. A desire to increase the fearfulness of my friends replaced my own trepidation.

46   Without warning, I leaped from the group and ran into the darkness of the hallway. So unexpected were my movements that Ray's light only caught a flash

of me disappearing down the hall. Everyone else stood in place, listening for some sign of me beyond their heavy breathing.

That's when I leaped out from the nearest crawl space in the broken wall with a howl. My friends screamed in unison, turned, and ran away with everything they had. I ran after them, slamming on the walls for additional effect. The light in Ray's hand wavered on the ceiling as they ran. They made it all the way to the mansion's entrance, and one by one were spat out of the house, panting.

HOUSE ARREST

I was right behind them and ready to begin laughing once I caught my breath, when the heavy door swung shut. I crashed full speed into it, the taste of the cider I had earlier punching from my stomach into my throat. Then the lock turned by itself, trapping me inside. In retrospect I suppose the rapid pace of my friends could have swung the door shut, its momentum closing the latch, but no matter how hard I pushed or pulled on the door, I couldn't get it to open.

Outside, my friends thought this was part of my prank. I begged for help, my frantic breathing fogging up the dirty glass of the window. They couldn't see

47

the desperation on my face, but they could hear the terror in my voice. Ray and Dave beat at the door, but their efforts proved little help.

Like a drowning victim, I reached a point where I just gave up. I turned around to face the darkness of the hall that swooped in to take me over and slid down the door on my back. It was as if the mansion was teaching me a lesson, and once it knew I had learned it, it let me go. I heard the latch move and felt the breath of air from the crack in the door. Now I was able to open it, and I quickly got out. Once in the car, we sped away from the Elberon House, still huddled together, our minds racing from the fear and adrenaline generated by the experience. But was it over yet?

From the backseat, Ray said he thought he smelled something like rotten eggs. Everyone's eyes lit up. Did a ghost follow us? Were we plagued by some poltergeist released from the mansion? I did not entertain this notion, as I was still thinking about the door that slammed on me. The smell was probably just some piece of doomed fast food that was left to rot on the car floor.

48

Terror Revisited

Exactly seventy-eight months and three days later, I found myself outside of the Elberon House again, taking pictures. The place is like supernatural flypaper, and apparently I wasn't the only thrill seeker attracted to it—every possible entrance was now boarded up with fresh plywood and long nails. I was hesitant about getting too close, and perhaps I wouldn't have at all if a friend hadn't randomly driven by and called my name. It seemed like an outside force was orchestrating things.

My friend and I crossed the yard, reenacting that long-ago night. The school desks were no longer on the back porch, and almost everything loose had rotted or been cleared out. My friend found the door that had once troubled me, but it looked less imposing in the daylight and behind clean wood.

I was glad for the lack of suitable entrances because I had no intention of entering again. As we were leaving, though, something cold and metallic slammed into my head: a chain-link ladder hanging from the second-floor porch. Thus, I found myself inside the Elberon House once again.

Enough light snuck past the few plywood-free windows on the second floor to keep us calm. Then, as we were about to go down the stairs, a closet door behind us began shaking horribly. We looked at each other in disbelief and hastily made our exit, but not before I snapped a few photos of the area where the noise came from. The door had an eye-level peephole cut into it, and we

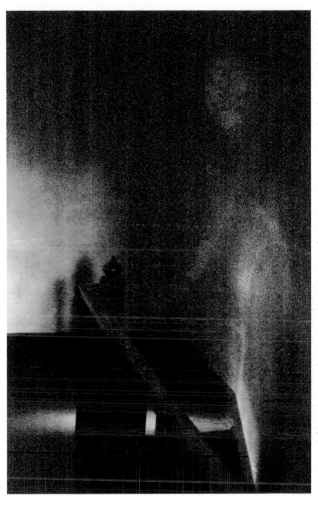

felt overwhelmingly that we were being watched. Later, we assumed that the noise came from a squatter in the closet who was trying to warn others below. It couldn't really be a ghost.

The next day I was downloading photos of my adventure when I stopped short on one in particular: The photo I took before we escaped. It showed a skeletal human figure walking up the stairs and looking straight at the camera. Had I seen the figure while still in the house, I wouldn't have needed the metal ladder to get back down to the ground. There would have been a "me" shaped hole cut clean through that wall.

NIGHTMARISH
NIGHTS OUT

"The toilet exploded!" —A woman running out of a haunted ladies' room at Ashley's Restaurant

SHOWER UP, GET DRESSED IN your finest clothes, break out the bubbly, and prepare yourself for a night on the town. . . . But not just *any* night. Sure, we'll stop at some taverns, get a nice meal in a restaurant, maybe even take in a show and some dancing, but there's going to be a paranormal element thrown into the evening.

For starters, we'll have a drink for the deceased owner of an Illinois inn whose ghost gets fresh with his female patrons and watch as spirits in a Washington tavern and Mississippi inn play tricks.

Next, we'll move on to some ectoplasmic eats—from the smell of haunted toast in a New Jersey restaurant, to dessert at a famous New Orleans restaurant that features a departed chef! Need to make a rest stop? There's something paranormally attractive about ladies' rooms in Florida as well as a men's room at a Missouri truck stop.

And on to the entertainment . . . Perhaps a ghostly stagehand will sit next to you in an Illinois theater, or you may hear the feet of ethereal dancers creak across the dance floor of a music venue in Oregon. All we know for sure is, by the end of *this* night out, the ghosts will have you screaming, "Check, *please!*"

CAPTAIN TONY'S HAUNTED SALOON

by Jeff Belanger

CAPTAIN TONY'S SALOON IN KEY WEST, Florida, is one happening place. The building's walls have seen both literary and rock royalty pass through. Ernest Hemingway frequented the bar while he lived in Key West, and Tennessee Williams and Shel Silverstein were both known to throw back a few at the saloon. Jimmy Buffett began his singing career on the bar's stage, and legends like Bob Dylan still show up for impromptu performances. It's the history above all else that draws so many spirits (living, dead, and the kind you drink) to this haunted hot spot—a history laced with lynchings, accidents, and murder.

Built in 1851, 428 Greene Street was originally home to two businesses operating under one roof: an icehouse stocked by ships sailing down the East Coast, and the city morgue. In 1865, a massive hurricane hit the Florida Keys, and the sea surged fifteen to twenty feet, smashing almost everything in the way. The building at 428 Greene Street took the hurricane's hit on the chin, sending doors, inventory, and fresh corpses drifting into the mucky aftermath.

"All of the bodies were missing after the hurricane hit, except one," said Joe Faber, the current owner of Captain Tony's Saloon. "According to some old Conchs that I spoke with when researching the history, they found one body that was near the outside of the building, which is now the inside of the building where the pool room is. They never found the others, so what the Bahamian people did is decide to make that an unofficial grave site. They buried the body they found, built a wall around the area, and put bottles full of holy water in the wall."

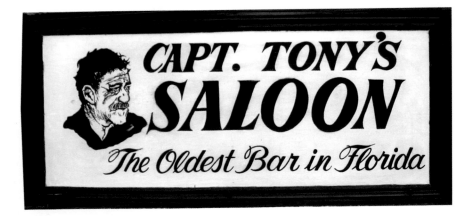

53

The Greene Street building has weathered many storms since then, and at different times has housed a wireless telegraph station, cigar factory, bordello, and speakeasy. The place went legit as prohibition ended, and the building entered its final incarnation as the saloon so many locals and tourists have come to love today.

Captain Tony's pub expanded throughout the twentieth century. Besides building around the hanging tree, owners expanded the saloon to include a billiards room, building over and around the wall containing holy water. In the 1980s, while taking up the old plywood flooring, the bones from between eight and fifteen bodies were discovered. A skeletal reminder of the find hangs behind the bar today. Also unearthed was the grave marker of a young woman named Elvira, which is now exposed in the cement next to a pool table.

LADY IN BLUE

See that tree growing through the roof of the building with bras and other miscellany hanging from it? Eighteen people were hanged from it during the 1800s, all but one of them for piracy. The one exception? In the latter half of the nineteenth century, a local woman brutally murdered her husband and two sons. She chopped their bodies into pieces and set the bloody chunks out in the backyard for the animals to dispose of. A neighbor caught a glimpse of the scene and called others over to investigate. They saw the carnage, and then

found the exhausted murderess inside her home wearing a blue dress covered in blood. The crowd turned lynch mob and dragged her to the hanging tree for some instant justice.

Today the legendary "Lady in Blue" is Captain Tony's best-known haunting. People spot a bluish blur passing through the room, or maybe see the apparition out of the corner of their eyes. Some have even claimed to photograph her. But the specter in blue isn't alone; there are others.

BLOODY BATHROOM BEHAVIOR

Joe Faber first came to Captain Tony's Saloon in 1976 when he was in college. He heard about some of the ghosts from Capt. Tony Tarracino himself, and although there are variations on the bathroom story, the gist of the legend dates back to the building's early days as a saloon. For instance, according to Faber, a woman brought her young child into the speakeasy, where she found her husband drinking and carousing. The mother snapped. "She killed her child in the bathroom, which is a pretty hairy thing, and she took the kid's body out under a blanket," Faber said.

In January of 2005, one of Captain Tony's female patrons had an eerie experience in the lady's restroom that left her rattled.

"I tried to go in the first stall, but it was locked. I figured someone was in there that I didn't notice, but then I heard the outside door close. Just before we left, I went in again. I again went for the first stall—the back one gave me the chills and an eerie feeling—and realized it was locked from the inside. While in the back stall, I again heard the outside door close and I looked around the corner. No one walked in. I was feeling strange but continued what I was doing when, all of a sudden, I heard that first stall door slam. I jumped out of the back stall and saw that no one was there, and that the first stall was still locked from the inside. I ran out and never looked back."

DON'T LEAVE

Joe Faber considers himself a skeptic. He's neither seen the Lady in Blue nor sensed a presence in the women's restroom. But he has had two experiences in the bar he can't explain: voices that seemed to offer a kind of warning of events to come.

"About eight or nine years ago, I'm in the bar alone at about four o'clock in the morning," Faber said. "I was sitting there doing paperwork, and someone . . . called

me. All I heard was, 'Hey, Joe.' I thought that was pretty odd, so I got up to look around to see who was looking for me. I walked out of the back of the bar, and the back doors were wide open. I had just been out there maybe half an hour earlier."

Faber described the back lot of the bar as being completely fenced in; there was no way someone could have come in or gone out that way. He figured that if the disembodied voice had any supernatural meaning, it was simply to lock the doors.

"I didn't think much of that voice until several years later," he said. "I was sitting at the bar at the end of the night doing paperwork, and I hear that same voice again, but this time it says, 'Don't leave.' Now I've got the chills. I got up, and I ran to the back to see if the doors were open. I checked, and everything was locked down. So then I checked the entire building, because I'm thinking this may be a warning that there's going to be a fire or something, but nothing was wrong."

Finding nothing amiss, Faber went home. A few hours later, his phone rang. "I get a phone call about six o'clock in the morning from the police saying that a girl, maybe seventeen or eighteen years old, committed suicide in front of the bar. Apparently the girl called her mother from her cell phone, said that she had just taken some pills to kill herself, and that she was in front of a yellow building that she thought was a bar, under a green awning. Her mother called the Key West police, who went from bar to bar and found the girl in front of Captain Tony's, dead. Had I stayed at the bar that night, maybe I would have found the girl and been able to help her.

"Now, do I know what the hell that is? Absolutely not. But I do know that I've been there twenty years, I've heard it twice, and it was meaningful both times. Everybody can speak about the Lady in Blue, the bathroom, and things like that, but it means nothing to me until I actively see it or hear it. But from what I've experienced, and the stories I've heard, I know something's going on."

Considering that a number of people were executed on the hanging tree, and lives were lost here by the storm surge, in addition to the other deaths that took place in and around the property, maybe something or someone is still around.

CAPTAIN TONY'S SALOON
428 Greene Street, Key West, Florida 33040

OLE ST. ANDREW'S INN
by Troy Taylor

ALTHOUGH IT'S KNOWN TODAY AS the Ole St. Andrew's Inn, this Chicago pub first gained ghostly notoriety as the "Edinburgh Castle Pub." The place has operated as a Scottish-themed bar since 1961, but before that, it was simply a neighborhood bar owned by Frank Giff, a colorful character whose spirit lives on in his beloved watering hole. But be forewarned: Frank's been known to get a little fresh with the ladies—from beyond the grave.

Frank had a taste for playing pool, joking, chatting with the customers, and vodka (not necessarily in that order). He loved to sample the tavern's wares and dipped into the stock every evening. He was always game for another drink with his patrons, until one night in 1959, when Frank drank himself to death.

The bar was never the same without Frank, and eventually his widow, Edna, put it up for sale. Jane McDougall, a native of Scotland, purchased the pub in 1961, brought in tartan carpet, Scottish memorabilia, and a line of ales and whiskeys from the old country, and dubbed the place the Edinburgh Castle Pub. But even with the changes, one thing about the place remained the same: Frank Giff.

As time passed, Jane noticed large quantities of vodka disappearing from the stock. At first she suspected the bartenders were stealing from her, and, thinking that she would catch them in the act, she started covertly marking the level in the bottles with a wax pencil. The levels continued to drop, and Jane was shocked when she realized the vodka vanished at night, when the bar was empty and no one was in the building.

Soon other events began to occur. Glasses started flying across the room and breaking. Drinks disappeared in front of startled customers. Ashtrays spontaneously slid down the bar. Cash registers and other electronic items often behaved erratically or stopped working.

The pub has been remodeled a number of times since 1961, and in each case, Frank has expressed objections. Paranormal activity is observed with some regularity in the area of the bar where Frank died. Today the spot is a booth in the dining area of the pub. Many people who have eaten here complain of a shifting cold spot, and have described feelings of numbness in their legs and feet. Attractive young women who sit in this area or other parts of the bar sometimes encounter a spirit that's a little too friendly! They describe feeling a cold hand touching or brushing up against their skin or clothing and gently

caressing them. Most of the women who've reported these close encounters have been blondes or redheads, and Jane McDougall believed that Frank might be mistaking them for Edna, who was a strawberry blonde.

The haunting has continued here over the years, despite changes in ownership and in the name of the place. Jane McDougall retired from the bar business and passed away in 1996, but Frank still remains, greeting customers from the other side. In his time and place, perhaps little has changed at all, or perhaps the afterlife offers an endless party for Frank and his spectral drinking buddies. So if you make it down to the Ole St. Andrew's Inn one evening, be sure to lift a glass in honor of that playful, inebriated spirit, Frank Giff.

OLE ST. ANDREW'S INN

5938 N. Broadway, Chicago, Illinois 60660

KING'S HAUNTED TAVERN
by Scott A. Johnson

NATCHEZ, MISSISSIPPI, HAS MORE ANTEBELLUM houses and plantations than any other place in the United States. King's Tavern, built in the latter half of the 1700s, is the city's oldest building and a popular destination among tourists looking for an "authentic" experience. You can feast on hickory-smoked prime rib or savory seafood, throw back a few beers, and relax in the pub's casual atmosphere. Don't be alarmed if you hear phantom laughter in the background or notice the lights flickering. It's not your imagination or the beer; it's just Madeline, one of the resident spirits of King's Tavern, making her presence known.

MADELINE

Around 1789 a young woman named Madeline came to work in King's Tavern as a serving girl. Beautiful and flirtatious, she soon caught Richard King's eye, and before long the two engaged in a brief, steamy affair. When King's wife learned of his infidelity, she hired thugs to murder Madeline and disposed of the body herself—the cadaver and murder weapon were bricked into the fireplace in the main room of the tavern.

Until the 1930s the story of Madeline was thought to be purely legend. However, when new owners began renovating the building, they made a grisly discovery. Inside the chimney wall, workers found the mummified remains of *three* bodies—two male corpses and one female.

Following the discovery, people began to notice strange things going on in the tavern. Waiters would find wet footprints across the upstairs floor, and lights would flicker at inopportune moments. Most startling, however, was that the old, out-of-commission fireplace would be warm, as if having been lit. This was the same fireplace in which Madeline and the other two were entombed.

Other eerie phenomena have occurred over the years: sightings of long, flowing shadows that pass through the stairwell, footsteps heard in empty rooms, and guests who experience tightness in their necks and shoulders. Video cameras with fully charged batteries often wind up drained in only a few minutes, and at times still cameras stop working completely, only to resume normal function outside the tavern walls.

Madeline may be the most recognized of the ghosts inhabiting King's Tavern, but she's far from the only one. Many patrons have reported seeing things that are "out of character" for the mischievous ghost—things that seem too aggressive. Dishes may move by her unseen hand, but it is rare for her to throw them. Most occurrences seem to happen at night, starting just before closing time and continuing until staff members arrive the next morning.

EERIE EVIDENCE

In November of 2000 a news crew from Natchez witnessed several flowing shadows without identifiable sources. Many of their cameras mysteriously malfunctioned, one of which did so only while trying to focus on a portrait of Madeline. A woman's voice was captured on tape in an empty bedroom, and one crew member experienced what he described as something dragging down his neck and poking him in the back.

A twenty-degree temperature drop, the most significant phenomena, was recorded in one of the bedrooms. The reporter, who was attempting to take a

61

nap, was shocked when alarms on the temperature sensors went off. She watched as the temperature fell steadily in front of her eyes.

King's Tavern still operates today as a restaurant and tavern and is a popular site on tours of historic Mississippi. They are open year-round, and the employees never seem to mind answering questions about Madeline or any of the other disturbances that occur there. The wait staff has, in fact, grown quite used to the tavern's spectral residents and regards them warmly.

KING'S TAVERN
619 Jefferson Street, Natchez, Mississippi 39120

SPOOKY TIDINGS AT THE OLYMPIC
by Jeff Davis

SHORTLY AFTER THE TURN OF the nineteenth century, Jack Scuitto purchased a burned-out lot in Centralia, Washington, and built the Olympic Club. At first, it was a no-frills men-only joint that catered to mostly lumberjacks and mill workers. Renovations in 1913 saw the addition of a large mahogany bar, Tiffany-style lampshades, and wall mosaics; and in 1916 a café and billiards tables were introduced. In 1972 the club opened its doors to women for the first time and then the McMenamins family purchased, restored, and reopened the Olympic in 1997.

A ghost named Elmer has haunted the historic club since the 1997 reopening. Ominous laughter echoes through the building; doors open and close of their own volition; and lights regularly turn on after they've been shut off for the

evening. McMenamins historian Tim Hills, who remains skeptical about the paranormal, has suggested that in life Elmer may have been Louis Galba, a German butcher who came to Centralia in the early 1900s. He rented a room at the hotel that once stood on the site of the Olympic Club. When the building caught fire, Galba was trapped in his second-floor room. He was badly burned but managed to jump to the ground below, where he broke several bones and sustained severe internal injuries. He was hospitalized for three months before dying. It could be Galba who returns to his ghostly room every night after a hard day's work.

THE OLYMPIC CLUB
112 N. Tower Avenue, Centralia, Washington 98531

BOOGEYMEN AT BRENNAN'S
by Fiona Broome

BREAKFAST AT BRENNAN'S IS A New Orleans tradition. Tourists and local residents flock to Brennan's Restaurant every morning for a perfect meal and an occasional visit from "the other side." Brennan's is in the heart of New Orleans' French Quarter and hosts a number of rather colorful ghosts that appear regularly—even in broad daylight.

Comte Lefleur is one of Brennan's oldest ghosts. According to legend, Lefleur, his new wife, and his college-aged son were visiting New Orleans in the mid-eighteenth century. He rented the spacious brick residence that later became Brennan's. To all, Lefleur appeared to be a mild mannered gentleman—until one sunny spring morning when Lefleur visited several New Orleans merchants to arrange for three funerals and three burials. Upon returning home, he went upstairs to the Red Room, killed his wife and son, and then hung himself from the chandelier.

63

THE FAMILY THAT HAUNTS TOGETHER . . .

Why did Lefleur murder his family? Nobody knows for sure, although some say his new wife and his handsome son were having an affair. Others suggest that Lefleur had been mad for some time.

Today the Red Room serves as one of Brennan's dining areas, and some people sense the presence of Lefleur in the corner of room. He appears as a shadowy figure, about five and a half feet tall and somewhat portly. You may catch a glimpse of him out of the corner of your eye, although the apparition usually vanishes if you look directly at him. The count's shadowy spirit has been observed flying across the room toward his haunted portrait, and the Red Room's gaslights have been known to flicker even when there's no breeze. Comte Lefleur's portrait, which hangs in the restaurant's Red Room, is one of New Orleans' most startling haunted sights. If you stare at the painting, Lefleur's moderate smile

slowly changes to a chilling—and some say evil—grimace. The effect can be very subtle, but it has been captured in photos.

The ghost of the count's wife also visits the Red Room. She remains close to where her portrait is displayed—near the fireplace along the southwest wall of the room—far from her murderous husband. Above the fireplace about a foot away from the wall, visitors detect a "cold spot" that remains about ten degrees colder than the rest of the room, even on a sultry day. Reach toward the spot and you'll feel as if you've reached into a freezer.

The painting of Comte Lefleur's son is haunted as well—his ghost regularly rustles the curtains on either side of his portrait. Some say that the curtains aren't making the noise; rather, the son's ghost is whispering.

ELDERLY ENTITY

Next to the Red Room, the Chanticleer Room hosts another dramatic haunting. In the late twentieth century, four painters intended to work overnight redecorating that room. However, as the evening progressed, one of the men was drawn to a window at the southeast corner. Looking out, he saw a grotesque face looking back at him. It appeared to be an old woman floating in midair outside the second-floor window.

The painter's coworkers saw him stumble away from the window and dashed to see what had frightened him. They too saw the menacing face and stepped back in horror. The ghost followed them, thrusting her face through the closed window and then chasing the workmen across the room. All four men raced downstairs and broke through two sets of locked doors to the street outside. They never returned to Brennan's—but the ghostly old woman never left.

The elderly woman's spirit has been observed outside the Chanticleer Room. Some even claim to have seen the ghost strolling the corridors late at night and describe her as five feet tall and dressed in a dark gown that almost reaches the floor. She's been called a cheerful spirit and no one knows why the painters angered her.

Visitors have also witnessed a paranormal distortion where her ghost appears. Standing near the entrance to the Chanticleer Room facing the wall at the back of the enclosed walkway, many describe seeing the surroundings twist slightly, as if seen through a fun house mirror. The strange visual effect often leaves observers feeling disoriented, and many have had to look away or place a hand on a wall to steady themselves.

CHEF BLANGÉ'S GHOST

Two other ghosts have been reported at Brennan's. One is believed to be the ghost of a slave and has been observed in the spacious two-story aboveground wine cellar, which in the eighteenth century served as slaves' quarters. The second is Brennan's most popular ghost, Chef Paul Blangé, who invented many of the restaurant's signature dishes, including Bananas Foster. Blangé achieved international fame for his outstanding meals and was well loved and respected by Brennan's owners and patrons. He often visited the dining rooms to greet the restaurant's guests and make certain that they were pleased with their meals.

After many years, Chef Blangé was diagnosed with cancer. As his health deteriorated, he was no longer able to work in the kitchen. However, his loyalty to Brennan's was such that he continued to supervise the kitchen and often sat at the restaurant's entrance dressed in his white chef's uniform greeting guests as they arrived. When Chef Blangé died in 1977, no one was surprised when staff and visitors began seeing his ghost around the restaurant. In fact, the chef's ghost stops by frequently, and Brennan's regulars look for him just inside the front door or strolling through the dining room.

The most reliable way to summon the chef's ghost is to order Bananas Foster. While the bananas cook at your table, glance around the room for the chef's translucent figure or look over your server's shoulder. The chef sometimes manifests as a brief sparkle. Or you may see just a slight distortion, similar to heat rising from a road in summer, in the shape of a man in a chef's hat.

Brennan's is known for world-class dining and fascinating ghosts. No matter where you're seated, you're never far from spirits of one kind or another.

BRENNAN'S RESTAURANT

417 Royal Street, New Orleans, Louisiana 70130

TIME STOPS AT THE ELEVATOR
by James A. Willis

FOR NEARLY A HUNDRED YEARS, it was perpetually 10:05 on North High Street in Columbus, Ohio—at least according to the old broken clock in front of the Elevator Restaurant. Rumor has it that the clock froze at the exact moment of a horrible murder that took place in 1909.

In 1909 Columbus was well on its way to becoming a booming metropolis. North High Street was home to all sorts of businesses, including several restaurants and taverns. One of the most popular was Bott Brothers' Billiards, located at 161 N. High Street. According to legend, one of the Bott brothers' regulars was Colonel Pritchard. He was well liked by the male patrons but also had a reputation as a womanizer prone to fits of rage. Those who knew the colonel could see that he was traveling down a dark road, and on a cold February night in 1909, that road hit a dead end in the entrance to Bott Brothers' Billiards. On that fateful night, Colonel Pritchard was just about to enter the establishment when he was stabbed several times by an unknown assailant. As the colonel staggered into the building and fell to the floor, the assailant ran off and disappeared into the dark night.

Billiards patrons tried to save the colonel, but his wounds were severe and he bled to death within minutes. Trying to locate the attacker, several others ran out into the street, following footprints in the snow that led away from the location of the attack . . . but then abruptly vanished. Upon returning to Bott Brothers, the patrons noticed that the clock outside the building had mysteriously stopped at 10:05, the exact time of the attack.

Since the colonel died almost instantly, he never had the chance to tell anyone if he recognized his assailant. A few patrons thought they saw a woman fleeing the scene, which led to the story that a former lover had murdered the colonel. An investigation ensued, but other than the footprints leading away from the crime scene, no other evidence was ever recovered.

As for the clock outside of Bott Brothers' Billiards, several attempts were made to fix it. A few times they were successful—at least initially. Repairmen dismantled the clock, found nothing wrong with it, and put it back together again. It would work for a period, but eventually the hands would stop, always at 10:05. Finally, the owners gave up and left the hands frozen at 10:05.

When the building reopened in 2000 as the Elevator Brewery and Draught Haus, the clock was taken down and totally remodeled, which seemed to do the trick. The hands of the new clock worked until recently, when the clock and its post were removed and the posthole cemented over. The clock is gone for good but the haunts remain.

A few phantoms haunt the Elevator, the first of which is believed to be the ghost of Colonel Pritchard himself. The colonel's ghost is rarely seen; most times, it is simply felt. People in the restaurant have reported feeling as if they are being watched, especially when they are downstairs near the antique billiard tables. When his ghost does make an appearance, he does so as a bright ball of light that moves through the restaurant.

67

The second ghost is thought to be Colonel Pritchard's unknown murderer. The assailant's ghost is rarely seen and never enters the restaurant. However, on certain nights—especially on the anniversary of the colonel's murder and if there is snow on the ground—ghostly footprints leading from the building's entrance appear in the snow. To this day, all attempts to follow the footprints have ended abruptly, just as they did in February 1909.

ELEVATOR BREWERY AND DRAUGHT HAUS

161 N. High Street, Columbus, Ohio 43215

ASHLEY'S HAUNTS
by Charlie Carlson

OVER THE LAST SEVERAL DECADES, an endless number of ghostly events have been reported at Ashley's Restaurant in Rockledge, Florida. And although strange things happen throughout the building, the paranormal pranksters seem to have an affinity for the ladies' restroom.

Sandwiched in a narrow strip between U.S. 1 and the Florida East Coast railroad tracks, this two-story, half-timbered, Tudor-style eatery looks much like an old English pub. It first opened in 1933 as Jack's Tavern, an upscale, coat-and-tie dining spot that featured steak dinners for a buck and the first jukebox in Brevard County. In 1946, it became Cooney's Tavern, followed by a string of name changes: The Mad Duchess, The Loose Caboose, The Sparrow Hawk, Gentleman Jim's, and for the last twenty years, Ashley's Restaurant.

"I know the place is haunted," insists J.S., a former employee. "I worked there when I was eighteen, in the kitchen. Things were always jumping off the shelf and breaking. One time a knife flew across the kitchen like somebody threw it, but nobody was there but me and the cook."

Ashley's has a long record of poltergeist-type occurrences, everything from dishes flinging across the kitchen, to lights turning off and on, to windows opening and closing by themselves. One patron recalled having dinner with her husband when the window suddenly opened. "The waitress came over, closed the window, and latched it. A few minutes later that window flew open again. What was really weird is that we never touched it; it just unlocked itself."

That's not as bad as the woman who came running out of the ladies' room, screaming, "The toilet exploded!" When the manager went to check, sure enough the commode was in pieces. Other women have seen images in the restroom mirror of a young girl dressed in roaring-twenties clothing, and there have been several instances of the toilet tissue spinning wildly off the roll.

Ashley's

Rockledge, Fla.

SINCE 1985
DINNER MENU
636-6430

68

Lynn, a bartender, related how she was fixing her hair in the ladies' room when the faucets suddenly turned on. In other instances, the water faucets would reverse, with hot water coming from the cold and vice versa. After closing one night, a former manager noticed a pair of legs, wearing old-fashioned high-button shoes, beneath one of the stall doors in the ladies' room. Upon checking, she found no one in the stall. The legs had vanished.

The strange restaurant has attracted several ghost hunters, as well as television crews looking for a good, haunted story. In 1998, filmmaker Ryan Lewis went there to shoot a documentary titled *Paranormal Florida*, only to find that something kept draining his batteries. Other TV crews have reported malfunctioning equipment and cameras capturing unexplainable images. When the famed psychic Sybil Leek visited the place with a film crew in 1993, she reportedly experienced "extreme cold bursts of air" and "sensed an unseen presence in one of the dining rooms." During the same time, a television crew allegedly witnessed a chair levitate from the floor, rotate in midair, and then move across the dining room.

In 1980, after the restaurant had closed for the night, the police responded to a disturbance at Ashley's to find the office looking like the aftermath of a hurricane. Books and papers were thrown about and the safe was standing wide open—with cash in it—but nothing was missing. The incident was written up as "suspicious."

Several spirits share the blame for haunting this fine restaurant. One account has the place haunted by a girl killed in an auto accident out on the highway. Another insists a boy was killed on the railroad tracks out back, and still others claim the building sits on an old Indian burial mound or the site of a burned-down depot. However, research of old newspapers and local history has failed to substantiate these theories.

ETHEL

"We used to call the ghost Sarah," recalls Jen B., a former waitress when the place was under another name. But according to historical documentation, Ashley's may be haunted by Ethel Allen, who was allegedly murdered in the storeroom—now the ladies' restroom.

Indeed, an old newspaper account revealed that in 1934, the partly decomposed, nude mutilated body of a girl was found in the Indian River near Eau Gallie, about thirteen miles south of the restaurant. She was identified as Ethel

69

Allen, a nineteen-year-old waitress who lived at a local boarding house. The 1930 census indicates that Ethel Allen came from a family of eleven siblings. When medium Susan Thompson was asked by the author to contact Ethel in the afterlife, the only name to pop up was "Bernice." This was chilling, because without knowledge of the census document, Susan had no way of knowing that Ethel's closest sister was named Bernice!

Ethel's picture hangs in one of Ashley's dining rooms, but her murder remains unsolved. Although there's no evidence suggesting she was killed in the storeroom, in 1934 the establishment, then called Jack's Tavern, was owned by Jack Allen—possibly a relative of the murdered girl. Ethel Allen's spirit may still linger in the shadows of Ashley's, but her body is in a simple grave marked by a homemade tombstone in the Crooked Mile Road Cemetery across the Indian River on Merritt Island. If you think Ashley's management is bothered by the ghostly happenings, you'd be wrong. They've learned to live with it, and include a brief story of it on the back of their menu.

70

ASHLEY'S Of ROCKLEDGE

1609 U.S. Highway 1, Rockledge, Florida 32955

OUR GHOSTLY PUBLICK
by Joanne Austin

THE PUBLICK HOUSE IS A venerable landmark that sits on Main Street in Chester, New Jersey. Built in 1810 by Zephaniah Drake, the building has served in a number of different capacities over the years. According to the book *Chester: Then and Now* by historian Joan Case, it was "the place to buy stagecoach tickets for the trip to New York and a favorite stop for refreshment and a change of horses." And like many old buildings that have seen an almost constant stream of humanity, the Publick House may have a few ghosts.

Paul Viggiano was one of a group of investors who bought the building in 2005. As the coordinator for the investors, Paul was in the building almost constantly, often alone, from January to September of that year. Being involved in every aspect of the renovations, he got to know the building—and possibly some otherworldly residents—very well.

Paul had worked at the Publick House as a teenager, and as an owner he was eager to learn about the building's history. In addition to being an inn, he found, the building had served as a brothel and a private boys' school at different times. There were also rumors that the house had been built on an Indian burial ground and that it had been the site of "a dozen murders" and "several hangings" in the backyard, as well as one in the foyer of a ten-year-old girl accused of being a witch.

According to another rumor, Zephaniah Drake murdered his first and second wives, one of whom was possibly buried downstairs. This is a pretty intense way to acquire a ghost or two, so *Weird Encounters* did some research. We could find no such murderous history at the local library, and according to *Chester, New Jersey: A Scrapbook of History* by Frances Greenidge, if Drake wasn't an upstanding citizen, he did a good job of hiding it. He was not only the innkeeper but also "proprietor of the first line of stagecoaches on the Washington Turnpike." The book also contains an old news item saying Drake participated in a posse that brought a robber back to Chester from the Philadelphia area. Another source, *History of Morris County N.J. 1739-1882*, published by W. W. Munsell, states that Drake was a justice of the peace from 1829 to 1834.

Zephaniah did have two wives, according to information found on a genealogy Web site. The first, Ruth Fairclo, was the daughter of the man who sold Zephaniah the property on which the Publick House was built. She was born the same year as Zephaniah and died shortly before her thirty-seventh birthday, in 1825. They had three children: Phoebe (1808-1809), Isaiah (1812-1839), and Elizabeth (1818-1834). Zephaniah's second wife was Martha Halsey, whose birth and death dates were not listed. Was murder involved in either wife's death?

Weird Encounters asked historian André Verge to clarify some of the more fantastic rumors about the Publick House. André has done Haunted Chester ghost tours for many years, and while he agreed the Publick House is spooky, to his knowledge there were no hangings or murders there. He said that when Zephaniah Drake built the original house in 1810, his mother might have been angry with him for putting a drinking establishment close to the churches in town. She wouldn't let up on him about it, and many think her spirit is haunting the place. Some say *she* is buried on the property, beneath what is now the parking lot.

ORBS AND ECTOPLASM

Regardless of how the ghostly inhabitants got there, Paul Viggiano's first experiences occurred after a contractor convinced the investors to take down the two wings and leave the main structure intact. One Sunday, Paul went upstairs to turn off the heat. Something didn't feel quite right, and when he turned to look at the stairs, he observed a bright white orb approaching him. Paul carried a digital camera with him at all times to keep track of construction progress and room contents, and he used it to catch a photo of the orb. The orb does appear to be moving, and it is unique in that most orbs don't show up until after the photo is taken.

There are many other photos that Paul and friends captured throughout the building, some showing orbs, others showing non-orb entities, such as various faces that appear in the wood molding of a doorframe or in window glass. But perhaps the best ghost photo in the bunch shows what looks like ectoplasm forming part of a face. Paul agreed. "That's in the front of the building. Something made me turn around and take the shot."

One bright, sunny Saturday afternoon, Paul heard chairs rumbling in the Tap Room, "which was the original old part of the hotel and the barroom." Alarmed, he left the building. It was the first time the ghosts had chased him out. He came back a few hours later with two friends: a priest and K. C. Daniel, the proprietor of a coffee shop (and former coffin shop!) in town. "All of the tables and chairs were upside down, all on top of one another . . . which was insane, I thought. And then they had—against the wall where the bar used to be—six chairs lined up, and two chairs facing them, as if they were having some sort of an interrogation."

A few of the more bizarre aspects of the haunting occurred upstairs in a room that Paul and his friends referred to as the Bible Room, because of an old Bible placed on a dresser in the room. "Every time I walked past it," Paul said, "the dresser would be pulled away from the wall." He'd frequently push it back in place. The room was always about twenty degrees colder than the rest of the building, and it "reeked of perfume," even though nobody had been in the room for more than a year.

One day, Paul, K.C., and local historian Joan Case toured the building, including the Bible Room. The dresser was—as usual—pulled away from the wall, so they pushed it back into place. At the time, K.C. "knew nothing about the history of the place," just that strange things had been happening there. While Paul and Joan talked, K.C. noticed the Bible. "It had been opened up to a page, and I decided to take a look to see if there was anything significant" in the words. But nothing jumped out at her, so she turned the Bible to another random page and left it on the dresser.

The three returned downstairs and continued to talk about the building's history. It was then that K.C. first heard the name Zephaniah Drake along with the wife-murdering rumors. According to Paul, K.C. asked them to repeat the original owner's name, and when they did, K.C. "just lost it."

K.C. recounts what happened next. "I ran upstairs, opened the door, and first of all, the dresser was moved out again—we had just moved it in. And the Bible I had opened was turned to page 911, and on the right-hand side, right up on the very top, it said 'Zephaniah' in big, black letters." Paul and K.C. have different theories about the message being from Zephaniah or his wife, but regardless, K.C. said the overall feeling she got from the room was ". . . peaceful. It smelled of perfume, and it was comfortable."

74

Other Ghosts

Paul and K.C. experienced other ghostly events at the Publick House. Some were minor and occurred frequently, like a vacuum that moved by itself down the hallway and a basement door that opened every time they entered the restroom. Another door would always open into the kitchen, even when there was no wind or other cause for it doing so.

On Mother's Day, Paul arrived at work, put his coffee down at his workstation, and made a quick trip to the restroom before turning on the lights. Upon returning, he said the lights were already on, "and it started smelling like toast."

Toast?

"When I was sixteen, I was the bagel boy, buttering the toast and the bagels right at that spot in the foyer. And since it was Mother's Day, maybe (the ghosts) felt sorry for me that I was late in seeing my mom. I had several hours of work to do, and that was kind of nice."

Historian André Verge shared the story of a woman who had worked at the Publick House as a waitress in the bar. It was late, and she was waiting for a young couple to finish so she could clean up. They left the room, and she briefly followed them out, but as she left she saw three men in business suits at the bar—each with a mug of beer—out of the corner of her eye. Thinking she had three more people to see out before she could finish up, she returned to the bar, only to find it empty. No men in suits. Just three empty beer mugs on the bar. They couldn't have left without her seeing them.

When the upstairs was a B and B, guests reported hearing noises in rooms next to them that were not occupied. Ghostly incidents seemed to occur most frequently in rooms 204 and 205. André Verge had two experiences involving Room 205, which was supposedly Zephaniah's mother's room. In the first, he had a rare chance to show a tour group the room, and while they were there, they heard somebody running around upstairs in the attic. They took a peek in the attic and saw kid-sized footprints in the dust on the attic floor.

A second time, André and his wife were at the Publick House, talking with a former owner about the building's history. The three went upstairs to room 205 while André's wife waited in the hallway to make sure that if anything ghostly happened, nobody was playing tricks. André and the owner both heard the door in the room slam shut and went back out into the hallway, where André's wife reported that the door had slammed shut by itself.

The three headed downstairs. It was a hot day, and very hot inside the building. Despite this, André's wife reached a step and said she was freezing cold. When André stood on the step with her, he felt a noticeable drop in temperature. The three quickly walked down the rest of the stairs.

Paul's partnership was never solid, and the investors disagreed on many aspects of the business. Both Paul and K.C. said that the spirits in the house knew that the group wasn't the right one to make the Publick House a success again. They feel that the current owners, who left the two wings on the building and want to create a more family-oriented business, are more to the spirits' liking. The Publick House was reopened in 2006, and you can legitimately enjoy its history—haunted and not—as a restaurant patron. Let us know if you can smell the toast.

75

PUBLICK HOUSE RESTAURANT AND INN
111 Main Street, Chester, New Jersey 07930

PARANORMAL PERFORMANCES AT LINCOLN SQUARE THEATRE
by Troy Taylor

THE LINCOLN SQUARE THEATRE, LOCATED on North Main Street in downtown Decatur, Illinois, is a labyrinth of a theater, with a sprawling stage, mezzanine and balcony levels, basements, and subcellars. It holds many secrets in its twists and turns, and according to some, many ghosts as well.

The theater was not the first building to stand on the site that it occupies. It was originally home to the Priest Hotel, opened in 1860. The hotel went through several ownership and name changes over time, finally becoming the Decatur & Arcade Hotel. Fire destroyed the hotel twice. The first fire was in 1904, but the hotel was rebuilt on the same site. The second fire, on April 21, 1915, was bigger. It damaged surrounding structures and killed a number of people. A few bodies were recovered from the ruins, but many were not. Many wonder if the fire victims' spirits lurk in the dark corners of the Lincoln Square Theatre.

Built in the wake of the ill-fated hotel, the Lincoln Theater's design included private seating boxes, massive ivory-colored columns, and 1,346 seats—all of which offered a splendid view and wonderful acoustics. The new theater was also fireproofed: Boilers were housed in a different building, a thick firewall was built surrounding the theater, and burn-resistant interior features were incorporated.

Silent movies, and then talkies, slowly replaced the stage shows and vaudeville acts of the Lincoln's early days. The theater was leased to different movie theater

chains over the years until December 1980, when the last chain lost its lease. After that, the Lincoln closed down, only opening occasionally for live music and poorly attended events. By 1990 the building was in a state of disrepair, abandoned except for the bats and pigeons that had taken up residence in the auditorium.

Thankfully the Lincoln Square Theatre is being restored. It still has a long way to go, but that hasn't stopped local and national acts from performing there, and show goers often encounter things that can only be described as well beyond the ordinary!

One-Armed Red

Stories have circulated about hauntings at the Lincoln Square Theatre since at least the 1930s. The most famous ghost is rooted in a legend from the vaudeville days. A stagehand named Red was deeply attached to the Lincoln, working long shifts and even coming to the theater on his day off to be among the actors and entertainers. A commanding presence with bright auburn hair, Red dreamed of becoming a performer himself, it was said, but he was simply too quiet and shy to ever take the stage. He thus contented himself to working behind the scenes.

One night during a performance, Red was working on the catwalks some seventy-five feet above the stage. He was accustomed to working at such dizzying heights, but on that fateful night, he slipped from the metal grid work and plunged downward. As he fell, his arm snagged on a pin rail, a sharp hook jutting from a piece of equipment, and was torn from his body. Red landed on the stage in a bloody heap, his arm still tangled on the rail overhead. He died moments later and Red's ghost has haunted his beloved theater ever since.

At least that's what the stories say. The truth behind the tale isn't nearly as exciting. There really was a stagehand nicknamed Red who worked at the Lincoln Square Theatre during its vaudeville days. Red had only one arm, but he did not lose it (or his life) in a horrific theater accident; rather, he lost it in combat during World War I. When he returned to Decatur, he took a job as a stagehand at the Lincoln and did all of his work with one arm. In fact, despite his disability, he was faster than many of the other stagehands at pulling the ropes and lowering the lights. Red was likable and completely devoted to the theater. This was perhaps the reason later generations of staff members remembered him as the "stagehand who never left."

Although Red wasn't killed as the result of a terrible accident, he did die at the Lincoln. One afternoon in 1927 he sat down to take a nap after his lunch and simply passed away in his sleep. When people began to speak of a ghost at the Lincoln Square Theater, they immediately assumed that it was Red.

Over the years, dozens of witnesses have reported strange sounds and footsteps in the otherwise empty theater—sounds that can't be explained away as acoustics. They have also reported whispers, strange voices, and even a shadowy apparition in the theater's balcony. However, this strange figure is not Red but rather a woman in a long, old-fashioned dress.

The Haunted Staircase

Countless reports of ghostly encounters suggest that an entire legion of phantoms haunts the Lincoln Square Theatre. Witnesses describe brushes with hazy forms and figures seen out of the corner of the eye, but none of those descriptions match! In addition to visual sightings, footsteps, and sounds, there have been inexplicable cold chills in certain spots of the building and claims of being touched by unseen hands. Several people say they've seen empty theater seats actually raise and lower, as if an unseen audience was watching the proceedings on the stage.

The haunted hot spot of the theater is the metal spiral staircase located in the back corner of the stage. Countless unexplained incidents have occurred on and around the staircase. During a 1994 performance, an actor was in the back corner changing his costume when he heard a voice whispering to him. He looked up and saw a shadowy figure on the steps. Although unable to describe the figure, he was convinced it was a man and so notified a staff member about what he saw. When they checked the staircase, it was empty—the man had vanished.

I personally had a supernatural encounter on this staircase one evening in October 1995. I was in the theater with a reporter and cameraman from a local television station. After an interview about the hauntings, I joined the cameraman, Robert Buchwald, for a trip up the spiral staircase, leaving the reporter down on the stage by herself. He took his camera along, hoping to film the theater's stage from this vantage point. It was a good thing that he brought it, because it was our only source of light.

The trip up the staircase seemed innocent enough at first. After we had climbed to the top, we soon heard the reporter's hard-soled shoes echoing on the metal steps as she followed us up the stairs. Realizing that we had the only portable light and that the staircase was quite dark, Robert leaned over the railing with the camera so the reporter would have some light to see by. Just as he did this, we heard a voice calling out to us from the stage. We looked and saw the reporter standing in the middle of the stage, dozens of feet from the base of the steps and much too far away to have been climbing the staircase just moments before!

The footsteps on the staircase had not belonged to the reporter. So, who was following us up the stairs? We didn't know, but when the sound finally stopped, we didn't stay up there long enough to find out. The eerie encounter was enough to convince a skeptic like Robert Buchwald that there may be more to the Lincoln Square Theatre than meets the eye!

Does the ghost of One-Armed Red really roam the dark corners and back hallways of the Lincoln Square Theatre? Or is he just a legend created to explain the generations of strange phenomena reported there? Is the theater home to a host of restless spirits that are somehow drawn to the building's tragic history? And most important, is the Lincoln Square Theatre really haunted at all?

I challenge skeptics to wait before answering these questions. Ponder them until some night when you have the opportunity to visit the theater and sit in the dark auditorium . . . by yourself. Listen. What do you hear? Are those the sounds of an old building settling in the shadows behind you or something else, perhaps not of this world?

LINCOLN SQUARE THEATRE

145 N. Main Street, Decatur, Illinois 62523

TRUCK STOP TERRORS
by Greg Myers

ON OLD ROUTE 66, AT the fork of Old Highway 100 and Highway AT in Villa Ridge, Missouri, is a historic landmark. Originally established as a fruit stand by Spencer Groff, by 1927 the site had become the Diamonds Restaurant, touted as "the world's largest roadside restaurant." In 1947 the restaurant burned down and Groff turned the business over to one of his longtime employees, who built the brick building that stands on the site today. Route 66 brought much prosperity to the Diamonds, but the completion of the interstates in the 1960s drew cars away from Route 66 and the businesses lining its sides. A new Diamonds was erected near the interstate in 1968, and the old icon was sold, becoming the Tri-County Restaurant and Truck Stop.

Employees and customers at Tri-County experienced a slew of eerie brushes with the paranormal during the 1960s and 1970s. In the 1980s and 1990s, employees became afraid to go into the basement after they witnessed mysterious shadowy figures and small objects moving on their own. The new millennium brought sightings of a translucent, ghostly man wearing a plaid shirt, unlocked doors that wouldn't open, and objects moving on the tables while customers were dining. When children started to report seeing a ghostly man and a bloody woman, a call was made to the Missouri Paranormal Research Society.

The ghostly residents quickly introduced themselves to the paranormal team. While they were dining, a full coffee pot levitated in midair behind the counter before crashing to the floor. That night, investigative meters acted erratically, temperatures fluctuated, and mysterious voices were captured on tape. Tom, the team photographer, captured one of the ghostly residents on film while in the men's bathroom, and his subject retaliated by later manifesting beside someone else using the urinal, causing the man to urinate on his own shoe. And in a subsequent investigation, the team had both a sixty-watt incandescent lightbulb and a rusty butcher knife thrown at them while in the basement.

Tri-County Restaurant and Truck Stop finally closed its doors, and it's now another faded memory along Old Route 66, vacant of the living. . .

TRI-COUNTY RESTAURANT AND TRUCK STOP

100 Old Highway 100, Villa Ridge, Missouri 63089
(Location closed at last check)

SPECTRAL SOUNDS
AT THE CRYSTAL BALLROOM
by Jeff Davis

THE TURN OF THE NINETEENTH century was not an easy time to open a dance hall in Portland, Oregon. There was a growing negative view of modern dancing and music (as well as liquor), and in 1913 a local women's suffragette coalition prevailed upon the city to pass temperance and anti-dance ordinances and to hire regulators to moderate all dance halls located within Portland.

But Montrose Ringler, a dance instructor in the area, was determined to buck this trend. His clients were wealthy and not willing to venture to the less-than-savory part of town in which his current dance school was located. He eventually convinced Paul Van Fridagh, the owner of property at the intersection of Northwest 14th Avenue and West Burnside Street, to build a large dance hall, music school, and society center on the site, and in January 1914, Cotillion Hall opened for business.

One of the hall's major attractions was the floating dance floor, made from a layer of maple planks that were laid on top of a series of wooden rocker panels. Ball bearings were attached to the ends of the rockers, which added a gentle swaying motion to the whole floor when people danced. The rocking motion

could be adjusted by a series of ratchet gears to enhance the floating motion for several different dances. The floor, which is sturdy yet creaky, may be the only one of its kind left in the United States.

Ringler sold his lease in 1921, and after Van Fridagh died in 1925, the building fell into disrepair. It was renamed the Crystal Ballroom in 1950 but had a hard time competing with newer, larger venues for popular bands. It didn't help that there were several dead spots located throughout the building where patrons had a hard time hearing the band play—a result of the building's asymmetrical construction.

81

It was closed as a music venue from 1968 until 1997, when the McMenamins chain purchased the facility and brought it back to life. At least, parts of it.

In 1998, manager Ed Lawrence and another employee were working late in the staff offices on the second floor (one floor down from the dance floor). Ed heard a noise from outside the room and looked up to see a man walking in the hallway heading toward his office. When he went to investigate, as it was late and nobody else was supposed to be in the building, he found no one in the hallway.

The hallway extended another twelve feet or so before ending at three offices and an exit door—all of which were supposed to be closed and locked. Ed walked down the hallway and checked to make sure the offices were locked and empty. They were. Ed returned to his office looking puzzled and pale. After explaining to his coworker what had happened, they decided to call it a night and promptly left the building.

82 GHOSTLY INTRUDERS

Christmas Eve 1998 was not a good night for Ed, either. While entertaining company at his home, he received a call from the Crystal Ballroom's security company. The burglar alarms had gone off, and Ed had to drive through the snow to check out the building.

When he arrived, Ed walked up to the second floor to where another set of stairs led to the ballroom's main entrance. He wanted to surprise any intruders, so he walked to the management offices, grabbed a flashlight, and then went up the performers' stairwell. He quietly let himself into the ballroom through a door in the back. There was no one there.

Ed then walked through the ballroom and headed down the main stairs to the second floor. He paused at the foot of the stairs for a moment, searching his pockets for his keys. Suddenly he heard voices talking loudly at the top of the stairs he had just come down. Then he heard their footsteps and voices grow fainter as if they were walking farther away. Ed believes there was no way a group of people could have followed him across the entire length of the dance floor without his hearing them. Having walked across the creaking floating floor myself, I'd have to agree.

Whether the intruders were ghosts or thrill seekers, there were too many of them for Ed's tastes, so he left. The following morning he checked the building and found everything in its place.

A Spirited Fete

More than a few other employees have been in the ballroom after hours and heard someone walking across the floating floor. On one occasion, an employee sitting in the mezzanine heard what sounded like a heavy book or box dropping on the ballroom floor. Again, no one was there.

Even the elevator seems to have a mind of its own. After a show, it can take several hours to break down the stage, and a band's roadies and the ballroom employees are usually packing things up until three A.M. Moving equipment outside involves several elevator trips down, and there have been occasions when roadies have unloaded the elevator, only to watch as its doors close and it travels back up to the third floor without any passengers—at least living ones.

During the winter of 1998, one of the assistant managers was using the men's room on the second floor. The ballroom was empty and quiet, but he could hear what sounded like people talking and laughing in Ringler's Annex, a pub located directly below the restroom on the first floor. He went downstairs to investigate and walked into a very quiet pub. There were only a few customers nursing their drinks, and he could clearly hear music playing over the pub's stereo system.

The employee asked the bartender if there had been a party there a few minutes prior to his arrival, but there hadn't been. He returned to his office shaking his head. Perhaps it was his imagination . . . or perhaps he heard the sounds of a party from earlier times, trapped in the walls of the building, just waiting for a quiet night to replay the revelry.

83

CRYSTAL BALLROOM

1332 W. Burnside Street, Portland, Oregon 97209

HISTORIC
HAUNTS

"The place is haunted. Eat your gumbo." —Polly to a customer at the Cayenne Moon in Memphis, Tennessee

HIGH GAS PRICES ARE making the family car trip a ghost itself. They still happen—albeit shorter in distance—and sometimes involve an educational stop to add value to the journey. But it's tough to get jazzed up about learning while vacationing. That's when you can drop the P-bomb: "Hey, know what I hear about *that place*? It has *ghosts*!"

P-bomb, as in "paranormal," you see. Now an educational pit stop is suddenly an adventure, or at least worth a leg stretch. And we've got a hodgepodge of haunted history in this chapter. There's the ghost of a little girl playing on a staircase at a Louisiana estate, and a different kind of "Big House" at a living history village in New Jersey, complete with a trickster ghost. In North Dakota, the Custer House and its surrounds offer ghosts of a tragic conflict between two nations.

Alas, a few historic sites can only be appreciated in walk- or drive-by mode for now: a house in Florida with a red-clad (dead) butler, and two homes with Civil War connections—one in Wisconsin holds a military collection, where the ghost seems to follow a tin cup, and another in Virginia that's home to a deceased but well-shod colonel. We've also got walking ghost tours. There's no guarantee you'll see a ghost, but we've got stories from two such tours where people have experienced bone-chilling brushes with the supernatural: the touch of a cold and unseen spirit during a town walk in Georgia, and an array of entertaining and educational encounters in Memphis, Tennessee.

Buckle those seat belts, and don't let gas prices get you down. This chapter has P-bombs aplenty and genuine ghouls standing by to greet you at the gates of our favorite historic haunts.

HAUNTED HOUMAS HOUSE
by Fiona Broome

At Houmas House in Darrow, Louisiana, the dead walk in plain sight among the living. From the majestic front gates to the cupola on top, this pre–Civil War mansion hosts ghosts who act as if they have every right to be there. Between its grand, turbulent history and its wide array of daytime ghosts, the house isn't just the "crown jewel of River Road," but a rich, profoundly haunted site for ghost hunters.

Built by Alexander Latil in the late eighteenth century on land purchased from Houma Indians, ownership of the aptly named Houmas House changed many times over the last two hundred years. In 1825, Col. John Preston acquired the property and expanded the original four-room house to accommodate his growing family. Colonel Preston, his wife, and their eight children spent many happy years at the house and then tragedy struck—one of the young girls passed away suddenly. Soon after, the grieving family moved to South Carolina and never returned.

The home's next owner was Irish immigrant John Burnside, who tripled the size of the Houmas House plantation lands to more than 300,000 acres, becoming the largest sugar planter in the South. Claiming British citizenship—Ireland was part of Great Britain in the 1860s—Burnside protected Houmas House from attack during the Civil War as Union soldiers burned many neighboring plantations. Burnside died a bachelor, and the house passed to Col. William Porcher Miles, a statesman and a Civil War legend who created the Confederate battle flag (the ubiquitous Confederate flag adopted in 1863, even though it was overlooked in favor of the "Stars and Bars" in 1861). Colonel Miles also lost a young daughter at Houmas House; she died unexpectedly at age seven and was buried in the family cemetery, in sight of the plantation home. However, in 1927 the Mississippi flooded its banks and displaced all the coffins in the family plot, dragging them to the river's watery depths. None of the bodies were ever recovered.

Since then, Houmas House has been as famous for its ghosts as for its magnificent antebellum architecture, furnishings, and gardens. The home's elegant and eerie setting may be why Hollywood producers filmed the classic 1964 horror movie *Hush . . . Hush, Sweet Charlotte* there. Enthralled by the ghostly legends surrounding this estate, the movie's star, Bette Davis, slept in Houmas House's most haunted room.

87

THE GHOSTLY GIRL

The room in which Davis stayed was once a nursery. Over the years, visitors to the Houmas House have reported seeing the ghost of a little girl appear as a reflection in the mirror or glass surfaces around the room and claim that the apparition disappeared when they tried to look at it directly. The ghostly girl, described as being less than five feet tall with shoulder-length light brown or dark blond hair, has also been spotted (and photographed) on a staircase that adjoins the room. In 2003, sightings of the little girl spiked when the current owner, Kevin Kelly, began restoring the house. On many occasions, workmen on

site reported seeing a little girl playing on the freestanding staircase at the end of a first-floor hall.

Witnesses say the young ghost wears a dark, old-fashioned dress and hides one of her arms, as if trying to conceal a disfigurement. Nevertheless, those who have encountered her claim she is a cheerful and pleasant entity. Who is this young spirit? Some say she is the ghost of John Preston's daughter, while others believe the apparition is of William Porcher Miles's young girl. No one knows for sure.

GHOULS AT THE GATE

I had a few otherworldly encounters of my own at Houmas House. The morning after an overnight stay at the house as part of a public relations tour, I saw a stout ghoul walking ahead of me. I followed him up a steep flight of stairs to the widow's walk, but I had to be mindful of my own steps and saw only his black, polished boots and crisp navy blue trousers a few feet in front of me. When I reached the widow's walk, I circled a few times looking around for the man, and was surprised to find that I was alone.

The stocky ghost has also been spotted standing at the railing atop Houmas House. He may be John Burnside, looking for Yankee ships on the river. However, some say the man is in uniform, and thus more likely to be Colonels Preston or Miles. This ghost appears at dawn, but he is also seen as late as eleven A.M., and again around dusk.

In addition to the stout ghoul, the ghost of a tall, slender black man may greet you at the historic main gate of Houmas House. Clad in simple, dark clothing and described as well over six feet tall, the ghost is always seen pacing—back and forth, over and over again—as if waiting for someone. I myself saw him as I looked down from the widow's walk encircling the house's cupola. He looked up at me, paused, nodded, and then resumed pacing at the gate. If he hadn't simply vanished after a few minutes, I'd have thought he was another visitor, or someone who worked at the house. The tall, pacing man can be seen in a picture displayed at Houmas House and some say his ghost appeared briefly in *Hush . . . Hush, Sweet Charlotte.*

APPARITIONS EVERYWHERE

If you tour the house, especially on foggy or rainy days, look out the windows on the upper floors. From there, you may see the shadowy outlines of Civil War soldiers gazing toward Houmas House. Approximately 250,000 Confederate soldiers died defending the flag that Colonel Miles created, and this historic connection may be why Houmas House's ghostly activity increases around April 9, the anniversary of the Confederate Army surrender. The soldiers are most often reported outside the fence, along the road by the river.

Some visitors sense ghosts in the oldest part of Houmas House. Latil's original eighteenth-century home—now the rear wing of the mansion—has been converted into a gourmet restaurant, Latil's Landing Restaurant. Café Burnside, another eatery on the property, was once part of a cotton warehouse. Today, visitors sip mint juleps and remark about "something odd"—and perhaps

ghostly—overhead. Nearby, especially around dusk, look for a ghostly figure at the doorway of Houmas House's wine cellars. At one time a water cistern, the building was recently converted to a home for fine *spirits*—more than a thousand cases of red and white wines.

Houmas House is located in Darrow, Louisiana, four miles from I-10 between New Orleans and Baton Rouge. It is open for tours seven days a week, and closes only on Christmas and New Year's Day. Ghost enthusiasts should visit late in the week or during the weekend, when the site is open until eight P.M. The widow's walk and cupola are, unfortunately, not accessible to the public, but this sprawling estate offers numerous opportunities for a ghostly encounter.

HOUMAS HOUSE

40136 Highway 942, Darrow, Louisiana 70725
225-473-9380, www.houmashouse.com

MAYPORT'S KING HOUSE
by Charlie Carlson

JOHN KING LIVED IN MAYPORT, Florida's haunted house for so long, eventually it took his name. The two-story wooden structure was built in April 1881 on the site of a boarding house destroyed by fire in the same year and, according to local lore that's a little short on facts, both houses were built atop an old graveyard.

In the 1970s, the colorful Mr. King gained folklore fame as the town's storyteller. Both locals and tourists attended his weekly sessions to hear tales from Mayport's past, which often included accounts of strange encounters inside the King house. Today, Mr. King is still seen around town, usually at sundown when the temperature cools. Locals regard him as one of the town's friendliest souls, even though he's been dead since the late 1970s.

The King House has been examined by various ghost-hunting groups and once by a visiting parapsychologist from the Rhine Institute. They all agreed that the house's atmosphere is ideal for a haunting and that it contained a presence of the supernatural kind, possibly connected to a violent past.

Indeed, history agrees with the "violence" connection. According to several witnesses, a green rocking chair in the house "rocked on its own," having once belonged to King's great-aunt, who died while sitting in it. It was a simple case of a pitchfork being thrust through her chest. The perpetrator is alleged to have

92

been her jealous boyfriend—a sailor, who evaded arrest by sailing out of town on a cargo ship.

RED, WHITE, AND BOO!

Some folks say they've seen apparitions of two different women in the house, usually in the hallway and kitchen. Those in the know claim one is John King's great aunt, but the other specter is clad in a flowing white gown. The most popular story has the "Lady in White" taking up residence after being killed on her wedding night in a car crash near the King house. Another account relates how she was killed at the jetty rocks along the river. Whatever the case, Mr. King said he was awakened by her cries the night she died. A few days later he saw her ghost standing in his kitchen, where she has been seen off and on ever since. Apparently she's been a good housekeeper, even washing dishes, cleaning the table, and putting things away in drawers.

The problem for Mr. King was that every time he hired a woman to keep house, the Lady in White would pull pranks such as opening and closing the stove or cabinet doors, or causing food to burn and cakes to fall. She may have also been responsible for opening closet doors in bedrooms or jerking quilts off overnight guests. Eventually hired help would get fed up and quit. "She didn't like other females in her kitchen," King liked to say about his ghostly housekeeper.

The King House also had its own spirit butler, known locally as the "Little Man in Red." Described as a short fellow dressed in a red uniform-style coat, he was full of humor and enjoyed pulling pranks. Sometimes he would answer the door and have guests wait for Mr. King in the parlor. When guests remarked about the courteous butler, Mr. King would answer that he had no butler, at least of the living variety. The Little Man in Red has also been in town, walking along the road, and a few times sitting in the backseat of cars parked in front of the King house.

There have been recent sightings of the Little Man in Red, and even a few of John King, on cool evenings near the ferry landing. If you drive through Mayport and catch a glimpse of a short fellow wearing a red coat, don't be surprised if he vanishes. If he appears in your backseat and tries to direct you to the King House, however, don't go.

THE KING HOUSE IS NOW A PRIVATE RESIDENCE.

COLONEL CUSTER'S GHOSTLY LEGACY
by Joanne Austin

DIE IN A BIG BLOODY battle, and you'll be the talk of the town for generations to come, particularly if your ghost haunts the site of the fateful event. Consider the case of Lt. Col. George Armstrong Custer and his 7th Cavalry, who perished well over a hundred years ago in the Battle of the Little Bighorn. Today folks around the Little Bighorn Battlefield National Monument in Montana swear that ghosts of Lieutenant Colonel Custer, his men, and even a Northern Plains Indian or two haunt the battlefield. Eerie events have also been reported hundreds of miles away at the former Custer family home in Fort Abraham Lincoln near Mandan, North Dakota.

On June 25, 1876, Libbie Custer invited some of the officers' wives to her home at Fort Abraham Lincoln. The women banded together seeking solace from their anxieties about the battle, although Libbie describes the overwhelming sense of unease that had settled upon the group in her book *Boots and Saddles:* "All were absorbed in the same thoughts, and their eyes were filled with far-away visions and longings. Indescribable yearning for the absent, and untold terror for their safety, engrossed each heart. . . . " Libbie and her friends somehow sensed the bloodshed afoot hundreds of miles away on the Little Bighorn battlefield. The women knew—by premonition, portent, or some other unexplained phenomenon—and when Libbie was notified of the tragic outcome of Custer's Last Stand several days later, she was already in mourning.

Fort Abraham Lincoln is now a state park about five miles south of Mandan. There *Weird Encounters* spoke with Tracy Potter, president and executive director of the Fort Abraham Lincoln Foundation, about the history of the fort and the alleged hauntings that occur there.

A Plague of Spirits

On-a-Slant Village, also part of Fort Abraham Lincoln State Park, is a re-creation of a community that inhabited the site from 1575 to 1781, before a smallpox epidemic wiped out about 80 percent of the population. "Many of my staff have reported at various times seeing people walking in the village and when they look again, they're not there. There's a feeling that the spirits are still walking around," said Tracy. He also mentioned that a group of investigators from United Tribes Technical College found a high level of spirit activity in three different locations.

Adding to the dark spiritual energy left over from this event are strange occurrences within the Custer House. The original house the Custers lived in no longer exists, but a reconstruction of it was completed in time for North Dakota's state centennial in 1989. According to Tracy, the new house is "precisely on the location of the Custer House. Even the same foundations are still there, and the basement is the original basement. It has been reconstructed based on blueprints of the building and photos that were taken inside the building in the Custer era."

At the time of the reconstruction and its re-opening there were already rumors of ghosts. Tracy adds, "Many of the staff and visitors reported feeling kind of prickly sensations at their neck and hair standing on end, somebody looking over their shoulder, and feelings of some kind of a presence in the place."

The staff took great pride in creating historically accurate rooms, but they would find things amiss. "They knew how they had arranged the rooms," Tracy said, "and they'd report that there was an impression in the bed that had been made and it looked like somebody had been sitting on it, and the hairbrush had been moved." These stories were picked up by the local newspaper and helped establish the ghostly lore of the house.

Tracy isn't liable to believe in ghosts and the supernatural, and he suspected that someone was playing tricks on the rest of the staff. However, the state tourism office went along with the stories during the centennial celebrations, and that's when he decided to stick it out for a night in the Custer House. He and the editor of *North Dakota Horizons* magazine received permission to stay "to see if the ghost of Tom Custer was going to come sliding down the staircase for us." Tom Custer was George Armstrong's younger brother, who also served in the 7th Calvary and also died at the Battle of Little Bighorn.

Tom never made an appearance that night, but Tracy and the editor took advantage of the billiard room to shoot a game of pool. Tracy noted an odd occurrence: "There was certainly an eerie roll to the shots on the table. They weren't rolling true: they were going all over the place."

Despite the ghostly events reported over the years, nobody really knows who haunts the house. What is known is that the staff at Fort Lincoln doesn't shy away from talking about the ghosts. Tracy said they enjoy it, and it helps promote the Haunted Fort, "a spooky Halloween thing that's very popular with the kids." And if the kids learn something historical while getting scared, *Weird Encounters* says that's good.

A SPIRITED STROLL
by Christina Barber

ONE BEAUTIFUL OCTOBER EVENING, MY family and I attended a "Spirit Stroll" that claimed to showcase some of the ghosts that haunt the historic town Newnan, Georgia. Near the end of the walk we came to a Victorian house called a Painted Lady, meaning it was painted in a style using three colors. For some reason, this house made the hairs on the back of my neck  rise. I didn't see any unusual movement on the grounds, but just looking into the home's windows made my stomach feel like it had dropped to my shoes.

I waited for our guide to talk more about this intriguing home. She said it was built in 1840 and renovated in 1890. Fires, deaths, and long-lost loves plagued the families who lived there. Anyone who came in contact with the house seemed to suffer in one way or another.

The rest of the group started to move on, but I remained on the sidewalk, holding onto the black iron gates in front of the home and peering through them. My family moved along to join the group, leaving me alone in front of the house. That's when I felt icy fingers grip my arm. I jumped, quickly removed my hands from the gates, and ran to join up with the group. I shivered even though the temperature was 60°F—a typical warm fall night in Georgia.

After the tour ended we started to head home, and as my husband and I chatted on the walkway, I felt something hit the calf of my jeans. I quickly turned, looking for a dog, cat, or child that had run past. There was nothing. I told my husband something had just brushed my calf; his face grew pale when he realized that nothing could have touched me. There wasn't anyone or anything nearby for hundreds of feet.

NEWNAN SPIRIT STROLLS are held during weekends in October at 7 p.m. and 9 p.m., or by special reservation with groups of ten or more. Strolls are run by the Newnan-Coweta Historical Society, 30 Temple Avenue, Newnan, Georgia 30263. For more information, please contact them at 770-251-0207 or visit www.nchistoricalsociety.org

ALLAIRE STATE PARK
by Jeff Heimbuch

THE CLANGING OF METAL FILLED my ears as soon as I walked into town. The blacksmith had started early, making nails for the nearby carpenter. I walked a few more feet, and the aroma of freshly baked bread permeated—the baker was at it, too. A few women from the village waved to me as I walked by. They were dressed appropriately for the 1850s, with hoop skirts covering their ankles and white bonnets keeping their hair out of their eyes while they worked. Nearby, the church bell tolled to let us know it was nine A.M.

So began another day in the Historic Village at Allaire—and no, I didn't hop into a DeLorean and travel back in time to see these sights. I merely got into my 2001 Oldsmobile and traveled down CR-524 to Historic Allaire State Park, located in Farmingdale, New Jersey. It's a living-history park where visitors can sample a slice of life from the early nineteenth century, with volunteers assuming the roles of townspeople and giving tours of the Howell Works—New Jersey's finest example of the bog iron industry.

And if the stories are true, you may experience some of the village's ghostly inhabitants as well. Before you can understand the paranormal populace, however, you need to know about their origins.

THE BIG HOUSE AND BEYOND

JAMES PETER ALLAIRE WAS A philanthropist, engineer, steam engine and boiler manufacturer, and all-around businessman. He purchased land in the Pine Barrens—a remote area in the heart of southern New Jersey—that became the Howell Works in 1822. The self-sufficient community Allaire developed in this isolated region eventually included a carpenter shop, bakery, blacksmith, various mills, a general store, a school, a church, and row houses for the workers and their families. Amazingly most of these buildings still stand today.

At the time of the purchase, the Allaire family lived in New York City. However, a cholera outbreak in 1832 made Allaire fear for his family's safety—especially his wife, Frances Duncan, who was ill with what was likely tuberculosis. He moved them to a large farmhouse at the Howell Works, which today is affectionately referred to as the "Big House."

The fresh air didn't help Frances Duncan's condition, though, and she died in the Big House on March 23, 1836. It hit Allaire hard, and he is said to have grieved by her empty bedside for two months after she passed. Business, along with the marriage of a daughter in June, eventually forced him out of mourning. After the wedding, Allaire fled the house that offered a continual reminder of his wife's untimely passing, journeying back to New York City.

Allaire suffered a series of financial setbacks in the following years, and shortly after 1849, the Howell Works Company was declared bankrupt. He lost his business and his New York home and retired to the Big House around 1851. His new wife, Calicia—whom he married in 1846—joined him along with their son, Hal. They lived out the rest of their lives on the Howell Works property, and on May 20, 1858, James Peter Allaire passed away quietly at the age of 73.

LINGERING SPIRITS

In 1941 the property was deeded to the state and renamed Allaire Village. Today visitors learn about the life and times of James P. Allaire, but what would any historical village be without a few of its former residents still lingering around? The park system doesn't officially recognize the existence of these otherworldly occupants, but many volunteers and visitors have witnessed strange occurrences in Allaire Village.

One of the most prominent ghosts is that of Hal Allaire, James's youngest son. He died on the property in 1901 at the age of 54, and is rumored to haunt the Big House. Hal's ghost is prone to paranormal hijinks, such as moving books and other household objects around or playing pranks on the costumed interpreters who work there.

I spoke to a few of the volunteers, and many were eager to share their ghostly stories. One woman recounted her experience of an evening when she was giving a tour of the Big House. A few of the visitors reported that a locked bookcase they had passed when the tour began was now wide open. The tour guide closed the case and resumed her stories about the house.

"After I regained everyone's attention, we noticed the candles were

flickering strangely. The flame would almost go out and then go bright again, repeatedly, like someone was taking all the oxygen away from it," she said.

"Instances like these happened often at the mansion. Other times, people would report seeing candlelight and faces looking back at them in some of the windows of the Big House, long after we had closed down for the night. We would also notice things going missing, chairs moved around, strange voices, and images in the mirror that weren't actually there. None of it was ever threatening, though."

A visitor shared a story with *Weird Encounters* about a tour guide who told his group the mansion was haunted. "Apparently," the visitor wrote, "the ghosts of two of Allaire's wives roam the place. In fact, the guide said that one day, while leaving the mansion for the evening, he said good night to the ladies of the house, as was his custom. But this time a disembodied woman's voice replied 'good night' in return."

The visitor's center is said to have some haunts all its own. Many ironworkers and their families used to live in the building, and visitors often complain of cold spots; some volunteers even refuse to go into the center's basement at night because they feel as if they are being watched.

Another ghost said to haunt the grounds is Oscar Cheesman Smith, a supposed former manager of the Iron Works. Oscar allegedly likes to play tricks around the manager's house by using the children's blocks on the second floor to spell out *Laura*, his former fiancée's name. One worker reported seeing him while she was waiting for her friend to come pick her up. Thinking it was her friend, she followed after him, only to see him disappear into thin air!

In addition to Allaire Village's rich history, the park boasts a small steam-powered train ride and nature trails. Caution: Though it's a state park, many areas are off-limits to guests, so please don't trespass. On your way out, be sure to say good-bye to the residents of the town—both the living . . . and the dead.

101

HISTORIC VILLAGE AT ALLAIRE
4265 Route 524, Farmingdale, New Jersey 07727
732-919-3500, www.allairevillage.org

HIS BOOTS WERE MADE FOR WALKING
by Paul J. Forti, Ph.D.

THE BATTLE OF BALL'S BLUFF occurred on October 21, 1861, in Leesburg, Virginia, and it was one of the first Civil War battles that tested the strength of the Confederacy. They did well, sending the Union Army running scared back across the Potomac. During the battle, Union colonel Erasmus Burt of Mississippi was seriously wounded. The evening of October 21, he was taken to an upstairs bedroom in Harrison Hall, a house located about a mile from the battle. Burt died the following day, and several years after the war rumors about his ghost roaming Harrison Hall were heard throughout the community.

Those stories continued into the current century, although ownership of the house changed several times. Once a private residence, it became a bed-and-breakfast, business conference center, a career management consulting firm, and then changed its name to the Glenfiddich House in the early 1990s.

For a period, the owner lived in the top floor of the home with his wife, whom I'll call Ms. Smith. The first time I stayed there, in the spring of 2006, she told me about her experiences with the colonel. During the late 1990s, back problems forced her to remain in bed for several months in the room where Colonel Burt had died. She swore she heard and saw the colonel on several occasions.

I didn't hear or see anything unusual during my stay. The owners gave me a tour of the home and told me its original owners were distant relatives of Gen. Robert E. Lee. Lee visited several times during the war, and in 1862 he planned the battle of Antietam in the dining room with his staff, including Stonewall Jackson.

The history intrigued me, but I remained skeptical about the colonel's ghost, even after hearing that other visitors saw him walking down the hall in his leather boots, rattling his sword. My feelings changed in August 2006, when the owners invited me to stay at the Glenfiddich House again.

This time, I had Colonel Burt's old room. After getting into bed at eleven P.M., I awoke two hours later to a strange sound down the hall. I attributed the noise first to heating pipes (before remembering it was summertime) and then to air-conditioning (it was a cool evening, and there was no need for it). I became concerned—I was the only person in the house and had no idea where the sound was coming from. I listened closely but didn't hear anything else, so I relaxed and began to fall back asleep. Fifteen minutes later I heard what sounded like footsteps coming down the hallway. As they got closer, I could hear the dull clang of metal as it rubbed against leather bootstraps. It sounded like the steps of a person wearing riding boots.

At first I was too scared to get out of bed, but I forced myself to do so, turning on the lights in my room. The sound promptly stopped. I grabbed a flashlight, opened the bedroom door, and walked around upstairs, but saw nothing. Back in the room, I left the light on and got back into bed. Ten minutes later, I again heard heavy boot-clad footsteps walking down the hall. I called out, "Who is there?" and the sound stopped. Once again, I got out of bed, opened the door, and shouted out, "Who is there?" but heard nothing.

I climbed back in bed and fell asleep, only to awaken to footsteps at about four A.M. I went through the same drill as before, but this time I stood at the door and shouted: "Go away, whoever you are!" It must have had an impact, because now I could make out the faint figure of a man walking down the steps to the first floor. I immediately turned on every light and went downstairs, finding nothing.

A few hours later I got dressed and went downstairs, where Ms. Smith had arrived with breakfast. When I brought up my overnight experiences, she said, "I guess you finally met the colonel." She told me he usually appears after he is comfortable with a guest, and though mischievous, he's not harmful. After her encounters with the colonel, he no longer bothered her.

I was alarmed and excited by what had happened, but I managed to finish my business in the area that day and headed home. A few weeks later, I received a certificate from the owners saying that I survived a night with the colonel.

I don't know where Colonel Burt is buried, but I can tell you where he's waiting for his next guest. As for me, I don't plan on being anywhere his boots will be walking again. Should I return to the area, I will stay someplace that has no ghostly claim.

THE GLENFIDDICH HOUSE IS HOME TO A PRIVATE BUSINESS AND IS NOT ACCESSIBLE TO THE GENERAL PUBLIC.

GHOSTLY BLUES IN MEMPHIS
by Joanne M. Austin

MEMPHIS, TENNESSEE, SITS HIGH ON a bluff overlooking the Mississippi River. Today, it's a major hub for FedEx, but in the past the prime river location made Memphis king of some strange bedfellows: cotton, mules, and music—especially blues and rock and roll. Because of the latter, the city's got an aura of unfeigned coolness about it that even its ghosts seem to have acquired.

In *Weird Hauntings*, we brought you the story of one of Memphis's haunted locations: the Orpheum Theater. But since then we've learned that there's more to Memphis ghosts, and we talked about some of them with Mike McCarthy (www.guerillamonster.com), a filmmaker who also conducts walking and pub crawl ghost tours for Backbeat Tours.

Mike shared stories about the ghostly stops on his walking tour, which goes for about a mile along Beale and South Front streets. Put on some comfortable shoes and join us as we hit up a few of these haunted hangouts.

105

HANDY PARK

Handy Park was established on Beale Street in 1933 to honor W. C. Handy, also known as the father of the blues. According to Mike, Robert Johnson—the man who claimed to have soul-selling dealings with Old Scratch at a crossroads—played in the park, as did B.B. King. So did many other guitarists, including one named Robert Dell, who, Mike said, never caught on. "He passed away under one of the

last remaining oak trees in the park, from exposure, which I think means 'dying outside from alcoholism.' His spirit kind of hangs around that tree."

Beale Street is a party street today, but revelers have to clear off by three A.M. "Afterwards, things get pretty quiet down there," Mike said. "But there are police reports that say they can hear guitar-playing coming from around the tree after that time." Nobody living makes that music.

THE ORPHEUM THEATRE

Mike takes people past the Orpheum Theatre, home to the ghost of a little girl named Mary. The theater was once called the Grand Opera House, and the story goes that Mary was struck down and injured outside by a trolley or carriage. She was dragged inside and passed away in the lobby from her injuries, and now manifests as a little girl ghost in a white dress with no legs or feet.

The Grand Opera House burned down in 1924 and was rebuilt in 1928 as the Orpheum. Mike doesn't think the four years the theater was in limbo mattered much to Mary. She likes to hang out in C5, a north box seat close to the stage, even though the original seats were torn out when the box was redone. Mary's still seen there by the cleaning crew and others, usually out of the corners of their eyes. When they turn to get a good look at her, she disappears.

106

A traveling production of *Fiddler on the Roof* came to the Orpheum in the mid-1970s. According to Mike, after cast members tried to contact Mary with a Ouija board they had horrible luck with the show—they were locked in their dressing rooms and the floodlights blew out. The cast reportedly tried to talk to Mary again, but she wouldn't speak, and they left town shortly after, without finishing their run and blaming the failure on Mary. "I think Mary is a bit of a critic," Mike said. "She's seen a lot of shows."

THE GAYOSO

Memphis is built in an area that was home to the Chickasaw Indians. There were Indian mounds farther to the south, according to Mike, and five Indian mounds near Riverside Drive, where the National Ornamental Metal Museum is today. The Union Army destroyed three mounds during the Civil War, and thus only two remain.

The Gayoso Hotel was built on one of the highest points on the bluff in 1842, possibly over many Chickasaw spirits. It was the biggest hotel in the mid-South when it was built. After burning down in 1899, it was rebuilt and then underwent several incarnations. Today it's an apartment building.

A woman is rumored to have died in Room 607, her body found several days later on the top floor of what is now called Gayoso House. She was a writer and an alcoholic. A person who worked in building management said she had read some of the woman's unpublished work, which was about "portals and things like that."

Like many a haunted room, Room 607 is no longer rented out. "No one can stay in it," Mike said. "They hear laughter, screaming, sobbing, and so forth coming from the other side of the door, and they don't really bother to check it anymore. I guess they clean it, but sometimes when I'm doing the tour, there's a

light on in the room. The tour group has no access to the building and can only see it from the street below."

On one tour, a woman insisted that someone appeared through the blinds and looked down. She said, "You set that up! Didn't you?" to Mike, but he swears not.

THE BUTCHER SHOP STEAK HOUSE

The tour also walks by the Butcher Shop Steak House, an upscale chain restaurant located in an 1860 building that was rebuilt in 1905 after a fire. Most businesses welcome ghost tours because they bring in customers, although Mike mentioned that the Butcher Shop is ambivalent about such tours—with relatively good reason.

During the Civil War, the building that the restaurant is located in had refrigeration, and when Memphis fell to the North in 1862, they stored dead Union soldiers in a cooler in the back. The scene Mike describes is grisly: "They crammed so many bodies back there; they were squeezed together and the blood ran down the back of the walls and into Riverside Drive."

That room and the top four floors of the building are no longer in use, although a candle or light sometimes appears in the middle window in the topmost floor, a custom borrowed from Europe during the Civil War to show you had a soldier off at war. Mike recalled a couple on one tour: The woman was trying to get pictures of orbs, and the man stood off to the corner, not saying anything. When Mike explained the theory behind the light, the man said, "That's not why there's a light in the window."

Mike asked if he'd like to tell the group why, and he did. "First of all, a boy or maybe a young man named Jay or James—I can't quite get it—that's the person who was killed in a construction or reconstruction of a building here, and that's the light in the window."

Mike asked, "How do you know that?"

The man said "James" had been talking to him for the last five minutes while he stood on the sidewalk. The group was a little startled, so Mike asked how he heard the voice. The man claimed it was through "radio signals or waves" and that it played out until he couldn't hear them anymore. Then he added, "Before James stopped talking to me, he did tell me that he didn't like you very much!"

Mike laughed at the time, but he now makes it a point to give a shout to James when he wraps up at the Butcher Shop because he doesn't want anything following him home.

THE CAYENNE MOON

The last ghostly stop on the tour is the Cayenne Moon, a Cajun-themed restaurant that's close to the former Cotton Exchange Building—now the Cotton Museum. The Cayenne Moon building was involved in cotton export, and at some point a man was killed there. It seems his spirit never left and now whistles in the basement. He's mostly harmless but has been known to throw objects or knock things over, poltergeist-style. A few employees have caught a glimpse of the ghost out of the corners of their eyes, but the ghost won't stick around for a better view. He reportedly has a Huck Finn look, with overalls, a straw hat, and no shoes.

Mike mentioned that almost every night he goes to the Cayenne Moon, owner Polly Hagedorn tells him about some new thing that's happened. Patrons' beers get knocked off the table with force. Glasses hit the floor but don't break. And sometimes, meals move on the table, unaided by human touch. One night, Polly brought a bowl of gumbo to a customer and turned to walk away, only to have the customer say, "Ma'am, my gumbo is moving across the table!" Polly slapped her hands down on the table, but the gumbo kept moving. She then told the customer, "The place is haunted. Eat your gumbo."

On Halloween 2007, a news team and some paranormal investigators arrived. They didn't find anything, but every time Polly went to the basement, the EMF meters lit up. Could the whistling ghost have a companion downstairs? Polly's husband, Larry, was her business partner, but he sadly died from a heart attack a few years back. Mike said he's missed dearly at the restaurant, and that Polly thinks maybe Larry is watching over things.

Mike's not sure how two ghosts share the basement, but that's where he experienced the paranormal himself, for three nights in a row in September 2007. The first night was a Thursday, and he had seven people in the basement sitting at a banquet table with the lights down low. Over the varied sounds of a busy restaurant, the group heard something knock on the table—two different times. The following night, the ghost did his signature whistling from the basement bar, right behind the group. But that Saturday night was probably Mike's creepiest experience in the basement. "I had twelve people sitting at the table, and the ghost grabbed my knee and let go of it. I asked the lady to my right if there was something under the table, and she said, 'Shut up!' then claimed her left arm was numb and she couldn't feel anything on her left side—as if he passed between us."

Nothing else has happened to Mike since then, but it has affected how he runs tours. "I become a different tour guide when I'm in that basement than when I'm just walking around talking on the streets. I think customers pick up on that. There's always a possibility that something's about to happen, and that makes it a really great last stop on the tour."

If you find yourself in Memphis and in need of a ghost fix, catch up with Mike McCarthy and Backbeat Tours at 140 Beale Street. The walking ghost tours and pub crawl ghost tours start at 7:30 p.m. You can find more information and make reservations through www.backbeattours.com.

Butcher—Moon Connection?

On another night in the Cayenne Moon's basement, an older woman was on the ghost tour with her family. After Mike told them about the whistling ghost, the woman said, "There was someone standing beside us when we were on the sidewalk up at the butcher shop." Her family started to comment about her clairvoyance, and she continued: "There was a kid standing there, and he had on overalls."

This blew Mike away—he hadn't brought up how the Cayenne Moon's whistling ghost looked. Could the James of the butcher shop sidewalk be the whistling ghost at the Cayenne Moon? It's possible, though Mike points out that Huck Finn–style overalls were common attire when the cotton industry was in full swing in the 1800s, and it's likely that similarly dressed workers died in different locations on Front Street. Or maybe James is taking those ghosts on a tour of Memphis.

A HAUNTING COLLECTION
by Linda S. Godfrey

FOR CIVIL WAR BUFF AND collector Michael Wozny, the two-story frame house just off the historic downtown square in East Troy, Wisconsin, fulfilled all the requirements of his dream home. Wozny and his wife, Sherry, needed a vintage place to display their Civil War uniforms and artifacts, and the Greek Revival, wood-floored house built on one of the oldest home sites in Walworth County still looked much the same as when it was built in 1857 by Dr. Levi Stebbins. What the Woznys didn't realize, however, was that Dr. Stebbins—and perhaps others among the nine inhabitants who died in that home—might never have left.

The Woznys began noticing strange things soon after they moved in. An antique, tin camping cup kept on the living room mantel tended to hop around by itself, for instance. Michael got eerie feelings while sitting in his office at the end of the downstairs hallway, and one day he turned to catch a glimpse of a man dressed in what looked like a Civil War–era frock coat.

The Woznys decided to research the home's history, and discovered their dream house had a dark background.

112

THE LONG CHAIN OF DEATH

First to die was an infant—the seventh child of Levi and Sabrena Stebbins. Their daughter died a few days after birth in August 1857, just a few months after the family had moved in. The baby's funeral was held in the front parlor of the house.

The second person to die was a Stebbins son, who was run over by a stagecoach. He was carried into the house, where he expired despite his father's desperate effort to save him. Daughter Laurie passed away elsewhere at age thirty-one in 1869, but hers was the house's third funeral. She was followed in death by her father, the doctor, who died in 1881 in his bed from pneumonia. Like his children, he was laid in state in the parlor. His wife, Sabrena, was the fourth person to die in the house, in 1887.

The next year, retired farmer Richard Brownlee bought the Stebbins estate and moved in with his son, David, and two daughters, Susan and Martha ("Mittie"). Richard died in his bed on October 9, 1907, and his funeral was held in the residence soon after. His children (David, d. 1934; Mittie, d. 1941; and Susan, d. 1942) became the sixth through eighth persons to shuck their mortal coils in the old house on Main Street.

Susan willed the house to her nephew, Ralph Brownlee, who in turn sold the place to a brother, George, and his two sisters, Alma Lazzaroni and Genevieve Cruver, who all managed to survive three years in the house before selling it in 1946. Perhaps they had good reason for moving, with eight possible revenants already on the property. The house changed hands a few more times in the next couple of years, and the ninth and final death occurred in 1954, when Mrs. Josephine Feuerpfeil succumbed to a heart attack in the master bedroom.

A succession of several more owners and tenants lived in the house of death before the Woznys bought it in 1996.

PHANTOM HITCHHIKER

According to Michael Wozny, it's possible that the chief spook on the premises, the man in the black frock coat, didn't pass away in the East Troy house. The shadow man may have hitched a ride with the Civil War memorabilia Wozny collected from all over the country. Wozny lived in an apartment with his antique paraphernalia for some time before meeting Sherry, he said, and at least two women he dated described seeing "something" that looked like a man in a long full coat and short-brimmed hat. When he met Sherry, she described the same thing.

Wozny also began having eerie problems with the tin Civil War field cup. "I'd leave the room and come back and find it sitting on the middle of the table," he said. "So I put it on the bookshelf. The next day it was completely gone, then I found it the following day inside a cabinet used to store other Civil War items, pushed in next to them."

The cup disappeared yet again, reappearing in the cabinet only when Wozny removed the other items that had been "crowding" it. The cup stayed quiet until the Halloween after the Woznys moved into their East Troy house, when it again "apported"—a term for the unknown means by which objects vanish and return on their own—by disappearing from the mantel and ending up on the windowsill.

Although Wozny never saw the man in the black frock coat while living in his apartment, he soon encountered the shadowy being when he and Sherry moved into the old Stebbins House. It was after the Halloween incident, about a year after they had moved in, and Wozny was sitting alone in his library, working. "I suddenly looked up and saw a black figure in the middle of the room," said Wozny. "It was like a shadow, only you couldn't see through it, and it was in the room itself—not on the wall. It had a long coat and a short, 'preacher's' hat. I started to get up and it turned to move away, breaking up into some twinkly stuff."

Wozny says he was surprised but not shaken. From time to time after that incident, he would catch glimpses of the figure out of the corner of his eye. "It was like a shadow person walking across the room, but not on the wall," he said.

HALF BOY AND OTHER GHOSTS

In February 2008, he spotted another figure—half a boy! A TV had broken, and he had moved it to the floor and left it there until he could get it out of the house. One day when he walked into the room, he saw the bottom half of what looked like a boy or young man wearing blue pants and black shoes and sitting on the TV. The figure trailed off into vapor above the belt. As Wozny came into the room, the legs stood up and walked away.

Wozny also had a strange experience while trying to drag a heavy board up the narrow stairs inside the property's two-story carriage house. He was having a difficult time of it, when suddenly it was as if someone picked up the other end and took most of the load. "It felt light as a feather," said Wozny. "I just said, 'Thank you, whoever you are.' That was weird."

There have been other incidents. A former upstairs tenant said he saw a figure he thought might be Dr. Stebbins standing in the hall. In the tenant's bedroom, the former master bedroom where several occupants died, the closet door would not stay shut—even when heavy objects were placed in front of it.

Wozny said that for some time, he was repeatedly awakened at night by someone insistently tapping one of his feet. It ended when he firmly asked the unknown tapper to stop it. And around Christmas of 2007, Mike and Sherry took some pictures of their front porch, only to discover the image of a lady in a white dress standing inside, looking out at them.

Despite all of this, the Woznys are not planning to move. Nothing much surprises them anymore, and they say they have no problem sharing their home with the mostly unseen inhabitants. After all, what could be more appropriate for a man who used to spend all his free time reenacting the Civil War, than hosting the spirits of those who actually lived it?

115

THIS HISTORIC HOUSE IS A PRIVATE RESIDENCE.

Fresh Air Phantasms

SPEED
LIMIT
55

"It's coming back!"—Woman screaming about a
hooded specter on a railroad track in Maryland

SOME GHOSTS THAT HAUNT the "inside" world probably like to get out and shake the dust from their bedsheets once in a while. They might have grievances to air, or perhaps they simply wish to share the freedom of roads, bridges, trails, and other outside areas with their living counterparts.

Wide-open spaces leave lots of room for interaction. Streetside, you may come across a hitchhiking volcano goddess on Hawaii's northwestern coast, or see the spirit of a Native American elder float-walking along BIA Route 15 in Arizona. Or maybe you'll chase after a horrid, cloaked specter that hovers along a railroad spur in Maryland, only to find it chasing after you.

And there are ghostly bridges to cross, like a bridge in Mississippi that's haunted by a serial murderer and the souls of his victims. Then there's a bridge in Maryland where a shadowy entity likes to shake up parked cars.

Now let's move off the road and onto wooded trails, like the Path of the Ancestors in Guam where spirits make side trips to knock on the doors of the living. On another trail at a Florida battleground, you might find the ghost of a confederate soldier still admiring modern contrivances around a campfire. Still another path takes you to an abandoned house where an invisible phantom gave literal chills to a trickster teen. And finally, you may not want to close the door on a New Jersey barn until after all of the ghosts inside escape.

Care to join us outside for some fresh air?

DESERT GHOST WALKER
David War Staff's story, as told to Antonio R. Garcez

IN FEBRUARY 1991, I ENCOUNTERED my first ghost at the age of seventeen. After a high school basketball game in Phoenix, my cousin Ralph and I left the gymnasium and headed to the town of Sells, Arizona, on the Tohono O'odham reservation, where I was to spend the weekend with Ralph's family.

We got on Interstate 10 and then switched to south Highway 15. About forty minutes into our drive, we were deep into the desert and surrounded by darkness. Suddenly a large javelina crossed the road, and before I could think about stepping on the brakes, I hit that wild pig with a big ol' bang! I knew we had some big trouble with the car because the radiator began to hiss and steam began pouring out of it. I immediately pulled over to check the damage. Sure enough, the animal had hit the front grill head-on, and a piece of metal had punctured my car's radiator.

Directly behind the car we could hear the pig squealing loudly. It was a weird experience to be alone at night in the desert, hearing the sounds of a dying animal just a few yards away. The pig kept up the terrible squealing for a long, long time. I had a flashlight, but knowing that javelinas can give a nasty bite when cornered, I wasn't about to go check on its injuries without a gun.

Ralph said, "You know, with a busted radiator, we're pretty much stuck here."

"Yeah," I answered. "I guess we're spending the night in the car, or start walking and hope someone picks us up."

We decided to stay with the car. After about a half hour, the javelina stopped crying. We sat in the front seat and waited . . . and waited. A few cars passed by, but none stopped. At 12:10 A.M., we turned off the car's radio to conserve the battery and decided to go outside and sit on the car's trunk to keep from falling asleep. By making jokes and talking about basketball we managed to keep each other awake, but after a while we ran out of things to say.

ENTER: BAREFOOT BOGEYMAN
I looked at my watch again: It was 1:40 A.M. *Damn,* I thought, *when are we going to get home?*

A few minutes later, I heard something in the bushes. Someone was slowly walking, breaking twigs and brush with each step. It was coming from the vicinity

119

of where the javelina was lying on the road. The moon was bright enough that I could make out forms in the darkness, but we were not able to see anything clearly.

Then, about twenty feet away, a barefoot man walked out of the bushes! I turned on my flashlight and focused the weak yellow light on him as I yelled, "Hey, what's up?"

The man stopped and turned to face us. Because of the weak batteries in my flashlight and the man's distance from us, it wasn't easy to make out his features. I thought he was a desert tramp. There are a few of those old guys living out there.

Ralph yelled, "Watch out, we hit a javelina and it's somewhere out where you're walking!"

Again he gave no reply. We both wondered what that guy was doing in the desert at this hour. It was not normal. A little scared, we both yelled, "Hey you, can't you hear us? Get away from there!"

The man stopped, turned in our direction, and looked at us. He took a few more steps toward the highway, and we both got a real good look at him. He was about five feet tall, elderly, and dressed in very little clothing. Around his thin waist he wore a tight-fitting, dark-colored cloth that draped down over one knee. Several long necklaces with large white beads or shells hung around his neck. He wore his hair short and greasy, with bangs above his glaring eyes.

Ralph and I yelled again: "Hey, you!" Without responding or even looking at us, the man continued to walk across the highway and into the brush on the other side, where he disappeared. I use the word *walk*, but though I could see his bare feet moving, he was floating about five inches over the asphalt!

Unlike before, we didn't hear any of the twigs breaking under his footsteps. Ralph and I looked at each other and jumped off the trunk, got inside the car, and quickly locked the doors. We knew this was no tramp.

A Lesson from the Spirit World

We spent the rest of the night scared that the ghost would reappear at the car's windows. Our imaginations kept us from sleeping. We kept the car's dome light on and the radio tuned loudly to a rock station.

Eventually we did fall asleep, and sometime before dawn we were awakened by two guys in a truck who were headed for Sells. They sure gave us a good scare when they knocked on the car's window, but we introduced ourselves, and they offered to tow us home. The guys told us they were artists from California on a photography trip, taking pictures of the desert and Indians for an art project.

We didn't mention the ghost to our rescuers, but when we arrived home that morning, we told my aunt and her family everything. Everyone agreed that what we had experienced was the ghost of an Indian from the spirit world. And since my ghostly encounter, I've decided—if at all possible—never to drive at night through the desert again.

BIA HIGHWAY 15 is located within the Tohono O'odham Reservation. Be respectful of the spirits (and living people) you may see while driving along the road, and look out for javelinas!

122

AN ANCESTRAL PATH
by Jeff Davis

SOME AMERICANS ARE BARELY AWARE of Guam's existence, much less that it is a part of the United States. The largest of the Marianas islands, Guam is only about 200 square miles in size, and is located about 1,500 miles east of the Philippines and 1,000 miles north of New Guinea.

The earliest Guamanians probably came from Indonesia or Malaysia, but over time they intermarried with incoming Spaniards, Chinese, Filipinos, Japanese, and, later, Americans to become the modern Chamorro. In 1950, Guam became a more formal part of the United States, and its people voting citizens. At the same time, the Chamorro have retained many of their traditions and cultural beliefs, including some ancient customs that acknowledge the presence of spirits.

The Chamorro traditionally lived close to the coast because many made their living as fisher folk. They buried their dead in cemeteries close to the villages, but not *too* close. Instead, they constructed special trails called the Paths of the Ancestors. At various times, villagers gathered and walked along these paths to their cemeteries, holding feasts and reunions that both celebrated their ancestors and reunited living relatives. The rest of the time, these paths were seldom used because people believed the *taotaomona* (spirits) haunted the trails and cemeteries.

As the population grew and became more urbanized, fewer walked over these traditional trails, though they celebrated this ritual in other ways. Towns grew, and parts of the old trails were paved over as roads. In a few places, people built houses or buildings over them.

KNOCK, KNOCK . . .

My friend Antonio is a Chamorro, and one day he received word from his brother in Guam about a strange happening at a relative's home. This family member lived with her children in military housing on one of the naval bases constructed after World War II. On many nights after her husband was deployed, she would awaken to the sound of someone knocking and banging on her back door. While no one broke in, the incidents frightened her. She contacted Antonio's brother, the nearest male relative, and he and his wife agreed to stay a few nights to investigate.

Antonio's brother was just settling in on the first night when the sound of someone knocking on the back door woke him. Grumbling, he got out of bed, walked to the door, and opened it. There was no one there. He walked onto the front porch and around the building, but didn't see anyone or hear any odd sounds.

Figuring he was mistaken or someone was playing a prank on him, he went back into the house, but a few minutes after he lay down, there was another loud knock at the door.

He returned to the back door and looked outside. No one was there. Then he walked around the building again with the same result. He wasn't sure what was going on but went back inside and closed the door. As soon as he did, however, there was yet another loud bang on it. He yanked the door open and was surprised, again, to find no one present. It would have been impossible for anything human to come onto the porch, bang on the door, and then get away in the space of a few seconds.

After some thought, Antonio's brother held the door open slightly and, in Chamorro, asked whoever was outside to stop knocking on the door and bothering the woman inside, since she had not done anyone any harm. He closed the door and waited beside it in silence. No one has banged on the back door since.

People with a more mundane turn of mind would suggest that the strange knocks were the work of pranksters. Others suggest that they originate from a restless spirit haunting an old village or portion of the Paths of the Ancestors that was covered over when the naval base expanded. Whatever the source, a stern warning in the Chamorro tongue is all that was needed to keep this mysterious visitor at bay.

PRIVATE PROPERTY

THE PASSENGER

by Rick Carroll, excerpted from *Madame Pele:*
True Encounters with Hawaii's Fire Goddess

MY DAY FULL OF STRANGE encounters began in Honolulu at the airport, when a security guard asked to inspect my carry-on. "Oh, I love your books," she said, finding several spooky titles in my bag. I handed her one, and she gave me a big mahalo (Hawaiian for "thank you") and waved me onward.

In line at Starbucks, a Charles Manson look-alike, one of the terminal's homeless denizens, hit me up for three bucks. He wanted "a wet, double tall, French vanilla latte." His outrageous request made me laugh. I gave him a buck.

While waiting for my coffee I was paged repeatedly: ". . . please return to the security gate." It turns out I'd dropped my ticket to Kona International during the security check. I ran to the gate only to find my plane was late, and then arrived at the Keahole airport to learn Budget was out of cars.

"We have a ten-passenger van," the clerk said. "You can have it for the same price as an economy sedan."

"It's only me," I said.

"It's all we have," the clerk said.

That's how I came to be all alone driving an air-conditioned, ten-passenger van on the Big Island's Queen Ka'ahumanu Highway on what felt like the hottest day of the year. My destination was Waimea School, where I'd been invited to read to children as part of the Marriott Waikoloa Outrigger's annual spooky "talk story" event.

SCORCHING SIREN

Queen Ka'ahumanu Highway is unique in Hawaii. The two-lane black asphalt not only runs through twenty miles of black lava landscape, it crosses over several layers of historic lava flows and under four of the island's five volcanoes: Kohala, Hualalai, Mauna Loa, and Mauna Kea. Pele, goddess of fire, land if there ever was.

I saw the hitchhiker on the highway just after leaving the airport. Since it was just me, all alone in the air-conditioned ten-passenger van, I stopped. She got in. Immediately something was wrong. The chilled van seemed warmer with her aboard.

"Where're you going?"

"Waimea," she said.

"Me, too. Do you live there?"

"No," she replied, "just visiting."

She was neither young nor old but somewhere in between. Her caramel skin, charcoal dreadlocks, bright clear eyes, and soft voice entranced me, but there was about her a distinct flammable odor. I thought for a moment the ten-passenger rental van had a gas leak.

As we crossed what looked like a bleak charcoal expanse, my fervid passenger knew and identified each and every lava flow with evident pride, as if each flow were an object of art in her private collection.

"Ka'upulehu flowed to the sea in 1801," she said as we passed under Hualalai volcano. "It filled Kiholo Bay . . . and the 1859 Mauna Loa flow ran from nine thousand feet near the summit to the sea . . . the Kaniku flow covered Waikoloa and ran into the fishponds at Anaeho'omalu . . ."

Her keen recitation startled me. "How do you know all this?" I asked.

"Just do," she said. "It's my hobby."

12 /

We rode in silence for a mile or so. I half expected her to ask for a cigarette—a common request of Pele, the fire goddess.

"Don't you want to ask me for a cigarette?"

"I don't smoke," she said, smiling.

We rode on in silence.

"Are you sure you're not Madame Pele?" I finally asked. I couldn't help it.

"Oh, no," she said. "I'm not Madame Pele."

"How do I know?"

"Believe me." She laughed.

"I'm not sure I do," I said.

In misty rain, we approached Waimea town. She said good-bye and thanks at the T intersection.

"I'll get out here," she said at the stoplight, opening the door and jumping out. She cut across the corner gas station, walking fast. I half expected the gas pumps to burst into flames.

128 That never happened, but something just as startling did. As I watched her walk away, she vanished in thin air. One minute she was there, the next she was gone—*li' dat*! I asked the gas station attendant if he'd seen the woman in white.

"No, brah, see nothing."

It suddenly felt real chilly inside my air-conditioned ten-passenger van.

I found the Waimea School library full of kids that Friday afternoon. The library was cool and quiet. I, by contrast, was hot and sweaty.

"Are you okay?" a librarian asked. "You look like you've seen a ghost."

"I'm not really sure," I told her, "but I think I just gave a ride to a woman who may have been Madame Pele."

The librarian had a sympathetic smile. "I know," she said. "It happens a lot here."

That night at a dinner party, I asked the other guests if they had ever seen that woman hitchhiking along the Queen's Highway or walking about their town. Now, Waimea is a very small town, and surely someone would have noticed a woman in a white dress with charcoal dreadlocks who knew a little too much about old volcanoes. Nobody ever had. At least that's what they told me.

QUEEN KAʻAHUMANU HIGHWAY is located in the northwestern corner of the Big Island of Hawaii.

HANGING AT STUCKEY'S BRIDGE
by Alan Brown

STUCKEY'S BRIDGE IS THE OLDEST iron bridge in Lauderdale County. It's located in a heavily wooded area twelve miles southwest of Meridian, Mississippi. The exact age of the 199.1-foot bridge is uncertain, but most estimates place the date of completion at 1850. However, other sources maintain that Stuckey's Bridge was built in 1901 to replace an older, wooden bridge that once spanned the Stuckey River.

Stuckey's Bridge spans the Chunky River, which was a "liquid highway" in the southwestern part of Lauderdale County in the first half of the nineteenth century. Traders floated down the river in rafts and boats laden with goods for sale. Many of these travelers fell victim to the cutthroats, gamblers, and robbers who operated on the shoreline. One of the most notorious of these scoundrels was an outlaw named Stuckey, a member of the Dalton Gang who ran an inn on the river's edge, just off a nearby stagecoach route.

129

The former historical preservationist for Lauderdale County, Fonda Rush, offered this description of Stuckey's activities: "The story goes that on the way back, when you had your pockets full of money from selling your wares and all, he would kill you and bury your body around the bridge. Supposedly, he killed around twenty people before he was caught." Stuckey's murderous deeds came to a halt in the early 1850s when he was apprehended, tried, and hanged from the bridge.

SINISTER SIGHTINGS

According to legend, as told by the young folks who hang out at the old bridge on the weekends and around Halloween, the ghost of Old Man Stuckey can be seen walking along the banks of the Chunky River on moonlit nights, swinging his lantern in an attempt to lure travelers to his inn. Some claim that on nights when the river is still, they hear splashing sounds underneath the bridge in the very spot where Stuckey's lifeless body fell after the authorities cut him down. A few people say they've seen Stuckey's corpse hanging from one of the iron girders.

Late one night in 2004, several members of the Meridian-based ghost-hunting group, Orbservations, drove out to investigate the paranormal activity that has been reported around the bridge for so many years. They were driving their car across the old bridge when they heard the spine-tingling squeal of metal scraping against metal. Concerned that the bridge might collapse, they backed their car off the bridge and began unloading their equipment.

Orbservations captured no full-body apparitions, but several members photographed orbs and a strange mist. The evidence collected that night was compelling—even chilling—but the scariest part of the evening, according to Gigi Ahrens, the group's director, was the way the iron bridge squealed in protest as they attempted to drive across it.

I myself had a very unusual—if not ghostly—experience on Stuckey Bridge on October 30, 2004. At eleven P.M., I accompanied Scotty Ray Boyd and Debbie Alexander—two disc jockeys from a local radio station—and their three guests on a trip to the old bridge. Because the bridge wasn't built to support the weight of SUVs, we parked at the foot of the bridge and sat quietly in the car, waiting for Stuckey to appear.

In the glare from the headlights, we could see a rope dangling from the middle of the bridge—tied there, no doubt, by some wag with the intent of instilling fear in the hearts of his buddies. We had not sat in the car for very long before we began seeing golf ball size lights flitting through the woods around the bridge. The lights were far too large to have been fireflies. When I explained that the lights could have been the souls of Stuckey's victims who are buried in the woods, the ladies in the group decided that it was time to go home, and we did.

Stuckey's Bridge was listed in the National Register of Historic Places in 1988. Although the old one-lane, twelve-foot-wide bridge is closed to vehicular traffic, people can still walk over it. Despite the decades of graffiti that adorns the iron beams, the sinister legacy of Stuckey's Bridge has been undimmed by the passing years.

131

STUCKEY'S BRIDGE can be found along the
eponymous Stuckey Bridge Road, in Savoy, Mississippi,
where it intersects with Meehan-Savoy Road.
Don't even think of driving over it!

JERICHO BRIDGE
by Joanne Austin

COVERED BRIDGES ARE ONE-LANE ANACHRONISMS in a multiple-lane world, imbued with a nostalgia that invites people to tour them, take pictures of them, and even write gushy romantic novels set around them. But with their age also come stories—some of the haunted variety.

Such is the case with Jericho Bridge in Kingsville, Maryland. Located on Jericho Road, it spans the Little Gunpowder Falls River, not too far away from Jerusalem Mill Village. It was built in 1865, and according to *Weird Maryland*, several ghosts haunt it. One is the mysterious, faded ghost of a woman in white who carries a basket of flowers while she walks through the bridge. Another is the ghost of a girl who burned to death near or on the bridge when hay in her father's truck caught on fire. And then there are the hanged ghosts—either runaway slaves, who you can also hear screaming, or "three young men" who committed suicide there.

Much of the bridge's lore involves parking your vehicle on the bridge, shutting it off, and then looking into the rearview mirror to see a ghost hanging from the rafters. Some claim their vehicles have trouble starting again or continue to roll along as if the ghosts are pushing them off of the bridge.

Paranormal investigations conducted at Jericho Bridge have indicated something odd about the location. One such investigation involved Catherine, a member of several paranormal investigation groups, among them the Paranormal Research & Investigation Society of Maryland (PRISMd) and Gettysburg Paranormal Investigators (GPI). Also known by the nickname "Paranormal Poison," Catherine specializes in electronic voice phenomena (EVPs) and has collected good photo evidence, too.

A GOOSE-BUMPY RIDE

Catherine's Jericho Bridge experience took place one October evening. "We weren't expecting anything," said Catherine. "We'd been to Jericho many times. We've taken our dogs back there hiking and we've been there many times trying to get something [paranormal]. This night we were not trying. We were just pleasing the kids."

Because of vandalism, visitors are no longer able to park on Jericho Road and walk to the bridge, so the family drove over the bridge, Catherine said, "Just to make sure there weren't any cars or anything coming that we could see." When they determined they were alone, they turned their van around, stopped on the bridge, and turned all the lights off, which had the desired "oh my gosh" effect on the kids.

Nothing happened, and eventually Catherine's husband said they were going to leave. He put the van's lights on. "And just as he started to go," Catherine said, "I looked in the van mirror and I saw this black shadow go from behind the van. It walked right into the bridge."

Catherine yelled for her husband to stop, telling him what she had just seen, but when they turned to look, the shadow was gone.

"We pulled onto the bridge again," Catherine said,

And [my husband] turned the lights off and [we] sat there. And we heard this noise on top of the van. We have a conversion van, so the top was high. And all of a sudden it was like there were people on our bumper. Our van just started hopping up and down, up and down. I've never seen fear in him, but I saw it that night. He said, "What is that?" And I said, "I don't know." And the kids said, "Go! Go! Go! Go!" So we left the bridge.

133

Catherine said her husband is more skeptical about the paranormal than she is, and more likely to offer up other explanations for what things could be. That he showed any sort of fear over what happened on the bridge demonstrates how genuine their experience was, and is a worthy addition to the evidence of Jericho Bridge's haunted quality.

134

THE JERICHO COVERED BRIDGE is on Jericho Road, Kingsville, Maryland 21087. Parking on the bridge isn't encouraged, so your best bet is to visit nearby Jerusalem Mill Village when it's open and walk a trail from the mill along Little Gunpowder Falls to the bridge.

THE CLOAKED SPECTER OF KEENERS ROAD
by Mike Smith

HAVING JUST SEPARATED FROM MY wife, April 1994 was a bad time for me. I was staying with friends and working at a convenience store in Dundalk, Maryland, when I met "Peggy." She shared my interest in the paranormal, and one night she told me about Keeners Road in Middle River.

When Peggy told me the story behind the haunting, I was certain it was an urban legend. Keeners Road, she said, was a lonely road that wound into the woods and was intersected by a railroad crossing, where a newlywed couple's car stalled and was hit by a train, killing them both. According to the legend, the woman's ghost haunts the tracks, looking for her husband's head, which was never found.

On the way to the site, Peggy told me about other ghostly things we might see, including glowing, disembodied eyes and dark, sinister men who suddenly stepped out of the woods onto the road. I was somewhat amused, but also skeptical that what she described was just another tall tale.

CHILLS

I turned onto Keeners Road, and as we passed some houses and condos I was nearly overcome with a feeling of absolute dread. The buildings gave way to woods, and then we came to the railroad crossing, marked by an old-fashioned wooden sign in the shape of an X. I was in a strange panic and, not wanting to get any closer to the tracks, I pulled over and lit a cigarette. When I finally calmed down, we crossed the tracks and continued down the narrow road and around a curve before turning around to leave. The bad feeling abated when we came close to home, but I still believed the road wasn't haunted. I didn't tell Peggy what I'd experienced, but I insisted that I was going to topple the ghost story.

My later library research turned up nothing about Keeners Road, but I spoke with a number of people who knew about it or had their own experiences there. A woman said she and her husband went there often, looking for a scare. One evening, they parked next to the crossing and sat in the back of his pickup. At first it was quiet, but after awhile they heard something drop out of the trees and then move through the leaves toward them. They left, but returned another night with a friend. The three built a fire and sat around it, and when the friend flipped a cigarette into the woods, it came right back at her.

A young lady told me she was walking on the tracks in daylight when two men dressed in dated Air Force fatigues approached. She claimed they had no eyes—just dark holes like zombies. *Zombies?* After that, I decided Keeners Road wasn't worth writing about. But I continued to make solo nighttime trips to the road, and every time I turned onto it, my blood ran ice-cold.

DREADFUL PURSUIT
One night in late April, I parked facing the crossing, about thirty yards away. My window was cracked open, and around one A.M. I heard a woman's voice coming from somewhere close to the tracks. She was yelling for a "Karl," and did so every ten minutes or so for hours. A few months later, Peggy and I returned. We hadn't been there long when someone stepped out of the woods near the crossing and walked toward us. The figure was backlit by the streetlight and we were scared, so I started the car, whipped it into reverse, and did a three-point turn to avoid the tracks.

Before I jammed the car into drive, however, I checked the rearview mirror. The figure I saw in it reminded me of a scene in *A Nightmare on Elm Street* where Freddy Krueger is walking down the street with six-foot-long arms. I couldn't make sense of what I saw; it was unbelievable. I screamed, "Look at it!" as I threw the car into gear and roared away. Peggy turned and saw it, too.

We went back on a Saturday night near the end of July. Peggy's son and daughter joined us, hoping for a thrill to break their boredom. I got chills as we turned onto the road, but we made an uneventful pass over the tracks and then went to the nearby 7-Eleven for sodas and smokes. At around two A.M. we returned for another try at the tracks, and this time something caught my attention. "Did you see *that?*" I asked the others. There was some kind of specter on the tracks, moving from right to left and away from the road as if it had just crossed it. It was a horrible thing, dressed in a hooded brownish gray cloak, the bottom of which was even with what should have been the thing's knees. There were no lower legs. Spookily, the hem fluttered as if in a strong breeze, even though the air was deathly still.

My companions agreed they had seen something horrifying, too, so we pulled over to get a better look. The specter was fast—it had moved farther away down the tracks than I thought possible. I got out of the car and beckoned to Peggy's eighteen-year-old son: "C'mon, dude!" Then I ran along the tracks after the cloaked specter.

PARANORMAL PREDATOR

I was about a hundred yards behind the specter when it turned around, pivoting as if it were on an axis—a completely unnatural movement. Behind me, Peggy screamed, "Mike! It's coming back!"

I turned and saw that Peggy's son wasn't with me—where had he gone? Even worse, I couldn't believe how far away the road now was. My knees turned into licorice sticks and I peed in my cutoffs. I looked back at the specter, and what I saw only deepened my horror. Inside the hood was only blackness. *There was no head!* Suddenly I sensed I was in great danger. I could feel pure evil radiating from the specter, and now it was pursuing *me*.

When I finally made it to the car and jumped in, everyone yelled at me for being so crazy. They said that the specter got close enough to grab me, but then vanished as if it couldn't enter the car.

Nobody said a word until I pulled into the McDonald's in Dundalk. As a

137

control, I asked the others not to describe what they had seen until I drew a picture of it. They then proceeded to describe the exact thing I had drawn.

I later read an article that claimed many ghost sightings are actually hallucinations that can be linked to nearby high-tension power lines, such as those that run parallel to the tracks off Keeners Road. For a while I wondered if this was true for me, but my friends had described the same specter. What are the odds of us all having the same hallucination?

There *is* a Ghost of Keeners Road. If you see it, stay in your car.

KEENERS ROAD is in Middle River, Maryland. To visit, take the exit off I-695 for Eastern Avenue. You'll pass Martin State Airport and shortly after passing a McDonald's, turn right onto Carroll Island Road and then left onto Keeners Road. It's okay to drive on the road, but residents don't appreciate people turning cars around in their driveways. The tracks belong to Conrail, and the land on either side belongs to Baltimore Gas & Electric.

OLUSTEE'S REENACTING REVENANT
by Charlie Carlson

FLORIDA'S LARGEST CIVIL WAR BATTLE was fought on February 20, 1864, at Olustee. It was at this bloody spot in North Florida that Gen. Joseph Finegan's 5,200 Confederates blocked Union Gen. Truman Seymour's advancing army. Seymour planned to march his 5,000 mostly black troops westbound across the state to cut transportation lines from central Florida that were funneling supplies to the Confederate forces in northern Georgia.

General Seymour had been warned by a defiant Southern woman, "Y'all will come back faster than you go." He found the woman's rant amusing, unaware it was a premonition of the fate awaiting his federal forces. The Battle of Olustee ended with a Confederate victory that left the woods scattered with the corpses of 203 Yankees and 93 Rebels.

Many of the battlefield dead were hastily buried in a makeshift cemetery. Stories about wild hogs rooting up the graves and eating the bodies persist.

Other folk tales casually mention people picking up scattered bones as souvenirs of the battle. Unsubstantiated or not, such stories are bound to rouse a few spirits.

In 1912 a historical monument was erected at the battle site, and for the past few decades a large reenactment has been held each February to commemorate the battle. Thousands of spectators flock to Olustee to watch reenactors bring the past alive, and it seems at times they have some paranormal help.

139

An Authentic Encounter

Orbs and ectoplasma ribbons of light have been caught in both digital and 35mm photos taken over the battlefield and during the event's annual Civil War Ball. Darting and floating orbs have appeared twice in video footage. To those who feel orbs are dust particles kicked up during reenactments, there's evidence that cannot be tied to dust, such as electronic voice phenomenon (EVP) recordings made at the site and fleeting glimpses of translucent apparitions in the pine forest surrounding the historic battlefield.

While playing dead during the mock battle, one reenactor recalled having an "eerie feeling" and "hearing a discarnate voice" that kept repeating, "Have you seen the elephant?"—a Civil War euphemism for experiencing combat. Another instance involves Ray Barlow, who in 2002 was helping a friend who worked as a sutler (vendor) at Civil War events set up before the Olustee reenactment. When they finished, Ray decided to walk along a trail that, he said, led to a very authentic encounter:

140

> I get a good ways down the trail and see this guy decked out in Confederate garb. I mean, he really looked the part, and on top of that he was barefooted. He was sitting next to a pine tree and had a small campfire going. So, he says, "Howdy," and I answered back but noticed he looked pretty skinny, like really ragged. I mean, he really looked the part. Of course, the reenactment wasn't until the next day.
>
> Anyway, he asked if I had a "chaw," so I pulled a square of chewing tobacco out of my shirt pocket. A lot of reenactors chew and spit—it adds realism to the whole business of reenacting. I handed it to him and he unwrapped the cellophane, cut off a plug with his knife, and put it in his mouth. Then he held the cellophane up and looked through it at the sun. He studied it for a bit and then asked me, "What's this made of?"
>
> I said, "It's cellophane." I figured he was making fun of me, having something that didn't fit the period theme. He didn't say much, but asked if he could have a piece of that cellophane. I obliged his request, put the tobacco back in my pocket, and went on down the trail.

Thirty minutes later, Ray went back to the spot by the tree to find no trace of the man—or the campfire. He told a friend about his experience, joking that he'd seen a ghost. Ray didn't see the man for the rest of the weekend, and when he got home, he looked up information on cellophane and learned it hadn't been invented until 1908.

"It really got me wondering," Ray said. "Maybe that guy had never seen cellophane; maybe he was in another time zone and somehow our paths got crossed up, because whatever happened to his campfire is beyond me."

OLUSTEE BATTLEFIELD STATE PARK

U.S. 90, Olustee, Florida 32072, 386-758-0400
www.floridastateparks.org/Olustee/

HEAVY-FOOTED PHANTOM
by Gregory Myers

IN 1982 MY FAMILY MOVED to a one-hundred-acre church camp where my grandfather had been sexton for decades. We did corrective maintenance on many of the buildings and equipment, and used a tractor and a Bush Hog to reclaim the fields along with an old dirt road on the property that had once connected the campground to the old highway. The transition from city life to country life didn't take long, and within a short time I would acquaint myself with the land and its inhabitants—both living and spectral.

The first time I cleared the road, the tractor's engine cut off cold. I tried to restart it several times before disconnecting the Bush Hog and slowly pushing the tractor over a small hill. It was then that I noticed an old, abandoned house about one hundred yards back from the road. It sat in an eerie little valley about a half mile from the home in which we were staying. I later noticed that most of the camp equipment didn't work well when used near the old house.

That summer, I explored the house with friends I'd made in the area. At that time of the year, dense vegetation blocked the two-story house from view. Most of the windows and doors were gone. There were no stairs to the second floor, and we quickly figured out that we could use the lathing boards to climb up into an open room with a vaulted ceiling and a square opening in the middle of the floor.

The house was still structurally safe—in my youthful opinion, anyway—and it became our clubhouse. I soon learned it belonged to former camp caretakers: a childless, married couple who were murdered in the house in the 1960s. The assailants had used a shotgun and were never captured, and the camp was closed for many years after the awful event. I never gave a second thought to the horrible events that occurred there until one frightful night the following summer.

A PRANK GONE WRONG

Within a year we had the landscape restored, and the following spring, the camp reopened. What had been a private playground for my family and friends now had to be shared with as many as fifty to seventy-five children, teens, and adults. Privacy was limited, except for a few secret dwellings I made hidden trails to— one of which was to the abandoned house.

One day I learned that one of the groups was planning to take a midnight nature hike on the grounds, and that their path would take them past the front of our clubhouse. My friends and I needed a plan to keep these midnight "trespassers" off our turf. In the end, our plan was quite simple: A friend and I would go down to the house before the group left for their midnight adventure and wait for them on the second floor. When they arrived, we would make creepy noises and give them the scare of their lives.

On that cool, summer night, the moon was bright enough that we didn't need much assistance from our flashlights to navigate the hidden trail to the house. We arrived at about eleven thirty P.M., climbed the wall to the second floor, and hunkered down to wait for our unsuspecting victims. After a few minutes, however, my friend and I heard odd shuffling noises from the first floor. We initially dismissed it as a four-legged critter that had found its way in, but the shuffling increased in volume and began to resemble human footsteps. We stuck our heads through the opening in the floor and shone our flashlights into all the areas below, but we found nothing in the vicinity, and there was no place to hide from our vantage point.

The footsteps were now those of a huge man wearing work boots, but we *still* couldn't see anything as they headed toward the staircase opening we had

143

haunted their grounds. The group brought in two psychics for a séance and filmed it for a cable show. Sandy had never participated in a séance before, but she found it quite educational. As she recalls, the psychics "found out the guy who we had seen there had a tannery. He made saddles. We used to smell cherry tobacco all the time, and we couldn't figure out why. The historians told us that sometimes the stench from the hides was so bad that these guys would smoke that to cover the smell."

Sandy's youngest daughter started to cough during the séance, appearing as if she were being crushed, and the

146

psychics determined that the man was crushed to death on the property. And while Sandy's son "never, ever saw anything, and didn't believe any of us," he may have changed his mind that night. He said he could feel the ghost of the little girl sit in his lap and play with his hair. The psychics also drew pictures of the tannery ghost and the little girl, which Sandy said were "exactly what we saw."

Perhaps the most mysterious ghost that came through during the séance was one who hadn't been previously sensed on the property. Sandy said,

> My son started gagging . . . he said, "I can't breathe, I can't breathe. I think I feel like my neck is really tight." So she (the psychic) asked him, "Do you want me to stop?" And he said, "No."

> She started talking to the (ghost) through him . . . she said, "I see people looking at me, they're all spitting at me, and I didn't do it." And

he was experiencing this little boy's hanging. It was apparently the last hanging in Flemington. It was a little black boy who was being hung at thirteen for killing his mistress. And he wanted everybody to know he didn't do it.

PROVING A STORY

Weird Encounters approached Allan Duncan, a former police officer turned counselor, historian, and contributor to other *Weird* publications, for additional information on hangings in Hunterdon County. He was able to confirm that a young slave, a boy of about thirteen or fourteen years named James Guild (or Guise, or Brown, depending on the source), was hung in Flemington, New Jersey, on November 28, 1828. The charge was murder, and the *Hunterdon County Democrat* reported the boy's execution the following December:

> The last execution was . . . in a field about forty rods west of the
> village, on the north side of the road leading to Stockton, or Centre
> Bridge as it was then called. It was that of James Brown, a colored boy
> aged about 14, who in Hopewell beat to death an old lady named
> Beaks with an ox yoke, because she refused to lend him a gun.

147

Duncan also found that a slave named Sylvia Dubois had witnessed James's hanging, as documented in *The Sourlands* by Jim Luce.

If the ghost at the séance was James, it's interesting that he claimed his mistress had been poisoned. Did someone else poison Old Lady Beaks, then beat her lifeless body with an ox yoke and point the finger at James? Perhaps, but Duncan suggested that even ghosts can be in denial, and maybe that's why James hasn't moved on. The newspaper account mentions that James was hanged in a field along the road to Stockton, and his story is not well known, even within New Jersey. Thus, for nonlocal psychics to pick James's spirit up in a Stockton barn without prior knowledge of his hanging is undoubtedly eerie.

PRIVATE PROPERTY

Creepy
Cemeteries

"No one is permitted inside the cemetery after dark." —A
sign outside of Logan Cemetery in Logan, Utah

THE GHOST RULEBOOK SAYS you can't haunt a graveyard or cemetery unless you meet one of two qualifications: you have died on that spot, or your grave has been disturbed in some way. Then you can start rattling chains and scaring the living.

Some ghosts follow protocol. Take the ones in a New Hampshire cemetery, rumored to be the site of an epic battle among American Indian tribes and several tragic farmhouse fires. Cemeteries in Ohio and California have been encroached upon by parking lots, streets, and sidewalks. And the desecration of a serial killer's grave site in Pennsylvania results in a lot more than a group of young men bargained for. Yes, the ghosts in these locations have every right to kick up a fuss.

Other spirits appear to have long ago tossed the rulebook. In New Jersey, a Ouija message brings unsuspecting teens to a tombstone with a tragic story. There are burial grounds in Massachusetts, Pennsylvania, and Utah in which nobody appears to have died, or haven't been rudely disturbed, moved around, or covered over to make room for progress, yet hauntings still occur. The ghost rulebook says there's no reason for ghosts to appear in many cemeteries, but they do anyway.

Who said ghosts follow rules?

NEW BETHEL CEMETERY
by Steve Weinik

KEMPTON, PENNSYLVANIA, IS A TINY town about two hours outside of Philadelphia, nestled at the base of Hawk Mountain. The currents that carry hundreds of birds of prey over the mountain, however, don't compare to decidedly stranger currents in the area. The Lenni Lenape tribe regarded the mountain as a sacred place, and archaeologists have uncovered evidence of ritual sites on its peak. European settlers had their own unusual relationship with the mountain, punctuated by the intensely dark legacy of a killer who once resided there.

The building that now houses the bird sanctuary off of Hawk Mountain Road was once an inn run by an eccentric and reclusive man named Matthias Schambacher. It was a popular way station where travelers could rest before setting out over Pennsylvania's rugged terrain—that is, if they ever managed to escape it. As it turns out, Schambacher was a serial killer, and on his deathbed he admitted to murdering—depending on the source—eleven to fourteen men before he lost count. Most disturbingly, he also claimed that the compulsion to kill was "caused by a great evil that lives on the mountain that whispered to him constantly, urging him to murder, even while he slept."

The murderous innkeeper was buried in Kempton at the New Bethel Church Cemetery. One summer day, spurred by a ghastly story I heard by a campfire years ago, I attempted a visit to his grave site.

RAISING HELL

The friend who told me this story is not prone to fanciful exaggerations or fabricated tales. He went to the mountainside two weekends a month to attend a survivalist-training camp. After a couple years of camping in the woods, he and his fellow survivalists experienced their fair share of strange things: unknown lights, screams in the middle of the night, and plenty of odd characters moving in the shadows. Their fear had nonetheless been gradually usurped by curiosity, combined with a confidence grown by their experience in the woods. So, one night after a few drinks, when someone suggested they take the short drive down the mountain to the "haunted" cemetery where the killer Schambacher was buried, no one flinched.

At ten thirty P.M., five young men pulled into the parking lot of the New Bethel Church. Only one knew where to find the unmarked grave site of Matthias

being watched, and even the bearded white figure holding a long-handled farm instrument, have appeared repeatedly in Kempton ghost stories.

Terrifying tales aside, I recently visited the New Bethel Cemetery. It was a strange, beautiful, and utterly peaceful cemetery in the Pennsylvania countryside, and my experience there was overwhelmingly calm and quiet—except for two small details.

The cemetery sits on a hill, at the top of which stands a grove of trees. During my visit, hundreds of crows—really, a murder of them—were roosting in the trees. I know that crows congregate in groups like this from time to time, but why there, and why

154

then? Nothing offsets my nerves like noisy crows, but I soon got used to them and enjoyed the late autumn afternoon in the idyllic countryside.

Mindful about leaving before sunset, I got back into my car and started on the trip home. The road darkened quickly, and I began to recall my friend's story. The moment I imagined what it must have been like in that other car, a jolt of electricity ran up my back to the base of my skull. Startled, I felt compelled to look out the passenger-side window, where I saw a fresh roadside memorial. At its base, among the wreaths, written messages, fresh flowers, and handmade cross, was a dead cat.

The jolt soon subsided, but my unease did not. It wasn't much—just an odd little coincidence, perhaps—but when dealing with Matthias Schambacher, you can never be certain.

NEW BETHEL CEMETERY

New Bethel Church Road, Kempton, Pennsylvania 19529

LOGAN'S CRYING LADY
by Janice Oberding

Situated on the western slopes of the Bear River Mountains some eighty miles north of Salt Lake City is Logan, Utah. Here you will find the University of Utah's main campus, and nearby, the weeping Logan Cemetery statue.

According to one legend, the lady statue sheds tears under full moons, while another describes the statue wandering through the cemetery in search of children who preceded her in death. Recently my daughter-in-law and I visited Logan Cemetery to see the solemn statue for ourselves.

It was late in the afternoon by the time we headed down North 1200 East to the cemetery, but as we pulled into the long narrow drive leading into the gates,

156

a sign caught our attention: NO ONE IS PERMITTED INSIDE THE CEMETERY AFTER DARK. Maybe too many people had attempted to prove or disprove the story.

Luckily it was the middle of summer, and we had several hours of daylight left. We found the statue easily enough and after photographing it from every angle, we set off on foot to admire and photograph other headstones. Before long, the sun had vanished beyond the horizon, replaced by a full moon.

As we neared the crying lady statue once more, we noticed a young woman kneeling at its base. Not wanting to intrude on her grief, we hung back and waited. Finally she stood. Tears sparkled in her eyes when she glanced our way. Then, brushing dried grass from her maroon skirt, she walked around to the other side of the statue. We crept closer, waiting for the gentle sobs that came from her direction to cease.

The crying continued, and I looked up at the statue, whose eyes were as dry as dust.

"I hope she leaves soon," I whispered.

"Me too," my daughter-in-law agreed. Then she teased, "I might love you, but being in here after dark, well, I'm not going to jail for you."

The sobbing intensified, so we stepped around to the other side of the statue. This poor woman was obviously in distress.

To our bewilderment, we found no one there.

"Where did she go?" my daughter-in-law gasped. "How did she get past us?"

"Maybe she went straight back the other way," I suggested.

"No. We would have seen her leave."

We looked up at the statue. The last streak of day had vanished from the sky, and we had no choice but to leave.

"Have you ever heard of a ghost brushing grass from its clothing?" I asked.

"Have you ever heard of someone vanishing into thin air?" she countered.

We drove through the cemetery once more. In the end, my daughter-in-law was right.

LOGAN CEMETERY

1000 North 1200 East, Logan, Utah 84321

KINGS ISLAND CEMETERY
by James A. Willis

BEGINNING EVERY SPRING, THOUSANDS OF people from Ohio and beyond make the trek along I-71 near Cincinnati to visit one of the best amusement parks in Ohio: Kings Island. Visitors delight in the rapid, stomach-dropping dips of such famous attractions as The Beast, but most are unaware that they may be in for one last thrill as they exit the park. After a long, exhilarating day on the Ferris wheels, coasters, and tilt-a-whirls, you might just catch a glimpse of a ghostly young girl skipping through the Kings Island parking lot.

Often described as having blond hair and wearing a blue dress, she is apparently quite playful. Some witnesses report that the little ghoul likes to play hide-and-seek among the cars, and park tram drivers claim she frequently darts out in front of the tram in a bizarre game of "chicken." The girl's identity and her reasons for haunting Kings Island have long been debated, but most agree that her ghost originates from a local attraction you won't find listed on any Kings Island park map: a small cemetery sitting quietly near the parking lot exit gates.

ENCROACHING ON THE DEAD

Over the years, the cemetery has been known by many different names, including the United Methodist Cemetery and the Dog Street Cemetery. For a long time, it was simply referred to as the Dill Cemetery or the Hoff Farm Cemetery to reflect the names of various landowners. In the late 1800s, the King Powder Company opened for business, and although it ceased operation in the 1940s, the King family continued to own the land until large portions of it were purchased to create Kings Island Amusement Park in 1972. Almost all of the existing buildings on the property were demolished to make way for the park's rides. The cemetery, however, was allowed to stay.

Today the cemetery sits quietly behind a wooden fence at the far end of the Kings Island parking lot. Since it is only about twelve feet from the pavement, a popular urban legend states that the girl's ghost arrived on the scene when her grave was inadvertently paved over. Another theory arises from the baffling disappearance of numerous gravestones over the years. In the 1980s, an unofficial count of the cemetery stones revealed that there were approximately sixty-nine stones within its confines, but in 2005, only fifty-two remained. What became

of the missing stones? In the field of paranormal research, it is a common belief that disturbing final resting places of individuals often results in a haunting as the spirit searches to make its grave "whole" again. Perhaps this is why the ghostly girl roams the grounds of Kings Island.

KINGS ISLAND AMUSEMENT PARK

6300 Kings Island Drive, Kings Island, Ohio 45034, 800-288-0808, www.pki.com. It's just off of I-71 northeast of Cincinnati, Ohio. The cemetery sits behind a wooden fence at the far end of the parking lot.

RESURRECTION MARY
by Jeffrey Wargo

DARKNESS CHANGES THE EVERYDAY WORLD into a realm where buildings are but black silhouettes against a moonlit sky, trees are imbued with the illusion of life, and reflections of light trick the eyes. But when a driver spots a young woman in white beside a deserted road or graveyard gate, who later vanishes into thin air, is it really just a trick of light?

The woman in white is a common motif in supernatural literature. In some tales, the woman is offered a ride but vanishes at some point along the journey; in others, she sticks around until the driver opens the passenger door to an empty seat. In yet others, the driver later visits the home of the mysterious passenger, only to hear from a baffled resident that the woman has been dead for many years. Another common plotline leads the driver and ghostly passenger to her address, where he encounters a cemetery.

160

The most famous of these tales involves an apparition known in local lore as Resurrection Mary, who haunts Archer Avenue in Chicago, Illinois. But Riegelsville, Pennsylvania, boasts two of its own Resurrection Mary stories.

THE FACELESS CHILD

On a cold, spring night, a young man and his friends decided to drive down the block to one of their houses off of Church Road on the southern end of Union Cemetery to pick up a forgotten item. It was approaching one A.M. as they climbed into the car at the northern end of the cemetery. Casual conversation ensued as they turned left onto Elmwood Lane and made a sharp right turn onto Church Road. At this juncture, heading straight down along the graveyard toward the churches at its far end, the driver was startled by an abrupt flash of a bright light about thirty feet ahead of the vehicle. Turning, he saw a young woman, short in stature and dressed in white, running out from the area of St. John's Church parking lot toward the cemetery wall on their right. The driver slammed on his brakes to avoid hitting her, but she had already reached the burial grounds. They rolled down the passenger-side window and stared into the cold night and darkness. There, peering in among the tombstones to see where she had gone, the friends were spooked to find that no one was in sight.

Comparing what each had witnessed, they agreed that it wasn't an animal or any trick of the eye. It was definitely the whispery white image of a school-aged girl wearing a frilled, formal skirt and some type of head covering. She had no visible face.

Could this be the same spectral child who had been seen along the cemetery wall across from the Riegelsville Academy, where boys and girls were schooled in the early days of the town's existence?

A CHARITABLE SOUL

Another spirit in town who shares the Resurrection Mary spotlight is believed to be that of Mary Louisa Aughinbaugh, a young woman buried in Union Cemetery. Mary Louisa was the wife of the Rev. George W. Aughinbaugh, who served as pastor of St. John United Church of Christ from January 1862 through July 1865 and from November 1865 through April 1873. During his second tenure as pastor, the couple lived in the Cyrus Stover house that served as the parsonage for the church until close to the turn of the century. It was in one of

161

the upstairs bedrooms of the Stover house that, on September 19, 1867, Mary Louisa succumbed to tuberculosis and died.

The church community was fond of Mary and erected a unique tombstone on her burial plot near the corner of the old Union Church site: a Victorian-style stone, with boulders from the Gettysburg battlefield forming its base and a faux wooden cross at the top, a symbol of faith and a life cut short in its prime. From the place where she is buried, one can see her beloved home and church, which some say she could never truly abandon.

Many folks in Riegelsville whisper about the woman in white seen walking the grounds of the Union Cemetery and along the Church and Delaware roads. About five years back, some teens and young adults were playing flashlight tag around St. Lawrence Roman Catholic Church and the bike path on the northern end of the cemetery. At one point in the evening, two of the teens were running down the bike path that extends between the woods and the community on the western edge of town and were startled when an otherworldly woman appeared on the path ahead. Like so many others before and since, they watched in astonishment as the whispery white woman disappeared into thin air.

Time passes, but the stories of the woman in white remain remarkably consistent. Why a child or benevolent preacher's wife would be denied their merited passage to a heavenly afterlife, however, presents another issue altogether. Perhaps they were simply not ready to depart when the light beckoned, choosing instead to wander the cemetery grounds where loved ones lay in final repose.

163

RIEGELSVILLE UNION CEMETERY
Church and Delaware Roads, Riegelsville, Pennsylvania 18077

PHEBE TALKS
by Walter O'Brien

ON THE NIGHT BEFORE HALLOWEEN in the early 1970s, I was among a dozen or so teenagers hanging out in a friend's basement in suburban New Jersey. With the likes of Black Sabbath and Coven blaring from the radio and talk of all things occult in the air, someone dragged out the Ouija board. My girlfriend and I decided to give it try.

"Are there any spirits in the room with us tonight?" I asked. The pointer suddenly acquired a will of its own and proceeded directly to YES. My girlfriend and I gasped in astonishment, each insisting no influence over movement of the pointer. A little shaken up, we asked the spirit's name. The pointer moved quickly to the letter P, followed in order by H, E, B, and E. None of us knew anybody by that name, but we joked about the spirit's poor spelling. Everyone there knew the name Phebe contains an O.

Next, we moved the pointer back to the middle of the board and asked, "Are you alone?" The pointer cut across to the number 2. We repeated the query, and this time I pressed my fingers a little tighter on the pointer and tried to move it to YES. It fought against me, however, and moved again to 2. At this point, the crowd noticed that something strange was going on, but I was still skeptical. I thus decided to take on the Ouija board alone—just *my* fingers on the pointer—to prove that there was no invisible third or fourth party present.

We asked the name of the second spirit, and despite my best efforts to hold the pointer steady, it slid directly to the NO space twice. Someone then suggested we ask the zodiac sign of the spirits. Letter by letter, the word *Sagittarius* was spelled out. When we asked the zodiac sign of the second spirit, the pointer quickly spelled *Cancer*.

More than a little freaked out at this point, the group unanimously decided that Ouija fun time was over. We ditched the basement and decided to take a road trip, which in those days meant driving around aimlessly and taking turns leading the pack of cars until we got bored. First we headed northwest up Morris Avenue. I took the lead and continued toward Springfield. As we turned one bend in the road, however, someone noticed an old Revolutionary War cemetery to our right. Already scared out of our wits by the evening's Ouija adventure, pulling into a deserted old graveyard at midnight seemed the sensible thing to do . . .

My girlfriend had some candles that we passed around as we wandered the cemetery, reading tombstones. It was a big thing at the time to take paper and crayons and do rubbings of the names, and one friend in our group had come prepared. After she gravitated toward a large obelisk-shaped monument in the middle of the yard, we heard her scream. As we ran to her side, my girlfriend took her candle and held it near the obelisk. There, in big letters across the top, was the word *Phebe*—followed by the words *loving wife and mother*, and dates somewhere in the middle 1700s. Someone pointed out the birth date: Phebe was a Sagittarius!

Casting our eyes farther down the stone, we discerned, in badly eroded lettering, the words *infant girl*. According to the dates on the stone, she had been born and died on the date of her mother's passing, suggesting that Phebe had died in childbirth before giving her daughter a name. That explained why the Ouija kept saying NO when we insisted on a name. To top it all off, the infant's date of birth made her zodiac sign a Cancer!

I've never seen a group of kids run faster than we did out of that cemetery.   *165*

BODIES BENEATH THE BOULEVARD
by James A. Willis

FEW OF THE VISITORS TO San Diego's Whaley House—reportedly one of the most haunted houses in the United States—realize that a mere two blocks away, some of the area's oldest ghosts are said to roam the cemetery they are buried in, as well as the road they are buried under!

Located in the 2400 block of San Diego Avenue in Old Town is the second oldest cemetery in San Diego: El Campo Santo ("The Holy Field"). Originally created to serve as the final resting place of the city's founders, records state that from 1849 until 1897 approximately 477 individuals were buried in El Campo Santo. And yet visitors to this adobe-walled cemetery will find less than one hundred markers. What became of the other graves?

Less than thirty years after El Campo Santo cemetery was opened, it became neglected and weed infested. Soon after, some of the graves were desecrated. For those reasons, several families decided to have the bodies of their loved ones relocated to better kept cemeteries. In some cases, tombstones were left behind while the bodies themselves were moved. Other times, neighboring grave sites were inadvertently disturbed while bodies were being exhumed. Over time it became quite difficult to identify exactly who was buried in El

REMEMBERING THE MORE THAN 20 MEN, WOMEN AND CHILDREN WHO LIE BURIED BENEATH SAN DIEGO AVE. ONLY ASSEMBLYMAN EDWARD L. GREENE WAS EXHUMED AND PLACED WITHIN THE NEW BOUNDARY OF EL CAMPO SANTO CEMETERY.

THESE GRAVES WERE DISCOVERED WITH THE USE OF GROUND PENETRATING RADAR IN 1993.

REST IN PEACE

THIS PLAQUE WAS PLACED BY THE HISTORICAL SHRINE FOUNDATION WITH FUNDS FROM THE SAN DIEGO COMMUNITY DEVELOPMENT BLOCK GRANT IN 1994.

Gate

San Diego Avenue

Campo Santo, and construction of a horse-drawn street railway along Old Town's main street in the late 1880s wreaked further havoc on the graveyard's remaining tombs. Builders ran the railway line straight through the cemetery. Some of the graves were relocated; most were not.

In 1933, in an attempt to officially stake out the cemetery grounds proper, the current cemetery walls were erected. However, because of all the moving and shifting that had already taken place, the locations of numerous grave sites were unknown. Thus, upon the completion of the wall, many graves that were once interred inside the hallowed cemetery grounds proper now lay outside them. But one of the saddest moments in the history of El Campo Santo came in 1942 with the creation of San Diego Avenue. Even back then, there was a public outcry over the possible paving over of burial sites, but local officials stood firm, stating that there was only one grave site in danger of being paved over: that of assemblyman Edward L. Greene. His remains were exhumed and placed inside the new boundaries of the cemetery. Then the asphalt was put down and the concrete for the sidewalk was poured.

167

Years later, in 1993, almost thirty-five graves were discovered underneath when special ground-penetrating radar was used along San Diego Avenue and the sidewalk in front of the cemetery. In 1994, a memorial plaque was placed at the entrance to the cemetery to remember "the more than 20 men, women and children who lay buried beneath San Diego Ave." At the bottom of the plaque is a diagram showing the approximate locations of the graves, and a second plaque at the back of the cemetery shows the locations of thirteen graves—mostly of children—buried underneath Linwood Street. Additionally, people walking past the cemetery on the sidewalk may come across simple circular metal markers embedded in the concrete reading, simply, "grave site."

A visit to El Campo Santo today is one filled with sadness. Inside the cemetery, there is hardly any vegetation—nothing but dirt and a few old trees. Some have managed to maintain the white wooden fences around the plots of loved ones, and a few have even erected biographies, but for most of the graves, there is nothing more than a small wooden cross or a few stones and bricks.

NOT YOUR USUAL SUSPECTS

With all of the sadness the desecration El Campo Santo has known through the years, it should come as no surprise that visitors to the cemetery have reported ghostly encounters. Within the cemetery, it is not uncommon to come across strange, unexplainable cold spots, even during broad daylight in the summer. At night, people have reported seeing strange lights moving inside the cemetery and ghostly figures floating above the ground. There is also a woman dressed in period clothing who is often seen standing near the cemetery entrance, gazing out toward the street.

The activity is not limited to the cemetery, either. Individuals parked in front of the graveyard often find that their cars won't start back up. Car alarms also go off for no apparent reason, as if unseen hands have pushed or touched them.

So with all this ghostly activity being reported at El Campo Santo, one question remains: Whose ghosts are they? One of the primary suspects is a gentleman whose spirit is also allegedly haunting the Whaley House: James Robinson. Better known as Yankee Jim, Robinson was convicted of attempted grand larceny and executed for his crime on the site where the Whaley House was erected years later. Whaley family members often reported hearing ghostly footsteps echoing throughout the house; and since Robinson's ghost is still apparently quite active, it makes sense that he would occasionally leave the Whaley House and head down to El Campo Santo Cemetery to visit his earthly remains, which are interred just inside the gates.

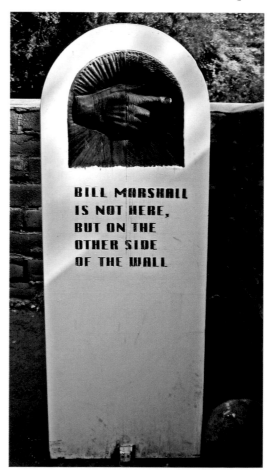

168

Another likely offender is Antonio Garra, chief of the Cupeños tribe. In the early 1850s, Garra took part in a planned uprising in response to taxation of the California Indians by the United States government. In December 1851, the uprising was quashed and Garra was arrested. After a short trial, he was sentenced to death, marched to El Campo Santo, made to dig his own grave, and then executed by a firing squad. If his violent death isn't enough of a provocation, there are some who believe the current marker for Garra's grave is in the wrong spot and that the chief is actually buried under San Diego Avenue.

Yet another possible culprit for the strange activity in El Campo Santo is William Marshall—at one point nicknamed the Wickedest Man in California. In December of 1846, there was unrest among the California settlers and the local Luiseño Indians. Things spilled over, and eleven Californians were killed by the Luiseño in what became known as the Pauma Massacre. Marshall was arrested and charged for his role in the massacre, and although he denied any involvement, was convicted and sentenced to death.

After being hanged for his crime, Marshall was interred inside El Campo Santo Cemetery . . . or was he? In what ranks up there as one of the strangest tombstones in history, Marshall's reads simply, "Bill Marshall is not here, but on the other side of the wall," complete with the etching of a hand pointing outside the cemetery wall. According to legend, Marshall was deemed so wicked that he didn't deserve to be buried on holy ground, though others believe Marshall

169

was originally inside the cemetery grounds until the wall went up. Whichever version you ascribe to, the controversy surrounding his grave-site location and possible false conviction certainly make him a prime suspect for such paranormal trickery.

The list goes on. Some people believe one of the ghosts belongs to Rafael Mumudes, a gravedigger who is also interred within the cemetery. Of course, we can't forget about the multitude of men, women, and children who are resting beneath unmarked graves, concrete, or asphalt. Whoever they may be, one thing is for sure: You never know when one of the ghostly residents of El Campo Santo will decide to make its presence known.

EL CAMPO SANTO

2410 San Diego Avenue, San Diego, California 92110

THE HALL FAMILY HAUNTING GROUND
by Sara Webb Quest

ON A BITTER COLD NOVEMBER day in 1983 when I was twelve years old, my mother escorted me and a friend through the woods of Dennis, Massachusetts. In front of us, an arched, wooden bridge led to the Cape Playhouse grounds, but on this day, we wanted to explore. Abandoning the fun and familiar for the thrill of the unknown, we strayed down a path running perpendicular to the old Hall Cemetery, a tiny family plot plum in the center of the woods. I glanced at the cemetery, where tombstones adorned with skulls and wings dated from the late seventeenth century, and spotted a thin woman in somber, Puritan attire walking among the graves. Moving with a distinctive straightness of posture, she seemed set on her destination. She wore a long dress, her gray hair was pulled back in a bun, and most jarringly, I could see right through her. "Look!" I said, pointing out the spirit to my companions, but she had mysteriously vanished.

As it turned out, mine wasn't the only encounter with the supernatural in Dennis, Massachusetts: A schoolmate of mine had her own account of the haunted Hall family cemetery. She had been walking in those same woods when she heard a woman's voice call, "Hellooo." Despite the voice's close proximity, no one was there.

THE HALL CEMETERY is located off Route 6A behind the Cape Playhouse grounds and is open to the public.

GILSON ROAD CEMETERY
by Fiona Broome

GILSON ROAD CEMETERY IS ONE of southern New Hampshire's spookiest sites. It's so haunted that in early 2001, the city of Nashua lowered the road in front of the cemetery to prevent accidents resulting from motorists witnessing ghostly activities behind the cemetery's ancient stone walls.

When I first visited Gilson Road, I was disappointed to find an ordinary, old New Hampshire cemetery: a dozen or so colonial headstones, a few newer ones, and some open areas. Then, to my delight, I spotted an opening in the cemetery's northeastern wall. In early American cemeteries, such an opening indicates the presence of "sinners" buried just outside the hallowed ground. If you're looking for ghosts, start there. With dusk fast approaching, I lingered, examining the gothic inscriptions on the headstones. "Prepare for Death / and follow me," one of them read. The chills really kicked in, however, when I encountered a sphere of icy air suspended above the stone marked "Jos. W. Gilson." I moved my hands through this frigid air, and felt as though I was reaching into a freezer—an indication of the drastic temperature discrepancy between the spot just above the headstone and the surrounding area. Filled with mysterious dread, I began taking photos of the headstones. The images revealed a strange mist around the older headstones—especially that of Rufus Lawrence—and an eerie haze surrounding the graves of the Fisk and Jewell families.

On that evening, and during subsequent visits to the site, I sensed something hostile at the cemetery's northeast corner. There, coffin-shaped depressions in the ground caused by the gradual decomposition of wooden caskets represent unmarked graves. On chilly nights, heat appears to emanate from some of the depressions, as if the graves are active.

GILSON'S HOODED GHOUL

The woods are well populated with chipmunks, squirrels, and other small animals, but—for no apparent reason—the area becomes totally quiet immediately before a paranormal event. That's when people suddenly see ghostly campfires and torches in the woods, and when the cemetery's infamous hooded figure appears.

For at least thirty years, people have encountered an apparition at Gilson Road Cemetery. A tall figure, well over six feet, emerges after dark from the woods behind the cemetery, sometimes leaping over the back wall. The ghoul has also

172

been seen entering the grounds through the opening at the northeast corner of the cemetery. According to witnesses, the specter wears a hood that conceals its face and often remains silent, although it has been known to shout at people on occasion. It chases people out of Gilson Road Cemetery and stops only when it reaches the cemetery's front wall. Then the specter vanishes abruptly. What happens to those who fail to outrun the hooded ghoul? No one knows.

SURROUNDED BY SPOOKS

Gilson Road Cemetery is wooded on three sides. Around noon each day, people sense figures creeping through the woods. When those figures are visible, they're often clothed in Native garb, such as buckskin loincloths. I saw a hooded figure in the woods about fifty feet away from me. The pattern of sunlight and shadows was visible across his shoulders as he walked, but he abruptly vanished after passing a slender tree. When I investigated the area, I found no signs of him.

A potentially dangerous phenomenon has been reported at the crest of the hill just north of Gilson Road Cemetery. People standing on the hill have described feeling as if an unknown force was pushing them toward the edge. Luckily no one has actually fallen off, although I highly recommend avoiding standing anywhere near the side where the hill drops off sharply.

One of the most reliable ways to detect paranormal activity at Gilson Road Cemetery is with an ordinary hiking compass. In theory, the compass needle should always point toward magnetic north. At Gilson Road Cemetery, however, you will witness the needle swing 35 to 90 degrees and then stop, as if north had changed position. And if you walk back and forth through the cemetery, north will change direction yet again. It's not magnetic ore in the ground or the effect of power lines: EMF devices measure brief spikes in electromagnetic energy and, no matter how many bars are displayed, cell phones frequently stop working within the cemetery walls.

SEEKING ANSWERS

Strangely, few records explain why Gilson Road Cemetery was built in the middle of nowhere. Even more strangely, most of the people buried at the cemetery aren't mentioned in any census or civil records of that era. It's as if they were forgotten . . . on purpose.

Though city records are sparse, local folklore provides some vivid explanations for the hauntings in and around Gilson Road Cemetery. Apparently the site was a battleground when rival American Indian tribes ruled parts of New England. Warriors from those Indian nations traveled hundreds of miles to fight in the surrounds of western Nashua, New Hampshire. Following one massacre in the area, a shaman reportedly embarked on a killing spree. Fearing that his spirit might seek retribution, the tribe chose to imprison him on a small island in the middle of a deep swamp rather than put him to death. During a drought some years later, the swamp drained. The shaman could have returned home, but he allegedly preferred the isolation of his new locale, where he could continue killing hunters and unwary travelers without detection.

According to another early legend, a colonial farmhouse on Gilson Road burned to the ground one night, killing everyone inside. Soon afterward, another family built a home on the same site. Mysteriously, that house also burned to the ground and everyone, likewise, died. When those graves were added to the property, it was converted into a formal cemetery. The stone walls around Gilson Road Cemetery are the same ones that once enclosed the doomed colonial farmhouses, a garden, and some animals. Today the bodies of both families are resting somewhere beneath the unmarked depressions at the back of the cemetery.

Could the murderous shaman be the hooded apparition spotted in the woods surrounding the Gilson Road Cemetery, whispering and muttering as he looks for fresh victims? Could the heat rising from the unmarked graves be a ghostly reminder of deadly infernos from centuries ago? Many continue to deny the existence of the paranormal, but evidence is mounting to suggest that tragic figures don't always go quietly into the night.

GILSON ROAD CEMETERY is located in Nashua, New Hampshire, about one-third of a mile north of the intersection of Main Dunstable Road and Gilson Road.

Hostel Environments

"At precisely the moment Jeff's hand touched the handprint on the wall, an inhuman, raspy sigh seemed to float off the tape." —Experience in a Pennsylvania inn

HAVE YOU ALWAYS WANTED to spend the night in a haunted house but just don't have the connections to do so? Well, we've got good news for you. Nowadays there are plenty of hotels, inns, or B and Bs that proudly offer the chance for guests to sleep—or not—with ghosts. When a haunted room is available, simply whip out the credit card, and you're in. Who needs connections?

Whether the rumored ghosts show up when you do is an entirely different matter. But if they do, you'll find they're a diverse bunch—just like the ghosts who appear in this chapter.

Pseudoroyalty walks the halls of a longtime hotel in Texas, and a ghostly maid and spooky dancers are among the many phantoms that appear in a swank New Hampshire lodging. A miner's ghost tweaks toes in a pet-friendly Arizona inn, and guests at a Florida B and B mingle with spirits ranging from long-dead millionaires to playful little girls to—gulp—evil clowns. The ghost of Alice makes visitors sick in a Pennsylvania rest stop, and the phantom of Fred will fix whatever's on the fritz at a California hotel. And though we don't know exactly who haunts another Pennsylvania inn, we suggest you don't touch the wet handprint on the wall of Room 6. You can even stay at a B and B where Lizzie Borden denied taking a few swings with an ax. . . .

We think these ghosts will certainly set your trip apart from the average hostelry experience. Instead of just staying in an anonymous room that holds your stuff while you head off to whatever else you're in town to do, a ghostly encounter can really define your stay. And a ghost is more fun than a mint on your pillow any day.

MONTEREY HOTEL'S REVENANT REPAIRMAN
by Janice Oberding

AMONG THE MANY STAFF MEMBERS of the hundred-year-old Monterey Hotel is an employee they call Fred. While most people are glad when their workday ends and it's time to punch out and go home, Fred isn't among them. In fact, he's still performing routine janitorial duties years after his own death.

I was on my first business trip to California's Monterey Peninsula when I booked into the haunted hotel. The place was luxurious, with ornate antique furnishings and a lavish continental breakfast, and—as I soon found out—a ghostly repairman. Prior to this I had always thought ghosts were nothing but a lot of nonsense, so Fred made a considerable impression on me when he helped fix some broken appliances that night.

OTHERWORLDLY INTERVENTION

It was after ten o'clock, and Alvarado Street was glistening after a winter night's downpour. Unable to sleep, I pulled on my raincoat and walked several blocks of the historic district, enjoying the mild, rainy weather. When I returned to my room, relaxed and ready for bed, I decided to catch the local news. I clicked on the television, but the screen remained black. I'd been in enough hotel rooms to know that maids sometimes unplug the TVs while vacuuming. I checked, and that wasn't the case.

The front desk will send someone to fix it, I told myself as I picked up the telephone receiver. There was no dial tone. After several attempts at calling, I stepped out into the hall and saw a man in a janitor's uniform standing by an ornate mirror. There was something about his demeanor that I sized up as strange, but I needed help.

"Do you work here?" I asked.

He nodded.

"Nothing is working in my room. The TV and the phone are on the fritz," I said, leading him back to my room. We stepped inside, and the temperature in the room dropped suddenly.

"The heat must have quit too!" I exclaimed. "I hate to change rooms. The view is wonderful from here. Can you fix it?"

He nodded and set to work on the thermostat. The temperature quickly climbed. Satisfied that he had solved the problem, he then tapped the back of the television and a crisp picture suddenly appeared on the screen. He smiled at me.

"I should have thought of that." I laughed. "Now if you can work wonders with the phone, we're in business."

He put the receiver to his ear a moment and listened before a smile spread across his face.

"It's working, isn't it?" I asked.

He nodded and headed toward the door. "Here, let me give you a tip," I said, digging into my trouser pocket.

He stopped, scowled at me, and was out the door before I could say thank you.

The next morning, over blueberry muffins and hot cocoa, I told the desk clerk about the helpful hotel handyman who had repaired the thermostat, phone, and television.

"You've got a real jack-of-all-trades in him," I laughed.

The smile vanished from the clerk's face. "No one like that was working last night."

"Well, he was dressed in a tan uniform, and   "

"Must have been Fred," the clerk sighed.

"Fred? I thought you said no one was working last night."

Now it was his turn to smile. "Fred's our resident ghost. He was the handyman janitor here years ago. He's been known to play pranks on some of the desk clerks, but he is always most helpful to our guests."

At this revelation, my mind suddenly recalled something awry about the repairman's appearance upon our initial encounter. "He was just there by that big mirror, almost like he was waiting for me," I said. "And now that I think of it . . . the way he was standing, there should have been a reflection in the mirror, but there wasn't."

A shiver ran down my spine. I'd just had my first encounter with a ghost—a helpful and handy haunt, at that.

MONTEREY HOTEL

406 Alvarado Street, Monterey, California 93940

www.montereyhotel.com

A SPIRITED INN IN BISBEE
by Ellen Robson

BISBEE, ARIZONA, IS A CHARMING city filled with Victorian-style homes, quirky businesses, and a potpourri of diners. You'll also find several hotels and bed-and-breakfasts scattered on its hillsides and narrow streets, but if you're looking to spend the night with a ghost or two, be sure to make reservations at the Inn at Castle Rock.

What is now a bed-and-breakfast with themed rooms and a pet-friendly policy was built in 1890 as a boarding house for miners. It is believed that one of those miners put in a hard day's work in the Copper Queen Mine, trudged back to his bare, rented room, and died. The dead miner's room is now called the Return to Paradise Room, and while you may find it homey, be aware that if you choose to sleep in the single bed instead of the double, you may feel your toes being tweaked during the night. According to legend, the culprit is the harmless ghost of the miner, wondering when he'll get his drab room back.

182

EERIE INHABITANTS

AT THE END OF DECEMBER 2000, Jennifer Baker and her cat, Morris, stayed in the White Eagle Room—directly across the hall from the miner's old room. Morris was fascinated with the room, not ". . . the least bit afraid, though. Whenever he was in the hallway and the door to the Return to Paradise Room was shut, he kept trying to squeeze under the door, meowing constantly. If the door happened to be open, he would poke his head in, glancing all around."

On the afternoon of December 29, Morris made a break for the room and dove under the single bed, scooting to the back where he couldn't be easily reached. No amount of coaxing or pleading worked—he was determined to stay put. Finally the innkeeper grabbed Morris by the scruff of his neck and carried him back across the hall, the cat complaining and kicking all the way.

An incident that happened two days later on New Year's Eve has Jennifer wondering if a ghost followed Morris back to the White Eagle Room. She was in a quasi-sleep stage when a shimmering light appeared at the foot of her bed. At first Jennifer thought some type of film over her eyes was causing the cloudy illusion, but even after rubbing her eyes and blinking a few times, the apparition remained.

"It was the size of a human, except it was more of an oblong shape, floating, very distinct and vague," she said. "It was just hovering and eventually disappeared. But for some reason, I wasn't the least bit frightened."

A guest staying in the Tasmanian Room shared his poltergeist experiences on several travel-related Web sites, prompting a soldier preparing for deployment to Iraq to make a reservation. The room had already been booked, however, so owner Jeannene Babcock suggested he stay in another room, silently pleading for the various ghosts not to disappoint him. They not only complied, but included all of the inn's guests in their activities. One guest felt someone observing her all night, while another claimed he was pinned down on his bed. Bob Stroub, who was staying on the second floor, was startled by a shadow that passed eerily by him in the hallway. A female spirit dressed in Victorian garb has been known to walk up and down the stairs, so perhaps her silhouette had crossed his path.

Employees have also encountered these "permanent guests." A maintenance man also had a run-in with two female apparitions dressed in old-fashioned

attire, and another employee brags that she glimpsed a small boy wearing period clothing. The cook has gotten used to having his pots and pans move spontaneously on the kitchen counter. When he gets tired of it, he asks the ghosts to please stop, and suddenly all is quiet in the kitchen.

Jeannene is content with the family of "protective spirits" that are watching over the inn, including that of her father, who converted the former boardinghouse into a lore-filled bed-and-breakfast. The spirits, she said, "are benign and fairly good, although one housekeeper felt the sensation of someone or something pulling on her hair in the Crying Shame Room."

Ghosts are so numerous at the Inn at Castle Rock that it doesn't matter which room you reserve. A ghost or two have even shown up in photographs, so make sure you pack your camera.

THE INN AT CASTLE ROCK

112 Tombstone Canyon Road, Bisbee, Arizona 85603
(520) 432-4449

PHANTOM SPASMS: THE U.S. HOTEL
by Matt Lake

"WE'RE JUST GOING TO INJECT you with something to slow your heart rate down. It will feel as though your heart's stopping. It's going to be scary, but you'll be okay. It's going to help. Do you understand what I just told you?"

From the gurney in the emergency room, I nodded my assent and wondered what it feels like when your heart stops. It made my already fibrillating heart beat faster and harder. It felt as if the thing was beating its way out of my chest. I struggled to slow my breathing, but it remained shallow and fast. All the time I was thinking, "This has nothing to do with the U.S. Hotel. It's just a coincidence."

Later that week, I heard that at the exact time I was in the ER with out-of-control atrial fibrillation, my friend Joel was doubled up with stomach cramps. This was odd. The two of us had been in good health the previous week, yet three days after we had visited Hollidaysburg, Pennsylvania's most haunted hostelry, we were both incapacitated by two very different ailments—at exactly the same time.

When I was released from the hospital, I looked back over the video footage we had taken during our trip and came to a startling conclusion. This had *everything* to do with the U.S. Hotel.

A Skeptic No More

I had gone along on that ill-fated trip to a small western Pennsylvania town because of my reputation among ghost hunters. They tend to call me ghost repellent because whenever I join them on a trip to a haunted place, we all come away disappointed. It had reached the point where if there was a ghost hunt on, they'd slip me a twenty and ask me to go somewhere else.

Joel was also a skeptic. When he visited the U.S. Hotel, he wanted skeptics with him so that he wouldn't be caught up in that spirit of wish fulfillment that makes some people see specters in every shadow. He arranged with the owners a visit to the hotel's abandoned upper stories and asked me to come along. I had heard one story about the second floor—something involving an ax-wielding man murdering a woman—but there were several others, and I stopped everyone who tried to tell me about them. I wanted to be free from the hint of suggestion.

We spent a couple of hours wandering about, taking video footage and photographs and feeling for vibes. Even to a skeptic, the place is a bit on the creepy side. In stark contrast to the cozy ambience in the restaurant downstairs, the upper floors were halfway through a remodeling project that had been going on for years. Drop cloths and building supplies lay everywhere. And even though all the rooms were furnished with beds and 1980s-era televisions, they felt old, untended, and unlived-in. Some of the doors were kept closed by chairs under their handles (to prevent them from swinging open and banging, according to the owner's granddaughter). By contrast, one of the third-floor doors seemed to be jammed, which I took to be the result of a warped frame or excessive paint. On the third push, however, it opened freely and showed no signs of sticking again. That particular detail made little impression on me at the time, but looking back on the green-tinted video footage from that night, I definitely should have avoided that room.

Heart-Stopping Scenes

"This is one of the more active rooms," said the image on my screen, the owner's granddaughter who had made a video about the hotel. "It's known as the Dying Mother Room. There's a woman lying on the bed dying and a girl in the closet. The door jams here. *A lot.*"

Oookay . . . that sounds like an excuse to fast-forward the tape a little.

"The ghost choked Al to the point when he passed out. . . ."

Maybe a little more . . .

"He smells like smoke and rotten meat. He followed me home once. . . ." 187

I paused the tape as my heart began racing again, and rewound it another few minutes. The images skittered across the screen until I saw the owner's granddaughter once again, sitting on the bed in a familiar room, flashlight in hand.

"Alice is an older woman who's dying of some sort of stomach illness. A lot of times when people walk in the room, they will get ill. . . ."

And here, I hit stop. The idea that two of us had entered a haunted room with a reputation for making people sick, and *both* had mysteriously fallen ill within three days was too much of a coincidence. This incident changed my outlook on ghosts immediately, and paranormal investigators have begun asking me along on their ghost hunts again. It's all very flattering, but the truth is, whenever I think of the injection I needed to slow my heart in the emergency room, I'm just not that keen on joining them anymore.

THE U.S. HOTEL RESTAURANT AND TAVERN

401 S. Juniata Street, Hollidaysburg, Pennsylvania 16648

www.theushotel.com

THE WENTWORTH WRAITHS
by Fiona Broome

NEW HAMPSHIRE'S WENTWORTH BY THE Sea hotel has been a favorite among fond-of-the-paranormal patrons since its construction in the late nineteenth century. Known to most as simply "The Wentworth," it has amassed a ghostly repertoire that includes appearances by former owners, guests, staff and servants, and even a few American presidents.

Sarah and Charles Campbell built Wentworth by the Sea in 1874 on land owned by Sarah's parents. The hotel cost about $50,000—a fortune in those days—and was financed by Sarah's cousin, rum tycoon Daniel Chase. However, in 1877 after several business reversals, Chase filed for bankruptcy, and the Campbells lost their hotel. Years later Chase recovered his wealth, but only his ghost is still tied to the Wentworth. His translucent figure is seen around the front stairs of the hotel. People sometimes mistake him for a staff member or servant because he wears an apron, which is actually part of his Masonic garb from when he was the Masons' first high priest in Somerville, Massachusetts.

When the Wentworth finally sold in 1879, Charles Campbell remained as the hotel's winter caretaker and night watchman. He remains at his post at the back of the hotel even today, looking as if he's about to get to work in the garden. You might recognize him by his handlebar mustache or by his rolled-up sleeves, and sometimes he has a shovel in his hand or near his feet.

Campbell's ghost may be looking for buried treasure to buy back his hotel. Starting in 1882, local newspapers reported a party of men searching for gold at Little Harbor, between Campbell's house and the Wentworth hotel. A reliable treasure map had been found, indicating the location of three chests of gold and a barrel of silver. However, the map indicated both a bridge and a stone marker that were no longer there in 1882, and the treasure was never found. By the late 1880s, the Wentworth was one of New England's premier hotels, but during the twentieth century its popularity declined, just as happened to many other grand but aging buildings.

HAUNTED HOUSEKEEPING

During the 1960s I spent many childhood summers as a guest at the Wentworth, playing hide-and-seek with the ghosts on the hotel's top floors. To me, the Wentworth was a huge, slightly decrepit castle filled with concealed staircases

and dusty, unused sanctuaries, and I'd frequently sneak off to explore the hotel's 189 many nooks and crannies. Sometimes I'd follow the hotel staff as they worked, especially on the upper floors where the guests' rooms were.

One dark morning as a thunderstorm raged outside, I noticed a woman in a traditional maid's uniform—a dark dress, black hose, a white apron, and a small white cap. Her outfit looked dated, like something from a novel, so I was determined to see where she was going. I carefully followed her through the corridors of the third floor, crouching in an alcove as she climbed a narrow staircase that I never knew existed, and then I crept up the stairs after her.

I peered into a few of the rooms that lined the unused top floors, which had once been the servants' quarters. Many displayed peeling wallpaper in pastel floral prints, and the few that were furnished had only a thin cot wrapped in a musty sheet, and sometimes a well-worn wooden chair. I followed the rustle of the maid's dress, but when I peered around each doorway, the room was always empty. I initially assumed that the echoes off the plaster walls and hardwood floors were disorienting me.

Finally I saw the back of her dress disappear as she entered a bedroom near the end of the hall. Caution flung aside, I charged after her, but that room was as empty as the others. This time I noticed that the hardwood floor was thick with dust, and when I returned to the hall, I saw only one set of footprints pressed into the ancient carpet.

Later that day, I told my younger brother what had happened. With two other children from the hotel, we found the stairs to the fourth floor, and I began to retell my story. I had barely begun to describe the maid when we all saw her sweep past the top of the stairs. We ran up, but nobody was there. Even in the limited daylight, we could see just one set of footprints on the carpet, and they were too tiny for an adult. We were thus left to conclude that we'd seen a real ghost, and to us, that was a prize worth far more than the hundreds of dollars being won downstairs at the bingo games.

As it turned out, that was only the first of many times I saw ghostly servants around the third and fourth floors of the Wentworth.

CELEBRITY SPOOKS

Over the years I saw other ghosts, too, especially around the first-floor ballroom late at night. They were translucent and elegantly dressed, and while some danced, others sipped beverages as they watched the other guests. When I first saw Disney's Haunted Mansion attraction years later, I immediately recognized the translucent waltzers in the ballroom—they were almost exactly what I'd seen at the Wentworth hotel.

Others who've seen the Wentworth's ballroom ghosts have reported former American presidents, especially Teddy Roosevelt and his cousin Franklin Roosevelt, among the partygoers. Some have identified actors like Marilyn Monroe in the hallway nearest the hotel's luxury shops, too. The spirits in these "classic" hauntings look almost exactly like ghosts in the old Topper movies—they're barely there when you see them, and they vanish into a gleam or sparkle suspended in midair.

I revisited the Wentworth site during its renovation in 2001. As I took pictures from the parking lot, I noticed someone looking down at me from a fourth-floor window. While it may have been a worker, I suspect it was one of the ghosts who kept a little girl amused many years ago.

191

WENTWORTH BY THE SEA HOTEL

588 Wentworth Road, New Castle, New Hampshire 03854

www.wentworth.com

GET WHACKED AT LIZZIE'S HAUNTED B AND B
by Jeff Belanger

Lizzie Borden took an ax / and gave her mother 40 whacks. /
And when she saw what she had done / she gave her father 41.

IT WAS SEVENTEEN (NOT FORTY) whacks that did in Abby Borden, and eleven (not forty-one) whacks with the same ax that killed her husband, Andrew. Regardless of the whack count, the horrific crimes captured America's attention and have held it ever since the jury acquitted Lizzie Borden of killing her father and stepmother more than a century ago. Today, the Fall River, Massachusetts, house draws fans of the macabre and the supernatural. Not only will you find pictures of the Borden family and crime scene inside, by some accounts you may find ghosts, too.

On August 4, 1892, the temperature soared to nearly 100 degrees. It was roughly eleven A.M. on this maddeningly hot day when family patriarch Andrew Borden lay down on the sofa in his frolic sitting room to take a nap. Moments later, someone took an ax and delivered eleven blows, leaving Mr. Borden slumped over and dead.

The killer then ascended the staircase to the second-floor guest room, where Mrs. Abby Borden was standing beside the bed. Before she could turn around, the assailant took an ax to her head. Seventeen blows later, Abby Borden lay in a pool of her own blood.

The victims most likely knew their killer, because there was no sign of struggle or break-in and nothing was stolen. Also, there were two other people home during the murders: daughter Lizzie and the housekeeper, Bridget Sullivan, whom the Bordens called Maggie, since that was the name of their previous maid. Evidence later implicated both young women in the murders.

A DAUGHTER'S BETRAYAL

Lizzie Borden claimed that around eleven A.M. she went into the backyard to pick some pears before heading to the second floor of their barn to get some sinkers for a fishing trip she was planning for the following week. Never more than fifty or sixty feet from the house, Lizzie estimated she was outside for about fifteen minutes and that the killer must have snuck in, murdered Abby and Andrew, and left during this short period. Lizzie and Bridget claimed they didn't hear or see anything while the murders were taking place.

The Borden house is a good-sized home, but one would hardly call it a mansion. How two people could be hacked to death without the other people in and around the house seeing or hearing anything would have been nearly impossible. All signs pointed to Lizzie, with Bridget as a possible co-conspirator. Lizzie's motive? She and her sister Emma stood to inherit the Borden fortune, and she may have been worried that her father would change his will and leave everything to her stepmother, Abby, with whom Lizzie didn't get along all that well.

What ensued was the trial of the century. Everyone believed that Lizzie was culpable, but the evidence was entirely circumstantial. Investigators found an ax head in the basement that may have been the murder weapon, and Lizzie burned one of her dresses in the oven on the day of the murder because she claimed she spilled some paint on it. Despite the obvious signs, the jury dismissed all the evidence as inconclusive and Lizzie was acquitted.

193

ANONYMOUS APPARITIONS

Many paranormal enthusiasts believe the murder and the events surrounding the Borden family left a permanent mark on the property at 92 Second Street in Fall River. The address is still infamous, and Lizzie's horrific legacy is recalled in the name of what is now a bed-and-breakfast. Eager to satisfy their curiosity about the legendary murders, visitors to this star-crossed residence often seek

more than a cozy place to sleep and warm breakfast rolls, but an unlucky few have come away with more than they bargained for.

Lee-ann Wilber, who has managed the Lizzie Borden Bed & Breakfast since 2004, has noticed that some of her repeat customers seem to be a magnet for paranormal activity, which includes windows slamming up and down on their own, voices, and disembodied footsteps. Audio recording devices have captured Electronic Voice Phenomena (EVP), including a disembodied voice in the basement that repeats, "Get out!"

The basement is also where a former owner claimed to see a misty apparition, and where Lee-ann herself experienced a ghostly encounter she will not soon forget: "My first experience was my first week here," Wilber said. "I had gone down to the basement to switch some laundry over, and when you come down the basement stairs, you step off the bottom step and you turn left to head toward the laundry room. As soon as I took a step forward, it felt like I had stepped into a walk-in freezer. I took two steps farther and walked out the other side of it [the cold], and as soon as I reached the door to the laundry area, it felt like somebody ran two fingers down my back. I stopped dead in my tracks, I turned around, and I went trotting right back up the stairs."

Strange noises and ghostly phenomena have become almost commonplace for Lee-ann. "While we were renovating and building the barn, my office was in the basement of the house in a little cubby hole—right below Mr. Borden's sofa," she said. "I was in the house one night, all alone on the computer, it had to be one or two in the morning. I'm down there tapping away and I clearly hear someone walk across the floor above me. And I'm alone in the house. It didn't sit well with me, but after a while you get used to it."

ANOTHER BORDEN TRAGEDY

Matt Moniz, a paranormal investigator with Spooky Southcoast, a southeastern Massachusetts–based radio program and investigative team, has witnessed a number of spooky phenomena there as well. In 2007 he was walking through the house on a tour when he saw an old framed photograph lift into the air, flip over multiple times, and then travel halfway across the room, as if tossed by an unseen force. On another occasion, he was filming the empty Hosea Knowlton Room when the camera turned itself about 45 degrees. An investigator came in to return the camera to its original position, and before he could leave the room, the camera turned itself 90 degrees.

During his many visits to the haunted bed-and-breakfast, Matt has also heard the guttural sounds of a disembodied male voice, as well as the voices of children.

195

In fact, the children may be the most omnipresent spirits in the house—and those children would be Andrew Borden's ill-fated cousins. As recounted in the August 5, 1892, Fall River *Daily Globe*, "Another horrible tragedy had been enacted in the vicinity of the Borden residence. In the yard of the house occupied now by Dr. Kelly . . . Between [18]39 or [18]40 . . . a woman named Borden had thrown her three young children into a cistern to drown and afterward jumped in and died with them."

The whispers, strange voices, and footfalls that haunt the former Borden house will continue to tempt our curiosity; and though we can't be sure of who or what are causing the occurrences, one can't help but think back to that hot August day in 1892 and wonder if the Bordens may still be lurking, demanding that justice be served.

LIZZIE BORDEN BED & BREAKFAST/MUSEUM

92 Second Street, Fall River, Massachusetts 02721
www.lizzie-borden.com

LIVELY GHOSTS AT THE LIVE OAKS INN
by Dusty Smith

BUILT IN 1871, THE STATELY structure at 444 S. Beach Street in Daytona Beach, Florida, was once the destination of choice among the city's elite overnight guests. Members of the Wannamaker, Gamble, and Vanderbilt families were regular visitors, as were the well-to-do railroad moguls, cattle barons, and lumber mill owners of the time. Now a historic bed-and-breakfast, the Live Oaks Inn's amenities include fourteen guestrooms, a spacious salon, breezeway deck—and a host of highbrow spirits who remain loyal patrons of the antebellum estate.

The Live Oaks Inn has a reputation among those in the paranormal community as a haunted hot spot. The Daytona Beach Paranormal Research Group, Inc. (DBPRG), which I founded in 1997, was doing an ongoing investigation at the inn when a production company contacted me, and I agreed to take part in a documentary focusing on the inn's hauntings.

196

GHOULISH GUESTS

Two nights before filming started, I received a frantic call at about three thirty A.M. from Rosanna, the woman who leased and ran the inn. She was staying

alone in the caretaker's building, located just behind the inn, when she had been awakened by a voice. Opening her eyes, she saw the shadowy figure of a man standing at the foot of her bed. She left the room in fright and headed down the staircase outside. As she fled, something pushed her down the stairs. I drove over to the inn to help, and when I went into Rosanna's room I saw that the lights were flickering. It was March and unusually warm outside, but the room had an eerie chill to it.

I returned to the inn the next day around sunset; as I pulled into the parking lot I saw a man standing in the window of the second-floor kitchen. When I told Rosanna what I had seen, she turned white. There were no guests in the building, and her fiancé was out running errands. Rosanna and I were the only people there . . . supposedly.

I bolted up the staircase and headed down the hall to the upstairs kitchen. The door was locked. Rosanna brought the keys, unlocking and opening the door. Nobody was in the room, but there was a heavy scent of cigar smoke and one of the gas burners was on full blast!

We shut off the gas and then checked all the rooms on the second floor. When we opened the door to Room 12, Rosanna gasped and said, "I was up here this morning and made all the beds, and now look. Someone has rumpled the pillows and blankets. . . ." In Room 14, the door slammed shut behind us. Then the TV turned on, and at the same time the phone began to ring. Rosanna said, "A call can't come through to a room unless I'm downstairs to plug it in from the switchboard." When I picked up the receiver, all I heard was static.

At the top of the staircase, we noticed that the pictures on the west wall were off kilter—a common occurrence at the inn. We straightened them out and I jumped up and down to see if my weight on the floor would move the pictures on the wall, but it didn't.

When Rosanna's fiancé returned, I said good-bye and told them I wanted to return the following night with equipment and a few team members to document the new activity. Since only two couples were staying at the inn, Rosanna agreed.

April Fools

The following evening, the crew split into teams of two and rotated through the various locations that had been identified as paranormally active.

There were two phantom phone calls in Room 14—one in which a guttural

197

growl was heard. In Room 12, a rocking chair rocked back and forth on its own, a small child's voice sang nursery rhymes, and the wrought iron bed frame made a squeaking sound, as if someone had sat or lain down on the bed. This sound was recorded, and at the same time the team members also documented a temperature drop and a reading on the EMF meter that indicated to us the presence of paranormal energy.

In Room 9, the ceiling fan kept turning on and off by itself, even after the room's breaker was cut, and two metal tile panels on the ceiling flew off toward the researchers, who were frightened but uninjured. The team members on second-floor kitchen duty smelled cigar smoke, and one experienced a severe headache that made her so nauseated that she had to leave.

By two thirty A.M., we took a badly needed break on the patio and sat down to talk with Rosanna. We were interrupted by one of the inn's guests, who appeared at the front desk, fully dressed, demanding his money back. He said his wife was upstairs packing because they awoke to see a clown standing over their bed, staring at them. A clown? I couldn't help but listen as he described it: six feet tall with a white painted face; huge, glowing red eyes; painted red lips with rotted teeth; a blue and white clown suit; and long fingers that reached out to the couple while they were in bed.

"Then he vanished!" The man yelled. "I don't know what kind of games you're playing here, but I paid good money to stay here and don't appreciate these kinds of tricks!" It *was* April 1, after all. Rosanna agreed and tried to calm the man as she scrambled to give him a refund. His wife appeared and told her husband to forget about the money—she just wanted to leave, and they did. In tears, Rosanna told me her other guests had left earlier that evening because the faucet in their room kept turning on by itself.

I went upstairs to the room from which the couple had just fled. I cautiously opened the door and swore I could smell greasepaint. The room was 103 degrees, the EMF meter readings went through the roof, and every photo I took captured a strange, red, misty blob hanging directly over the bed.

By five A.M., we were beat, but we planned to return later in the day for more filming and investigating.

PSYCHIC CONFIRMATION

After a short rest, I began a room-by-room tour of the property with a psychic and the film crew. We started at the inn, and the psychic gave her impressions of who was haunting it and why. At the top of the staircase, she felt the spirit of a young girl who sang nursery rhymes and played pranks on guests and staff. When she looked at the pictures on the wall, she said the girl liked to turn the pictures around. I was impressed.

We moved on to Room 9. The phone rang and when the psychic answered it, all she heard was static. She offered help to whoever was at the other end of the line, and then suddenly pulled the receiver away from her ear. We all heard a deep growling sound, and the room got very cold. On the second floor, the psychic felt the spirit of a man who, in life, liked to start fires with his cigars.

As we left the main building, one of the film crew looked up at a window above the restaurant and asked, "Who is that up there?" We all looked up, saw a woman standing at the window, and quickly made our way there. The door would not open for the psychic, but others opened it with ease. The room was frigid. As the film crew entered, a rocking chair began to move, and the bed looked as if someone had been sitting on its edge. We heard footsteps on the attic stairway, and as we walked up the narrow stairwell we heard low, muffled singing. Upstairs I pulled out my flashlight, and the three of us saw the figure of a woman walk through the wall to the attic.

When our group descended the main staircase into the bar area of the restaurant, the psychic went into a trance and began speaking about many men gathering in the room toward the back of the bar for secret meetings: "I

199

don't know what all of these secrets were about but they had a ring, a book, a symbol, and held these meetings." I wondered if maybe it was a meeting place for Freemason members. From the bar, we heard glasses clinking together and noticed that bottles of liquor that were *behind* the bar when we first entered the rooms were now *on* the bar.

It took nearly three hours to walk through both buildings, and with what we knew and had experienced previously at the inn—now confirmed by the psychic—we were confident about getting some hard evidence for paranormal activity.

FLOUR POWER

We tried to capture the footprints of the little spirit girl at the top of the stairs. To do this, I laid out a couple of large black garbage bags and sprinkled them with flour. The framed photos at the top of the stairs were all leaning in different directions again, so we straightened them and headed back downstairs to wait. We heard footsteps and when we arrived upstairs to inspect, there were three small footprints in the flour! This was awesome evidence of the little girl. Additionally, one of the pictures we had just straightened out was off-kilter again.

Rosanna finally came to terms with the spirits at the Live Oaks Inn and embraced them to the point of promoting it as haunted; but she was still leasing the building, and the owner didn't feel the same way she did. The inn was closed and sold to new owners, who reopened it in December 2007. They have since reported some otherworldly experiences at the inn, and only time will tell which direction they'll take in promoting, or denying, the existence of the spirits at the Live Oaks Inn.

LIVE OAKS INN

444 S. Beach Street, Daytona Beach, Florida 32114

www.liveoaksinn.com

THE LOGAN INN: ROOM 6
by Ryan Doan

TO MY BEST FRIEND, JEFF, and me, there was nothing more manly than a good old-fashioned ghost hunt—especially in a place with such well-documented hauntings as the almost three-hundred-year-old Logan Inn of New Hope, Pennsylvania. One of the oldest continuously run inns in the country, it has hosted a number of spirits, particularly in Room 6. There ghosts have manifested in many ways, including visually as white misty shapes or images of a man or small children, audibly as a man or woman sobbing, and through the smell of lavender perfume—the favorite scent of a woman who supposedly died in the room.

One summer night, Jeff and I arranged to stay in this infamous room. We had all the proper provisions: a notebook, camera gear, audio recorder, and other paraphernalia. We also had a thick textbook on parapsychology containing the documented history of the bed-and-breakfast.

201

The book also listed the name of the kind woman who still worked the front desk—a woman I'll refer to as "the Proprietor." It was she who initially held the most mystery for us. Regal in demeanor and stature, the Proprietor seemed every bit the lady, but every time we had met with her in the weeks leading up to our visit, a different piece of finery hid her neck from sight. It was no different on the night we finally checked in: she wore a scarf wrapped around her neck—in the middle of August.

When the Proprietor saw us, she called us by our names and calmly ushered us to Room 6. Jeff wanted to keep our motives quiet, but on the way to the room I couldn't help but tell her our plans and the fact that she was written about in a credited book on the paranormal. The mountain of gear we carried—cameras and tripods—gave us away, anyway. We were either there to investigate ghosts or to do something worse.

THE HANDPRINT

The room was very small, and we could see the history of the place just hidden under the skin of new amenities. But there was nothing odd or supernatural—no scent of lavender, no misty forms.

After setting up our gear, we went down to the porch for dinner and laughed at the sign that swung overhead. It read FINE FOOD, LODGING, AND SPIRITS. So far, we had two out of the three. Upon returning to our room, we found the Proprietor waiting for us. With a smirk, she told us that the foreboding portrait outside of Room 6 was that of the owner's grandparents, and it was the owner's mother who was said to haunt the room.

We were only gone from the room for maybe an hour, but when we returned we saw a wet handprint with elongated fingers centered on the far wall. Alarmed but skeptical, I began to describe this finding in my microrecorder as Jeff went to compare his hand to the handprint. A few minutes later I replayed the recording, and as I listened my heart leaped with horror. At precisely the moment Jeff's hand touched the handprint on the wall, I heard an inhuman, raspy sigh emanating from the tape.

I played the tape back to Jeff, who then almost burned a hole in the hardwood floor with his frantic pacing. We had come looking for evidence but didn't really want to find it, and we ran several variable tests to see if any other ambient noises could have made the sounds on our tape. Even when pointed directly at the traffic on the street below, the recorder didn't pick up anything remotely like what we heard.

Jeff and I left the room with an overwhelming sense that something was in there, and we did everything we could to avoid returning to it that night. The Proprietor wished us a good night's sleep with a toss of her scarf and a wide grin on her face. We climbed into bed at about four thirty A.M., carefully maintaining the boundary we'd outlined between us, but sleep didn't come for a long time. Wide-eyed, we stared into the dark, trying to focus on the continental breakfast awaiting us—should we survive the night.

Very manly, indeed.

THE LOGAN INN

10 W. Ferry Street, New Hope, Pennsylvania 18938

www.loganinn.com

Dead Lights

Rock of slow torture.
Ernie's domain.
Hell on earth—may New London Ledge's light shine on
forever because I'm through.
I will watch it from afar while driking a brew.
  —Tribute to Ernie, resident ghoul of New London Ledge

DEATH HAS ITS DARK moments, but it can also be full of light. The journey isn't always a straight shot to the other side—some souls complete the passage, others return, and some spirits get lost along the way. . . .

Maybe in the confusion, ghosts look to any old light as a way out. Lighthouses, for example, offer guidance for the living but attract their fair share of the dead, too. As far as we can tell, the country is full of such lighthouses: Young ghouls and shadowy men haunt a lighthouse in Florida, and another in Connecticut hosts a departed lighthouse crew member with a story to tell. Oregon is full of beacons that attract the dead, including two with dual spirits just four miles from each other, and another that's home to a tidy spirit named Rue. There's yet another neatnik spirit—a sea captain—in a Maine lighthouse, plus a multispecies haunt in Ohio.

Other lost souls might become flashes of energy themselves, appearing as "ghost lights" in fields and along lonely roadways and train tracks. The lights seen in a Colorado cemetery might be those of dead miners, and the beacon on a Texas prairie may well be the thirsty soul of a man buried without his favorite alcoholic spirit. Then there's the light that appears along railroad tracks in Virginia—possibly the spirit of departed railroad worker, or even a ghost train.

Go into the light? Some ghosts might welcome the suggestion, but to paraphrase J. R. R. Tolkien, "Not all ghosts who wander are lost." Entering the lighted tunnel might simply be a choice best left to the spirits.

THE SPECTRAL LIGHTS
OF SILVER CLIFF
by Troy Taylor

ONE MILE SOUTH OF THE little town of Silver Cliff, Colorado, sits an old graveyard that has become one of America's greatest sites for unexplained phenomena. During the day, Silver Cliff Cemetery is a tranquil place, giving no outward indication of the unsolved mysteries that have plagued it since 1880. When darkness falls the cemetery becomes quite eerie and the "ghost lights" begin to appear. Located in the Wet Mountain Valley, Silver Cliff now boasts only a few hundred inhabitants. In its heyday, however, it was a bustling town of more than five thousand people. Once the mines stopped producing, the population dwindled, but the ghost lights in the old miners' cemetery remained.

In earlier days, stories about the lights spread by word of mouth, but in 1956 the *Wet Mountain Tribune* published an article about them, and it wasn't long before people from all over Colorado began touring the small cemetery. Visitors' reports were remarkably similar, describing tiny dim lights that flashed on and off, popped up and then vanished. Sometimes they'd be little more than a twinkle, and other times they'd move about horizontally. If a visitor tried to approach them, they'd move just out of reach.

Skeptics dismissed the lights as nothing more than reflections, but in the older parts of the cemetery where the lights usually appear, there are no reflective stones. To counter this explanation, residents of Silver Cliff and nearby Westcliff once agreed to shut off their lights—including the streetlights—for an evening. The area was plunged into blackness, "but the graveyard lights still danced," recalled Judge August Menzel.

In May of 1895, Denver scientist Charles H. Howe journeyed to Silver Cliff in the company of a photographer and an electrical engineer to study the phantom lights and identify their source. The three observed the eerie lights for a week, noticing them on two overcast nights when there were no light reflections from town. More recently Silver Cliff resident Bill Kleine observed them on foggy nights, helping refute the theory that the lights are merely reflections of stars overhead.

Another explanation maintained that the lights were "swamp gas" or "will-o'-the-wisps"—effects caused by marshy places and decaying matter. Ray de Wall, former publisher of the *Wet Mountain Tribune*, adamantly disagreed, pointing out that the cemetery was located on a dry ridge and that yucca and cacti grew on the graves. This refuted the theory that wet conditions caused the lights to appear.

Many local old-timers believe the ghost lights have a supernatural explanation. According to legend, the cemetery was the burial ground for many men who died while working in the mines of the region. The flickering lights are said to be the small lights worn on the miners' hats as well as manifestations of the miners' restless souls, which are still looking for the bonanza they never found during their lifetimes.

FAMED PHANTOM FLICKERS

The Silver Cliff lights gained national attention in August 1967 when an article about them appeared in *The New York Times*. Then *National Geographic's* assistant editor Edward J. Linehan featured a piece about the lights in the magazine's August 1969 issue.

Linehan drove to the cemetery in the company of the aforementioned Bill Kleine. The two parked, climbed out of the car, and stood in silence for several minutes.

"Do you believe it?" Linehan asked. "About the lights in the graveyard?"

"I've seen them plenty of times," Kleine replied. "This is a good night for them—overcast, no moon."

They walked closer to the old cemetery and, slowly, the vague outlines of the tombstones appeared through the haze. That was when Bill Kleine whispered harshly, "There! And over there!"

Linehan looked and saw the lights appearing. "Dim, round spots of blue-white light glowed, ethereally among the graves," he later wrote. He and Kleine scurried about in the cemetery, pursuing one elusive ghost light after another for the next fifteen minutes.

Strangely the lights remain just as evasive today as they were in 1969. Even the most persistent skeptics have been unable to explain the origins of the lights. Nobody can get close enough to examine them; and despite many attempts, the lights remain unphotographed. Until a logical explanation can be reached, romantics among us continue to watch and wonder about the lost miners. As Linehan wrote in the conclusion of his article, "No doubt someone, someday, will prove there's nothing at all supernatural in the luminous manifestations of Silver Cliff's cemetery. I know I'll feel a twinge of disappointment. I prefer to believe they are the restless stirrings of the ghosts of Colorado, eager to get their Centennial state on with its pressing business: seeking out and working the bonanzas of a second glorious century."

209

SILVER CLIFF CEMETERY

Mill Street, Silver Cliff, Colorado 81252

OWL'S HEAD LIGHTHOUSE
by L'Aura Hladik

THE LIGHTHOUSE IN OWL'S HEAD, Maine has stood high up on a rocky promontory since 1825 and over the years has been the site of a number of strange phenomena. At the keeper's house in December 1850, a "frozen couple" was miraculously defrosted from a block of ice and revived after a raging winter storm sent a stranded schooner crashing into the rocks. The house was also home to Spot, a fog-bell-ringing springer spaniel credited with preventing a mail boat from smashing into the rocky shore during another storm in the 1930s. Neither incident is associated with a ghost, but several eyewitness accounts suggest the presence of a certain maritime phantasm haunting the lighthouse and surrounds.

Why a ghostly sea captain made the lighthouse at Owl's Head his permanent residence is unknown, but he has presented himself to people in various forms. The Andrews family, who resided at the keeper's house, had the first documented ghostly encounter. Mrs. Andrews witnessed a mysterious swirling light upstairs in the house, and her father found his bed shaking one night for no apparent reason.

The spectral seaman gave himself a more identifiable human form one night in 1980, when former lighthouse keeper John Norton awoke to see the captain staring at him. He also observed footprints in the freshly fallen snow that began in the most peculiar places and ended much the same, without incurring more prints on either end of the mysterious trail.

Gerard Graham, a Coast Guard officer in charge of the lighthouse, lived in the same house with his wife, Debbie, and three-year-old daughter, Claire, from 1987 to 1988. Like many young children, Claire had an imaginary friend at Owl's Head . . . or so her parents thought.

One night, Claire's imaginary friend woke her and instructed her to tell her parents to sound the foghorn, as there was a fog rolling in. Claire left her room—which was always colder than the other rooms—and did what she'd been asked. Debbie was certain at this point that her daughter's imaginary friend was more ghost than imagination—why else would a three-year-old child wake from a sound sleep and tell her parents about the incoming fog?

The ghostly sea captain did more than leave tracks in the snow and issue fog warnings; he also allegedly polished brass fixtures in the house. The keeper

worked diligently to ensure the light functioned continuously; his wife was responsible for keeping the house perfectly clean in case of unannounced inspections. After all, they didn't own the property. Both keeper and wife appreciated a ghost that pitched in.

According to author Bill Thomson, there is another ghost residing at Owl's Head Lighthouse. The Little Lady is said to occupy the kitchen, slamming doors and rattling silver- ware. Malcolm Rouse, the last Coast Guard lighthouse keeper at Owl's Head before it was automated in 1989, didn't elaborate on the ghost or activity, but likewise insisted that the place was haunted.

Today Coast Guard personnel occupy the keeper's house, which, along with the lighthouse, is off-limits to visitors. The surrounding area, however, is a state park, so bring a picnic basket and enjoy the views. You just might catch a glimpse of the sea captain's ghost, on the lookout for imperiled ships.

OWL'S HEAD LIGHT STATE PARK

Lighthouse Road, Owl's Head, Maine 04854

THE PHANTOM FELINE OF FAIRPORT
by James A. Willis

FAIRPORT HARBOR, OHIO, ON THE eastern bank of Lake Erie, is home to two lighthouses, one of which holds the unusual distinction of being home to ghosts of both the two- and four-legged variety.

The original Fairport Harbor lighthouse was erected in 1825. Crowned with an octagonal iron lantern, the tower stood roughly thirty feet high. Next to the lighthouse, a two-story home was built for the lighthouse keeper and his family.

212

A mere forty-three years after the first buildings were completed, it was decided that both structures needed to be rebuilt, and when construction was completed in 1871 the new lighthouse was an imposing sixty feet tall—double the size of the original.

The first head keep of the Fairport Harbor Lighthouse was Capt. Joseph Babcock, who lit the new lighthouse for the first time on August 11, 1871. He moved himself; his wife, Mary; and their young family into the house next to the lighthouse, and over the years, several children were born there. Sadly their son Robbie died at the tender age of five, just months after the family moved in.

The lighthouse was decommissioned in 1925 and slated for demolition, but because of local protest it was left standing, alone and abandoned. Fourteen years later, the Coast Guard officially took control of the building and turned the lighthouse into a maritime museum. And that's when things started to get interesting.

GHOSTS OF THE LIGHTHOUSE

As soon as people starting moving artifacts into the museum and cleaning it up, they began feeling that they were not alone. What started out as a general sense of uneasiness grew over the years until many people began to sense the melancholy presence of a young boy. Although he is felt throughout the building, his favorite spot appears to be the first-floor hallway of the museum. Many believe the ghost is that of little Robbie Babcock, but if the stories are true, Robbie's ghost is not alone.

When Captain Babcock operated the lighthouse, his wife was reportedly bedridden on what is now the second floor of the museum. To help elevate his wife's spirits while she was sick, the captain gave her several cats. When Mary Babcock passed away, her husband continued to care for the remaining cats, with one exception. According to the legend, shortly after Mary died, her favorite feline—a big gray kitty—disappeared. After several days of searching, the captain gave up and the cat was never seen again . . . at least, not alive.

Many years later, museum curator Pamela Brent was given permission to live in the upstairs quarters where the Babcock family once resided. Shortly after moving in, Brent heard her staff whispering about a ghostly gray cat roaming the building. After initially dismissing the reports, Brent herself caught a glimpse of the feline phantom darting back and forth across the kitchen floor. Things got even stranger when, one night, she felt something jump onto her bed. She could feel the weight of a cat pressing down on her, but there was nothing in sight.

Still, many people dismissed the idea of the feline phantom, until one afternoon in 2001 when someone decided to venture into the basement.

GRISLY DISCOVERY

In late 2000, Lighthouse Trustees decided to air-condition the house. The following spring, Bryan Smith, one of the men installing plumbing for the new system, went down into the basement. While climbing into a tight crawl space to run plumbing over the air-conditioning system, Smith caught a glimpse of something to his left—the face of a mummified cat staring back at him.

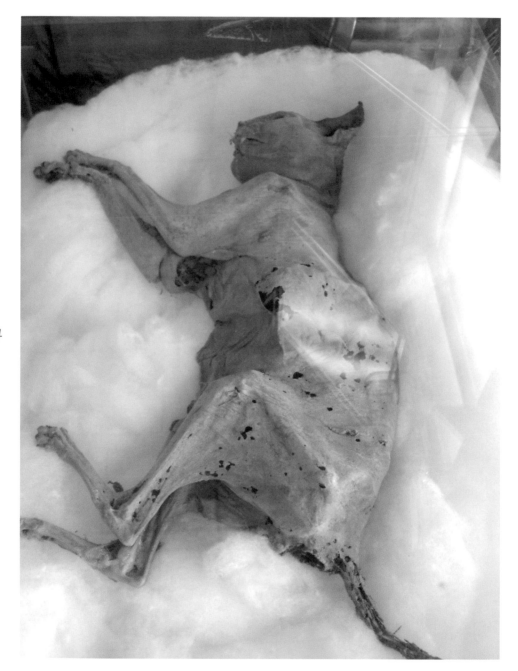

Once he overcame his initial shock, Smith gathered up the courage to remove the cat from the dark, damp crawl space. Even though the cat appeared to be well over one hundred years old, it was almost completely intact—right down to the claws and whiskers. Not knowing what to do with the mummy, Smith simply left it on the basement steps for the lighthouse staff to frightfully discover later.

The mummified cat was initially put on display in the museum, propped up among all the other memorabilia, but it began to creep out both the patrons and employees, so it was removed. And then it vanished. For several years, rumors abounded that the mummified cat had been lost or thrown away, but in 2007 it was discovered inside a giant glass case in the mayor's office.

In the spring of 2008, the remains of the cat were moved back into the lighthouse museum, but its return has done little to appease the phantom feline, which is still spotted from time to time roaming the halls of the museum. The young boy's ghost is still felt in the hallway, too. So, between a ghost cat, a ghost boy, and the mummified cat remains, there's no telling who or what you might bump into when you visit this haunted lighthouse of Fairport Harbor.

FAIRPORT HARBOR MARINE

MUSEUM AND LIGHTHOUSE

129 Second Street, Fairport Harbor, Ohio 44077

www.ncweb.com/org/fhlh

BAILEY'S LIGHT
by Scott A. Thompson

ONE NIGHT, A YOUNG MAN spotted what he thought was a burglar's flashlight in a grove of trees in Brazoria County, Texas. He stopped his car to investigate the strange glowing orb, finding—to his horror—that there was neither a flashlight nor a body attached to it. As he approached, the bouncing ball of light stopped abruptly and began to move toward him.

The panic-stricken man ran back to his car, with the fiery light less than a breath away. He made it into his car, only to find that it would not start. The ball of light circled the vehicle, pausing by the window as if observing him. Relief arrived a few moments later, when it backed away, shot straight up into the hanging willow branches, and vanished. No sooner had the light disappeared than the car's engine roared to life, and the man sped away. Shaken but otherwise unharmed, he phoned the police and recounted the terrifying ordeal. The voice on the other end of the line laughed heartily and congratulated him: He'd just met the ghost of Brit Bailey.

A NEFARIOUS REPUTATION

In Texas, a man's dying wish is gospel. Deny a dying man's final wish and his soul is doomed to walk the earth for eternity. This seems to be the state of affairs, anyhow, in the case of Brit Bailey.

James Britton Bailey was an original settler of Texas. He arrived from North Carolina in 1818, situating himself and his family near the banks of the Brazos River. Brit was not well liked by any measure—stubborn, eccentric, and grumpy are among the more polite terms used to describe him. In truth, he was an argumentative fellow whose life revolved around hunting, drinking, and getting into drunken brawls. Stories of his nefarious behavior are near legendary in south Texas.

On one occasion, a traveling preacher showed up on Brit's property looking for a place to stay for the night. Bailey, who feared no man, much less God, gave the preacher a dark smile and invited him in for supper. Like a sneaky predator, Brit lulled the wayfarer into a false sense of security and then pulled his shotgun from beneath the table. He proceeded to humiliate and terrorize his guest, and by the end of the evening, the preacher was naked and dancing on the table to the merry tune played by one of Bailey's slaves. It wasn't wine or happiness that moved the guest to such carousing, but a few well-placed shots from Brit's shotgun by his toes. Bailey eventually tired of the sport and allowed the preacher to get down. The trickster—drunk on whiskey at the time—then found the tables turned on him when the preacher snatched his gun and ordered a similar performance. Without much choice in the matter, Bailey complied. Rather than get angry, however, the whole event struck him as funny, and he and the preacher became good friends.

Eccentric in life and in death, Bailey left behind a will in 1832 that included precise burial instructions: His body was to be interred standing up, facing north, under a large pecan tree with his rifle, favorite pearl-handled pistols, hunting knife, favorite dog, and . . . his beloved whiskey jug. His widow, Dorothy, saw to it that all his wishes were carried out, until one of his slaves attempted to place the jug of whiskey at his feet. Dorothy claimed that her husband had imbibed enough in life and would not greet Saint Peter with whiskey on his breath. With that, she threw the jug out the window, and he was buried without it.

Some years later, John and Ann Thomas bought the Bailey house, and it was Ann who first reported seeing a roguish revenant about the premises.

Shadow and Light

Ann never liked the house, finding it oppressive and downright creepy. One night in 1836, while her husband was away on a business trip, she awoke from a deep sleep to find a shadowy man at the foot of her bed. She screamed and covered her eyes as he reached toward her, but when she drew the blanket down moments later, the shadow stood at the door to her room. The phantom soundlessly approached her, then disappeared when she screamed, only to form again next to the door. The shadowy figure materialized and vanished several more times that night. After that, she refused to sleep in the room, as Ann learned her bedroom had been Bailey's own.

When John Thomas returned from the neighboring town, he was angry to find that Ann had moved out of the master bedroom. He told her that it was foolishness, that he would spend the night in the room by himself, and that if Bailey did show up, he would gladly shake his hand. When his scream cut through the night air, however, it was clear that there would be no handshaking.

The spirit of Brit Bailey first appeared as a shadow of his former self, but he is usually identified as a large ball of white light that floats only within the boundaries of Bailey's Prairie. Though many have tried to follow the glowing spirit, it eludes capture by rapidly changing directions and then soaring upward into the trees of the pecan grove.

The most entertaining—and frightening—reports of Bailey's light, though, are the ones in which the glowing orb has chased people. Witnesses also recount instances where the orb has floated across the highway, causing several wrecks, and even chased a police car to the county line. According to legend, Brit Bailey is still out on his lands looking for the jug of whiskey his wife threw out.

Bailey's Prairie is a quiet place, where the locals are quite familiar with their spectral celebrity, who has appeared every seven years since the first recorded sighting in 1936. Though the prairie is quiet during the "off" years, the ghost is sighted quite often throughout the seventh. If he keeps to his schedule, the next year of sightings should be in 2013.

Mark your calendar.

BRIT BAILEY'S TEXAS HIGHWAY HISTORICAL MARKER

is located west of Angleton, on State Highway 35, in the vicinity of Bailey's Prairie.

A TALE OF TWO GHOSTLY LIGHTHOUSES
by Jeff Davis

DRIVE ABOUT FOUR MILES ALONG the central Oregon coastline near Newport and you'll come upon two historic lighthouses each rumored to contain at least two different spirits. For ghost hunters, that's a baleful bargain.

The Yaquina Bay Lighthouse, located where Yaquina Bay meets the Pacific Ocean, is the second-oldest lighthouse in the state. With its two-story caretaker's house and attached square lighthouse tower on top, the atypical landmark is one of only four Oregon lighthouses built in this style. It was first lit in November 1871 but decommissioned in 1874 in favor of the brighter—and equally ghostly—Yaquina Head Lighthouse. Various state and federal agencies used the building until 1934, and over the next few decades there was much debate over demolition, but a concerned citizens' group successfully lobbied to save it.

MacClure's Misadventure

According to legend, Yaquina Bay's first ghost is that of a large, redheaded sailor with an emaciated, skull-like face. Sources attribute the frightening apparition to Evan MacClure, captain of a Yankee whaling ship. The horrifying tale began in 1873, when MacClure and his first mate, Bill Brewster, fought over a woman in Hawaii. MacClure cut off Brewster's ear during the skirmish, and when their ship sailed again, Brewster led a mutiny that put MacClure over the side of the ship in a small boat.

In January of 1874, there was a violent storm along the Oregon coast. Locals were standing on seaside cliffs watching the storm waters break over the Devil's Punch Bowl near Yaquina Bay, when they saw a small boat wash up on the rocks. In horror, they observed a man with an almost skeletal face and red hair climb out, but quite suddenly a wave washed over the rocks, taking the boat and man with it. While the boat was recovered, the man was never seen again.

That spring, the local sea rescue team was launched several times to answer calls for help, but no shipwrecks were ever found. Stories up and down the coast told of people hearing the clanging of chains and seeing doors open and close on their own, but other sightings were much more sinister. In one instance, a tall, gaunt man with red hair entered a Newport bar and ordered a beer, only to disappear when it was served. A man fitting the same description also appeared to a frightened farmer's wife. He told her he needed two things to find his eternal rest: a place to stay, and someone to share his otherworldly existence.

He may have found both at Yaquina Bay. As the story goes, when the lighthouse was shut down in 1874, MacClure's ghost moved in. Many people claimed to see the lighthouse beacon lit, even though the oil reservoirs that powered it had been empty for weeks.

Blood and a Hidden Door

Legend has it that the same year, a ship landed at Newport, and a man named Trevenard came ashore. He arranged for his daughter Zina (or Muriel, as some accounts refer to her) to stay in the small hotel in town until he returned a few weeks later. Zina quickly mixed in with the local youth and didn't seem concerned when her father failed to return as promised.

In December of 1874, Zina and her friends decided to investigate the deserted lighthouse. While looking around, they discovered a secret wall panel and metal door in the third-floor closet. Upon removing the door and wainscoting, they found a tunnel or chute leading downward but decided not to investigate further, leaving the door and wainscoting on the floor. The group was locking up when Zina realized she had left her handkerchief in the lighthouse. She reentered the building in search of it, and after several minutes her friends grew impatient and walked back toward the lighthouse. That's when they heard screams.

The group entered the austere building looking for Zina, but she was nowhere to be found. Instead, to their horror, they discovered a pool of blood on the floor in one of the upstairs bedrooms. A trail of blood droplets led to where the hidden door had been found earlier, but the metal door and wainscoting had been replaced. Zina was never seen again, and interestingly, her father never returned for her, either.

222

Rumors continued about strange lights and figures seen at night in the old lighthouse. In 1982, a hitchhiker camped on its porch was awakened in the middle of the night when the front door opened. In the yellow light that shined from inside, he saw a woman walk toward him, followed by a large man who stopped at the door. The woman told the traveler, who happened to be looking for a job, that he'd find work in town. Then she and the man went inside. That same evening, the captain of a tugboat and small plane pilot both reported seeing the lighthouse beacon on.

Walt Muse, who oversees activities at the lighthouse, recalls reports of people experiencing eerie sensations when walking through the building or seeing a light in the second-floor room late at night. Muse believed it was all due to overactive imaginations until he saw the same light, which he attributes to the beacon on the top floor shining through loose floorboards into the second-floor rooms.

Today the secret door and tunnel are open to the public, but the bloodstains are covered by paint. Harder to explain are the photographs of the lighthouse that tourists have taken and sent to Muse, showing filmy figures passing in front of the camera lens.

COMING TO A HEAD

The Yaquina Head Lighthouse lies a few miles north of the one it replaced at Yaquina Bay, and it's an imposing sight. The beacon shines from the top of a ninety-three-foot-tall tower, which is built on a high rock face. Inside, 114 steps lead up a spiral staircase to the top.

This lighthouse's story begins in tragedy. During construction of the giant structure, workers were filling the space between the inner and outer walls with rubble when one of them accidentally fell in. Having no means to rescue him, his coworkers were forced to finish filling in the space, entombing their friend within. Some people believe the man survived long enough to realize what was happening to him and that he still hammers against the inner walls of the lighthouse in an attempt to free himself. The hammering sound may be explained away as the normal creaking of the huge tower as it gradually settles, but the second ghost is harder to explain.

One night in the 1930s, the head lighthouse keeper had to take a trip into Newport and left the first assistant keeper in charge. The first assistant used the opportunity to get drunk, however, leaving the second assistant keeper, Henry Higgins, to look after the beacon that night. Sometime after dark, the head lighthouse keeper returned to find that the beacon was out. He rushed to the lighthouse, found his number-two man passed out, and then ran to the spiral staircase to get the beacon working again. That's when he discovered Henry on one of the staircase landings, dead from an apparent heart attack.

The surviving assistant keeper managed to keep his job and was more attentive to his duties, with one exception: Believing that Henry's ghost haunted the stairs, he would never ascend them unaccompanied either by another person or his pet bulldog. Does Henry's ghost still try to climb the stairs to light the beacon and fulfill his sacred trust? Several years later, lighthouse keepers standing watch over the beacon swore they heard sounds of someone walking up the eighty-foot spiral staircase, but when they looked down, no one was there. Since the lighthouse was opened to the public, many have felt something strange on the stairs or heard disembodied footsteps.

Might the strange energy on the stairs arise from the restless spirit of an entombed worker? Could the disembodied footsteps belong to a dead lighthouse keeper repeating his last ascent? Perhaps visitors to this imposing structure allow their imaginations a bit too much liberty. Before you jump to conclusions, you could pay a visit to the Yaquina lighthouses and experience the freakish phenomena for yourself.

THE YAQUINA HEAD LIGHTHOUSE

Yaquina Head Outstanding Natural Area Interpretive Center,
N.W. Lighthouse Drive, Newport, Oregon 97365.

YAQUINA BAY LIGHTHOUSE

Yaquina Bay State Recreation Center, off U.S. 101, Newport.
www.yaquinalights.org.

COHOKE CROSSING LIGHTS by Ryan Doan

FOR SOME PEOPLE, STANDING ALONE at midnight on a series of train tracks several states away from home would seem rather foolish. For me, it's just another night out.

I arrived in the town of West Point, Virginia, a little ahead of schedule. Ghost lights, even the famed Cohoke Crossing Lights, aren't visible in broad daylight—floating paranormal lights are ornery like that. So I stopped at a little Italian restaurant to wait out the setting sun, and when I mumbled to some strangers about the lights, everyone in the place erupted with stories of what they had seen. Some believed the source was a long-dead train brakeman searching for his decapitated head after a tragic accident. Others attributed the lights to a lost train eternally carrying injured Confederate soldiers. Whatever the source, the Cohoke Crossing Lights are phenomena in which the locals truly believe.

Later that evening, I stood for several hours on the silent tracks in the pitch black and took numerous photos with extremely long exposures. My camera acts like a security blanket at times like these, taking the fear out of what I witness through the viewfinder. I saw lights appear and flicker out far down the tracks, but I passed them off as odd reflections. It wasn't until I arrived at the hotel later that night that I noticed in several photos a form of some kind over the tracks. I shot many angles with the same long exposures, and the "shape" only appears in one direction. The fact that none of the other shots picked up anything of interest led me to conclude that the light was not an ambient reflection caught on film. In truth, I do not know what it was—but that, in the end, is half the fun.

THE COHOKE CROSSING LIGHTS are located on railroad property and trespassing is not recommended.

NEW LONDON LEDGE: ERNIE'S DOMAIN
by L'Aura Hladik

UNLIKE MOST LIGHTHOUSES, WHICH ARE constructed from cast iron, the New London Ledge lighthouse was built from bricks, in keeping with the lovely homes along the shore of Connecticut's New London Harbor. This "manmade island," constructed on a concrete base in 1909, provided the perfect campground for solitude—even if not all the keepers enjoyed their stay. When the U.S. Coast Guard took over the lighthouse in 1939, they always had three men on duty for three weeks at a time, followed by a six-day shore break. It was rumored that if any two of the men got into a fight during their watch, the third was there to break it up.

According to some, the New London Ledge Lighthouse is also home to a ghost named Ernie, who has made his presence known over the years by closing and opening doors, turning off the television, and swabbing the decks. He's even been blamed for sounding off the foghorn at odd times and setting docked boats adrift.

Ernie may be the product of a fantastic yarn spun by a keeper to keep boredom at bay while serving at the lighthouse. Ernie, as the story is told, was the lighthouse keeper in the 1920s or 1930s. While he did keep the light blazing, he did not manage to keep his wife, who ran off with the captain of the Block Island Ferry. Ernie was supposedly so heartbroken and distraught that he committed suicide by throwing himself off the roof of the lighthouse.

EXHUMING THE FACTS
I spoke with author and East Coast lighthouse expert Jeremy D'Entremont about a night he spent at the lighthouse in August 2006 with Ron Kolek and Maureen Wood of the New England Ghost Project and *Ghost Chronicles* radio show. Maureen is a psychic trance medium with more than twenty-five years' channeling experience. She's also a seasoned paranormal investigator, having completed more than a hundred ghost hunts with Ron, founder of the New England Ghost Project.

On that ghastly night, after setting up some recorders and other ghost hunting equipment, Maureen began to channel the spirit of a man. Her demeanor transformed completely into that of an angry, violent spirit, and at one point, she struck her cohost while flailing her arm in an accusatory motion and screaming in a deep voice, "You lie!"

Jeremy said that statement was about all he could make out from the mumbled and indiscernible ranting.

After several tense moments, Maureen came back to herself and told Ron and Jeremy what she had experienced. The spirit that came through her was angry because the story about a lighthouse keeper killing himself was a cover-up for an ill-fated prank. The spirit claimed to be a former worker at the lighthouse who slipped and fell to his death after his fellow crew members decided to play a joke on him, locking him out on the wet lighthouse roof. He claimed that the truth about what happened to him was buried along with his corpse long ago.

Whoever he is, perhaps this vengeful ghost can take some comfort in the fact that the last entry in the lighthouse log, written in 1987 by a U.S. Coast Guardsman, pays tribute to him:

> *Rock of slow torture.*
> *Ernie's domain.*
> *Hell on earth—may New London Ledge's light shine*
>   *on forever because I'm through.*
> *I will watch it from afar while drinking a brew.*

227

THE NEW LONDON LEDGE LIGHTHOUSE

rises up from the New London Harbor and is only accessible by boat. Visit www.oceanology.org for information about public lighthouse cruises.

HECETA HEAD'S GRAY LADY
by Joanne M. Austin

THE HECETA HEAD LIGHTHOUSE IS *not* haunted. The Oregon Parks and Recreation Department, which owns it, wants to make sure people understand that.

But the keeper's house at Heceta Head is a different story. It originally stood by the lighthouse, making the short move to its present location in 1939. The U.S. Forest Service now owns the building, which serves as an interpretive center offering free tours to the public. It has also been leased out as a bed-and-breakfast since the winter of 1995–1996. Whether you tour or stay at Heceta Head, current co-owner Steven Bursey advises that you keep an eye out for a ghostly resident by the name of Rue, a.k.a. the Gray Lady.

Steven researched the house and found there was no mention of it being haunted before 1970, when Lane Community College took over the keeper's house as a satellite campus. The house was a duplex, and when the college removed the wall between the two dining rooms, they may have awakened something. Throw some inebriated college kids into this equation, and you can imagine the stories that evolved. And although there's no definitive proof that a woman named Rue ever lived in the keeper's house, Steven contends that residency records weren't

228

carefully kept that first decade, and it's possible she might have lived there between 1894—when the lighthouse first operated—and 1904.

Rue's Spooky Debut

Steven first encountered Rue in a 1975 newspaper article, which began with the story of a man hanging insulation alone in the attic one evening. When he took a break, he looked out a window, saw a reflection behind him in the glass, and, turning around, "saw this lady with gray hair, in a dress, floating towards him." The terrified man didn't move as Rue floated *through* him, but then he ran out of the house, leaving all of his tools behind. Once in town, he rationalized that there was still work to be done on the outside of the house, where he thought the ghost couldn't bother him. He returned the next day, put a ladder up against the side of the house, and was working near a window when the gray specter reappeared, floating toward him as before. "In his haste to get down the ladder," Steven said, "he broke a windowpane. The glass fell into the attic, and he ran off and never set foot on the property [again].

"The caretakers came home late that second evening and went to bed. They both woke up to a strange sound: glass being swept in the attic. They knew they were the only ones in the house, so the next morning they went up to investigate, and the glass from that broken window had been neatly swept up into a little pile." Rue seemed to be maintaining the white-glove cleanliness standards held by lighthouse keepers.

The Associated Press picked up the story, and the keeper's house was included in an article entitled "Terrifying Tales of Nine Haunted Houses" in the November 1980 issue of *LIFE* magazine.

"Ever since that point," Steven said, "we've been known as a haunted house."

Victoria's Room

Rue is just a matter of course for Steven, who said he's not "really into ghosts" himself. He tries to find logical explanations for things he has experienced, though sometimes it's hard. Steven hasn't seen Rue, but in the seven years he lived there, he stayed in most of the rooms and "had quite a span of time to experience the mood of the house."

Most of the ghostly happenings seem to occur on the first assistant lightkeeper's side of the house—especially in Victoria's Room. One common

occurrence is the scent of old-fashioned lavender perfume in the air. Steven and his wife, Michelle, closed the bed-and-breakfast for a few days of vacation at one point, and upon their return opened up the rooms to air them out. When Steven went into Victoria's Room, however, "I was almost knocked over by the smell. . . . It was like a woman had just doused herself in perfume. It was really pungent."

The room also tends to heat up for no reason, and other ghostly evidence has manifested on the bed. Steven, under his mother-in-law's tutelage, became an expert at making beds. One day, he made the bed in Victoria's Room and then attended to an adjoining room. On his way back through Victoria's Room, he said, "I noticed an indentation, as if someone had sat on the bed. At first I thought my coworkers or Michelle were pulling a trick on me. I realized after a while that there wasn't anyone upstairs. This happened maybe half a dozen times." These occurrences in Victoria's Room tend to come in groups and then stop for a while.

THE STORIES CONTINUE . . .

Once guests check in and are familiarized with the bed-and-breakfast, they have the run of the house until the innkeepers provide a seven-course breakfast the next morning. That meal is often where guests share whatever ghostly encounters they may have had the previous evening. Steven keeps a "ghost log" of these stories, which he plans to someday assemble into a book on the Gray Lady.

Former students from the house's college campus days have reappeared to mention frequent coastal power outages that occurred in the 1970s. "People would drive up the dark coast and they'd see a light in the attic, even though there was no electricity going to the house," says Steven. "A couple of these people would investigate, and they'd open up the attic and a light would go off. . . . " Whenever stories of Rue run in a newspaper or magazine, there's a new array of people who visit the B and B, hopeful for an encounter with its famed otherworldly occupant.

Rue or no Rue, the Heceta Head lightkeeper's house is a stunning place to visit. It is open five days a week during the winter, and seven days a week from the beginning of May to the end of November.

HECETA HEAD LIGHTHOUSE

92072 Highway 101 South, Yachats, Oregon 97498

www.hecetalighthouse.com

ANASTASIA ISLAND Apparitions
by Charlie Carlson

St. Augustine, Florida, has racked up quite an inventory of spooky sights since it was founded in 1565; and according to those who dare to dabble in the ethereal, the lighthouse on Anastasia Island ranks in the top five. Having been featured in several paranormal television documentaries, it might even "outshine" all the other ghostly places in the ancient city. Built in 1874 directly across Matanzas Bay from the Castillo de San Marcos National Monument, this lighthouse is the last in a line of light towers dating back to the 1500s, and it's also the alleged domain of a portal to the afterlife. No wonder St. Augustine is crawling with ghosts!

The 165-foot-tall lighthouse is believed to harbor numerous souls—mostly of lives that ended within the tower or somewhere on the grounds. There are many contrived ghost stories concerning the lighthouse, among them a tale about thirteen pirates who were executed and buried on the grounds, as well as the story of a former lighthouse "owner" who remains earthbound to revenge himself on the government, which confiscated his property under eminent domain. Albeit intriguing, none of these yarns have any historical basis, so let's stick with the haunting facts.

Smoke and Shadows
The most frequently seen phantom—usually observed on the tower's catwalk—is of a little girl who wears a blue dress and a bow in her hair. People have also been unnerved by the disincarnate laughter of children late at night. Investigating mediums attribute these phenomena to three young girls. Records indicate that when the lighthouse was being built, construction supervisor Hezekiah Pittee resided on the site with his wife and five children. On July 10, 1873, while playing with a handcart on a track used for hauling building supplies, two of the Pittee children and a playmate were drowned when the cart ran off the rails and into the bay.

The lighthouse is also known for its cigar-smoking ghost, which some believe is an earthbound soul named Peter Rasmussen, a former keeper remembered for being very fussy when it came to managing the lighthouse. Although Rasmussen has never been seen, visitors often report smelling cigar smoke in the old fuel house and basement.

233

Historical records indicate that several people died at or near the lighthouse, including lighthouse keeper William Harn in 1889, and the wife of another keeper in 1894. There were two deaths at a lighthouse that stood near the location of the present structure—one in 1853, when keeper John Carrera fell from the tower, and the other in 1859, when Joseph Andreu fell while painting the lighthouse.

Perhaps one of these departed souls is the shadowy figure seen roaming the grounds or on the tower's spiral staircase, where The Atlantic Paranormal Society (TAPS) filmed an undisputable moving human figure that mysteriously vanished as they hastily pursued him to the top. In lighthouses, the stairs are the only way up or down—did he jump to his death, or vanish through a portal into the ethereal world? The St. Augustine Lighthouse and Museum offers you a chance to reflect on this conundrum on its Dark of the Moon after-hours paranormal tour.

SAINT AUGUSTINE LIGHTHOUSE AND MUSEUM

81 Lighthouse Avenue, St. Augustine, Florida 32080

www.staugustinelighthouse.com

Educated Entities

"You old black crows!"
—The crabby neighbor to the holy men
at the University of Portland

THE QUEST FOR KNOWLEDGE is never ending for many people, and some particularly dedicated spirits continue their scholastic pursuits in the afterlife. Such academic apparitions may appear to a college freshman living away from home for the first time, or to a graduate student studying on campus late at night. Highly educated haunts can even creep up on those just visiting the local library.

Sometimes it's just one ghost that will get your attention, like that of a young woman murdered on the campus of Marist College in New York, who is now rumored to haunt the residence hall in which she once lived. At the former Monticello College a beloved lilac-scented educator watches over a chapel-turned-library, and an oversensitive actor named William haunts Hart Chapel Auditorium at Clarion University in Pennsylvania. In Tennessee a ghost dressed in academic-style tweed competes for your attention at Lincoln Memorial University. Dressed in old-fashioned bathing garb and joined by the spirit of a crabby old neighbor, Paul (or is it Peter?) haunts the oldest building on the University of Portland campus in Oregon.

These ghosts teach afterlife lessons that don't result in a degree, but their mere presence often reveals what we really need to know about life in general.

MARIST COLLEGE'S GHOSTLY FRESHMAN
by James A. Willis

THE HISTORY OF MARIST COLLEGE begins with a religious order known as the Marist Brothers. Located primarily in France, the order was known throughout the world in the 1800s for its educational work. In the early 1900s, a small group of Brothers relocated to the Hudson Valley area in upstate New York, settling along the eastern bank of the Hudson River just outside the city of Poughkeepsie. In 1905, after purchasing more property, the Brothers renamed the area Saint Anne's Hermitage and began preparing men for a life dedicated to, among other things, prayer and work. These things would later become the basis for Marist's school motto: *Orare et Laborare* (to pray and to work).

Over the next few years, more Brothers arrived to help with the expansion of the hermitage, and more buildings were constructed on the site. In 1946, New York State officially granted a four-year charter to the Brothers, establishing Marist College.

237

Another twenty-two years passed before women were admitted at the college and allowed to enroll in day classes. Today there are close to five thousand students at the 180-acre campus. It's a beautiful, tree-lined landscape with grottoes and streams. Few students realize that, as they make their way to the dining hall, they might be walking in the footsteps of a cold-blooded killer.

BLOODSHED

On the afternoon of February 18, 1975, freshman Shelley Sperling decided to walk to the campus cafeteria with a friend. Having graduated from high school the previous spring, she was enjoying her newfound freedom at college, much to the dismay of her ex-boyfriend, Louis Acevedo III. They had been high school sweethearts back in Mahopac, New York, but Sperling had broken things off before leaving for Marist.

Shortly after fall classes started, Acevedo visited Sperling and attempted to reconcile with her. Sperling refused, which sent Acevedo into a violent rage. He attacked Sperling with a brick and fractured her skull. Acevedo was arrested and charged with felony assault and released on bail. Sperling alerted campus security of the attack, and they assured her they would remain on the lookout for Acevedo.

One day, as Sperling and a friend neared the entrance of the cafeteria, Acevedo stepped from the bushes out onto the walking path. Sperling sensed danger, told her friend to run, and took off toward the cafeteria, Acevedo following close behind. The two women made it to a small office off the main cafeteria, where several employees were taking a break. She grabbed a nearby telephone and was frantically trying to dial campus police when Acevedo entered the room. The first shot rang out, sending Sperling's friend and the cafeteria workers running. Shortly thereafter, several other shots echoed through the quickly emptying cafeteria.

STANDOFF AND AFTERMATH

When campus police and local officers arrived, they roped off the area surrounding the cafeteria and attempted to initiate contact with Acevedo. Not wanting to start a gunfight with the disturbed gunman, the officers decided to take their time. Two hours later, seeing no movement from inside the cafeteria and still unable to make contact with Acevedo, the officers moved in to take a closer look.

As they entered the building, they came across the body of Shelley Sperling sprawled across the entrance to the cafeteria's office. Moments later, they located Acevedo. He was sitting nearby, quietly looking at photographs of Sperling. He was arrested without incident.

Several days later, Sperling's memorial service was held at the Marist College Chapel, attended by hundreds of students and faculty. Her body was later interred at Ivandale Cemetery in Brewster, New York. The following year, Louis Acevedo III was found incompetent to stand trial and sent to the Mid-Hudson Psychiatric Center for further evaluation. He was later transferred to the Harlem Psychiatric Center in Dover, New York, where he remains to this day.

GHOSTLY ACTIVITY

During her short stay at Marist College, Shelley Sperling lived on the third floor of Sheahan Hall, the college's very first residence hall. According to many of the students who live there today, she never really left.

Freshmen living in Sheahan Hall have reported an array of strange activities inside the building, especially on the third floor: toilets flush on their own, faucets turn themselves on and off as if by unseen hands, electronic devices such as TVs and stereos turn on and off at will. Sperling's specter has even been known to play around on students' computers when no one else is around.

Sheahan Hall residents sometimes awake in the middle of the night to the sounds of a door opening and then slamming shut. At first, students were understandably frightened, but over time many found themselves reassured by the ruckus, taking it as a sign that Sperling's spirit was making the rounds at Sheahan Hall to ensure everyone's safety. So many people have reported seeing, hearing, or otherwise sensing Sperling's spirit in the residence, in fact, that former Marist College student Christina Hope created a small Web site chronicling several people's encounters with the specter.

But while Sperling's ghost seems to have made Sheahan Hall her home, she's in no way a homebody. The specter has been spotted on campus at the Novitiate Grotto of Our Lady of Sorrows, erected in the 1920s in memory of Marist College students who passed away.

239

MARIST COLLEGE

3399 North Road, Poughkeepsie, New York 12601

www.marist.edu

HANGING AT HART CHAPEL
by Todd Pfannestiel, Ph.D.

EVERYONE HAS WITNESSED AT LEAST one poor theatrical performance in which the actors "die" on stage. Yet few actors literally die there, leaving their spirit behind to foil others who work the same stage. Of the several ghost stories related to Clarion University, in the foothills of the Allegheny Mountains in scenic northwestern Pennsylvania, the story of one such actor has become legend at the institution.

Founded in 1867 as a Methodist seminary, Clarion University became a teacher's college in 1887 and later a comprehensive four-year undergraduate university. One of the oldest buildings on campus still in use today is Hart Chapel Auditorium. The building served for many years as the center of worship on the college grounds as well as the primary location for assemblies, commencement ceremonies, and other gatherings.

240   In the early 1930s, the building underwent significant renovations to transform it into the roughly four-hundred-seat auditorium it is today. Since then, the auditorium has hosted theatrical and musical productions, guest speakers, film presentations, and several large student classes. Many students, faculty, and patrons attending these events have related stories about William, the spirit who haunts Hart Chapel.

DASHED HOPES

William's story began like that of any other aspiring actor. Dreaming of Broadway and a career on the professional stage, he set out from his home in Ohio in 1934 with his new "one-man show," a scrapbook for his clippings and reviews, and determination. As he worked his way through the Ohio Valley, William learned

of the newly renovated Hart Chapel Auditorium and its mission to introduce new cultural elements to the local community. He booked a date and arrived in town in the fall of 1934.

Whether due to nerves or overconfidence, William's solo performance did not go as intended. The audience booed him mercilessly until he fled the auditorium before finishing his act. Feeling that his theatrical career had died that night, William chose to end his mortal life as well. He left his hotel room on Main Street in the middle of the night and re-entered the auditorium through the locked side doors. With a rope slung over his shoulder, William crept to the stage-right balcony. Slowly he crawled along a thick wooden crossbeam to where a large light fixture was suspended from the uppermost peak of the roof. There he tied one end of the rope to the bracket supporting the light and formed a crude noose with the other end. He placed the rope around his neck and leapt from the beam.

William may have been a questionable actor, but he was an even worse physicist—he made the rope too long. Rather than dying from asphyxiation or a broken neck by hanging, William decapitated himself, his body continuing its plunge to the seats below while his head fell to the wooden stage. Several stories relate the pools of blood discovered by auditorium personnel the next morning, including one noticeable puddle on the stage where William's head lay.

Supernatural Stain

In the seventy-five years since William's death, other actors, musicians, teachers, and students have performed upon that same stage—some worthy of applause, others not so much. Yet only William took the vocal criticism to heart and ended his life. His soul thus trapped in the theater, he observes the events occurring therein and at times makes his presence known.

Visitors to the auditorium today can see the plaster repairs on the wall where the crossbeam from which William jumped was removed long ago and the round white bracket from which the large light fixture was previously suspended. Most eerily, remnants of the large bloodstain downstage center where William's head allegedly came to rest are still visible. Despite repeated efforts to buff, sand, stain, paint, and even replace the wooden stage (twice!), this one significant stain reappears again and again.

OTHERWORLDLY ACTOR

William is also responsible for several poltergeist events in the auditorium, most often when individuals tell his story incorrectly to visitors and prospective students. Auditorium and public safety personnel tell stories of lights mysteriously switching off and on, and of microphones and other equipment being moved from the stage to the balcony from one night to the next. Students attending class in the building frequently report mysterious movements in the shadows of the balcony surrounding three-quarters of the auditorium. In the fall of 2007, less than a week after a professional paranormal investigation of the building,

William apparently disrupted one class video presentation by illuminating a theatrical spotlight on the screen for twenty minutes before turning it off. Investigation of the light booth revealed no one present.

Since 2004, the Hart Chapel Auditorium has been the focal point for an annual ghost tour conducted by the student members of the university's History Club. One year, less than five minutes before the doors opened to a crowd of nearly five hundred patrons, the fire alarm mysteriously engaged, delaying the event's start.

In 2007, paranormal investigators labeled the building the most haunted they'd encountered, with several photos revealing orbs as well as shadows and outlines passing by windows. Audio recorders revealed footsteps in the stairwells—despite the fact that the building was completely vacant—and twice recorded "shhhhh" when the investigators attempted to ask questions and seek responses from William by using dowsing rods. Subsequent amateur investigations have added to the photographic evidence, including pictures of mist in the shape of a human head in the stairwells leading to the balcony.   243

Is William's spirit trapped in the building where his body perished, or is this a ghoul craving the attention and applause he did not receive in life? Perhaps the phantom of William is simply the conjuring of the overactive imaginations of thousands of students, faculty, and other individuals who, for seventy-five years, have remained convinced of the otherworldly actor's presence in the building. Regardless of whether William is a fabrication or a real ghost, one thing is certain: Clarion University residents don't take chances. They steer clear of the stain that continues to bleed through on the stage. They're cautious but not alarmed by the shadows they see moving in the balcony through their peripheral vision. They tell William's story accurately. And, most important, they applaud long and loud when they feel his presence.

HART CHAPEL AUDITORIUM

Clarion University, 840 Wood Street,
Clarion, Pennsylvania 16214,
www.clarion.edu

HAUNTED BALL STATE
by Christopher Chambers and Colleen Boyd, Ph.D.

BALL STATE UNIVERSITY IN MUNCIE, Indiana, is like many colleges in the Midwest: stately ivy-covered buildings surround the tree-lined quad, where students sit outdoors to study on warm spring days. When winter storms blow and the winds howl, students and faculty walk briskly across campus, anxious to get indoors. Sometimes, however, what awaits them inside is colder than an Indiana snowstorm in January.

According to folklorist Elizabeth Tucker, author of *Haunted Halls: Ghostlore of American College Campuses,* students entering an exciting, volatile, and sometimes anxious time in their lives delight in spreading spooky tales in classrooms, dining halls, dormitories, and on the Internet. Several such stories exist at Ball State University, including the one about the infamous ghost of Elliott Hall.

THE ELLIOTT HALL GHOST

244

Ball State University is named for the Ball brothers, leading industrialists in Muncie who funded many good works, including the university. Built in 1938 as a tribute to Frank C. Ball's son, Frank Elliott Ball, who died in an airplane accident in 1936, Elliott Hall is one of the oldest residence halls on campus. It is a replica of the residence young Frank lived in while attending Princeton University.

Despite the hall's tragic origins, it is not the ghost of Frank Ball that keeps students whispering. The spirit of a Ball State student is said to wander the hallways of the four-story residence building on the south edge of campus.

In the days following World War II, William Schamberg was one of thousands of young men who returned from the battlefield eager to take advantage of the federal GI Bill and attend college. Sadly, by the time he arrived at Ball State, Schamberg was scarred, disfigured, and something of a social recluse. Rejected by his girlfriend, he lived alone, became severely depressed, and ultimately ended his life in Elliott Hall's fourth-floor library. It is said that he still roams the hallway, engaging in paranormal trickery and frightening students.

John, a recent resident of Elliott Hall, encountered William's ghost during a long holiday weekend in the dead of winter. John awoke in the middle of the night freezing, and was surprised to find the room's windows wide open. Certain that he'd closed and locked the windows and door before going to bed, as he always did, he got up to check his door—it was locked. Puzzled, he shut

the windows again, taking great care to lock them, and returned to bed.

Once again, after John had fallen asleep, he awoke chilled to the bone and found the windows wide open. This time John asked William to leave him alone, explaining that he had work in the morning and needed to rest. Nothing happened, according to John, for the rest of the night.

John's encounter with Schamberg's specter is just one of many paranormal events that have been reported over the years. Some students have had books and other items hurled at them while they slept; others describe hearing strange sounds of objects moving on the fourth floor where William died. Julie, who was studying on the fourth floor one evening, claims she heard someone calling her name repeatedly. She dismissed it at the time, thinking it was one of her friends playing games, but later learned that no one else had been on the fourth floor that night.

GHOSTLY INQUIRY

The E. Fay Kitselman home, one of Muncie's architectural landmarks, was donated to Ball State in 1956. Constructed in 1927, the building is now equipped with twenty-first-century technology, although its period furnishings and style

remain virtually untouched. In 2000 the Virginia B. Ball Center for Creative Inquiry moved into the house, creating a place where BSU students could immerse themselves in learning projects. Work and study continue around the clock, and it isn't unusual for center staff to find students sleeping there when they arrive in the morning for work.

Both students and staff have reported eerie experiences at the center, especially during the evenings. Strange vibes and sensations of being watched are the most common complaints; whispers and disembodied voices are also known to occur. Spontaneously slamming doors that lock themselves have been reported and in at least one case, a student discovered she could no longer gain entry to the center with the key that had been provided. She assumed the locks had been changed for some reason, but when she tried the key again the following day, the doors opened perfectly.

E. B. and Bertha C. Ball Center

The Balls donated their family home to the Ball State University Foundation in 1975 and it remained vacant until 1986 when it became the E. B. and Bertha C. Ball Center for University and Community Programs. Today it serves the entire community as a venue for adult education classes, conventions, banquets, and meetings. It's also the home of the Magna cum Murder conference, an annual conference that brings together murder mystery writers and fans from all over the world.

According to local lore, one of the Ball children died at a young age in the building. Staff members of the center have reported feeling as though they're being watched and some claim to have been touched by an entity. Ghostly figures have been spotted throughout the facility, although the basement is where most of the eerie encounters have taken place. Staff members refuse to go into the basement at night.

247

The Shively Hall Bathroom Ghost

A playful spirit allegedly torments student residents of Ball State's Shively Hall. Apparently students sharing a Jack and Jill bathroom between rooms will sometimes find the doors locked on both sides. This is impossible to do unless someone is inside the bathroom. Or is it? According to students who have experienced the phenomenon, it is the Bathroom Ghost . . . at play again.

BALL STATE UNIVERSITY

2000 W. University Avenue, Muncie, Indiana 47306
http://cms.bsu.edu/

SCHOOL SPIRITS:
LINCOLN MEMORIAL UNIVERSITY
by Larry D. Thacker

OTHERWORLDLY RUMORS AND TALES ARE common fare in residential college communities like Lincoln Memorial University in Harrogate, Tennessee. Shadowed by the ancient Cumberland Gap, the LMU campus offers a unique opportunity to examine a microcosm of lore-threaded lives. Few are left to verify or quash the accuracy of these interesting, mysterious, and romantic stories, but there seems to be an endless number of volunteers bent upon breathing life into such tales. Add 110 years of LMU history, and there are almost too many ghost stories to track. Literally every building on campus, even the newer facilities, has its share of stories—playful tales, innocent fantasies, and a handful of more sinister legends.

248

HONEST ABE APPARITIONS

Finished in 1977, the Abraham Lincoln Library and Museum is home to a significant number of items much older than the university itself, and it's the site of some truly haunted happenings. The most famous tale is of a tweed-clad academic whose specter examines the building's collection.

SPOOK HALL

Dedicated in 1928, the Duke Hall of Citizenship offers the most architecturally spooky details on campus. The old radiator systems hiss and clank. The expansive theater and stage provide more shadow than light, long exaggerated echoes, and nooks and crannies galore. It's by far the easiest campus building in which to feel suddenly "accompanied."

Tales of Lincoln's form wandering the deserted corridors of Duke Hall were popular when the Lincoln Room on the third floor housed the university's collection (before the artifacts moved permanently to the Abraham Lincoln Library and Museum). And rumor has it that a true Lincoln relic—a fragment of his jawbone kept in the collection—calls the great president to the campus in search of what rightfully belongs to him.

Another well-known Duke Hall story concerns its long unused set of organ pipes. People claim the pipes have a musical life of their own at night and that moving lights are seen in this stately building as well.

AARON AT STOPINKSI

The LMU bookstore, located on the second floor of the Student Center is known for several strange "tricky occupants." A six- or seven-year-old paranormal prankster known as Aaron has been blamed for objects falling off shelves, displays falling over, and computer problems. He reportedly giggles to himself, speaks the names of employees, and darts around corners, just out of sight. On one occasion, his name appeared finger-written on the outside of a second-story window.

The third floor of the Student Center building also has its share of eerie issues: Objects move of their own volition and go missing, and mysterious moaning winds blow through the rooms, keeping many from venturing to this floor when it's completely dark.

HUFF'S ELUSIVE BLUE LIGHTS

Just left of the main entrance to the campus is Huff Tower, LMU's oldest intact structure. This landmark is reputed to be an indicator of local deaths: during fatal disease outbreaks in the 1920s, tales abounded of strange blue glowing lights floating around or shooting from the top of the thirty-foot tower whenever a student, faculty, staff, or community member succumbed to smallpox or typhoid.

According to Beth Gibson, LMU activities director in 2002, campers staying in the base of the tower saw the lights for themselves. "They woke up in the middle of the night and felt pebbles falling on them. . . . They looked up and saw small lights coming from the holes in the walls. The lights began to go in a circular motion until they formed one big circle, and then they suddenly shot out of the tower."

250

LAFRENTZ-POOLE HALL HANGIN' TREE

A slave-owning Confederate sympathizer, Capt. David Huff, owned much of the property that is LMU's present campus according to Joseph E. Suppiger, author of *Phoenix of the Mountains: The Story of Lincoln Memorial University.* Shortly before the Civil War, Huff buried a slave somewhere just southeast of a tree that either now stands or once stood to the front of Lafrentz-Poole residence hall. Legend has it that this was the tragic place where lynchings occurred.

Some say the silhouettes of swinging bodies appear on certain nights. Inside the residence, reports abound of unexplained noises and the undeniable cries of an infant child. Residents describe waking at night to the disturbing cries, and although searches take place and security officers are sometimes paged, no child is ever found.

This building reportedly also has a closed-up room, where a student was found hanging from the rafters. The story continues that, though the room's window is visible from the outside, all entrances to the space no longer exist.

The Office of Student Services and other organizations continue to search *251* out, collect, and preserve these many tales. Who knows how many stories have been forgotten, which details of existing but fragmented stories are lost, or how many stories have combined themselves over the years, creating unique mixes of strange fiction and nonfiction? No matter one's belief, LMU continues as a hotbed of haunts.

LINCOLN MEMORIAL UNIVERSITY

6965 Cumberland Gap Parkway, Harrogate, Tennesssee 37752
www.lmunet.edu

Of DROWNED BOYS AND BLACK CROWS: THE UNIVERSITY Of PORTLAND
by Jefferson Davis

THE CAMPUS OF WHAT WOULD eventually become the University of Portland first opened as a Portland University, a Methodist college, in 1890. West Hall (later called Waldschmidt Hall) was the first large building constructed: a five-story brick building of Richardson Romanesque style. After the college closed its doors in 1900 because of financial difficulties, the Catholic Church bought the property and in 1901 reopened the school as Columbia University, hoping to make it the Notre Dame of the West. The Fathers and Brothers of the Holy Cross have run the facility since 1902, though in its early days it was a boys' preparatory school. West Hall was the major facility: The upper floors were used as dormitories and the lower floors were a combination of classrooms, dining facility, and chapel. It is during this time that one of the campus's ghostly legends begins.

PARANORMAL PETER

A ghost called Peter reportedly haunts the fourth and fifth floors of the hall. He might be the ghost of a boy named Paul (not Peter) Hillgen, who arrived on campus from Dufur, Oregon, on September 15, 1923.

It was a Saturday, and after Paul checked in with the administration and took his bags to the fifth floor, he and some of the other boys decided to go swimming down at the Willamette River. They likely took a stairway from the bluff that overlooks Swan Island to the river below; and, while the details aren't known, Paul drowned. His bags were sent home without ever being opened, and his ghost was said to haunt the hall and the bluff outside of it, looking for his bags.

Over the years, people working on the upper floors claim to have felt young Paul's paranormal presence, literally feeling his touch. Others, while gazing down from the hall's upper stories, have seen a strange-looking teenage boy standing on the bluff.

A few years ago, Waldschmidt Hall was renovated, and the fifth floor was converted into offices for university officers and staff. During construction, two campus security guards were inside the hall when they saw a boy standing outside on the bluff, looking down to the river. They noticed he wasn't wearing the typical clothing of a student; he was dressed in knickers and a tank top, like an old-style swimsuit.

Concerned that the boy might be contemplating suicide, the guards hurried

outside. They approached him from different sides, talking to him but getting no response. When the guards got close enough, they both sprang at the boy, only to run into each other. The boy had vanished.

If this was indeed the ghost of Paul, it was his last reported visit. The changes to the hall must have upset him and he hasn't been seen around the building since.

You Old Black Crows!

When the university began as a Methodist facility, the plan was to divide the property around the campus and sell it when money was needed. Frank Houston was a neighboring landowner and fellow Methodist who did not favor the changes when the campus came under ownership by the Catholic Church. He put up a fence along the common property line, which ran through the bluff overlooking the river. The university tried to buy the land from Houston, but he refused. He would patrol the property line yelling, "You old black crows!" as the Brothers and Fathers passed by. When he died in the 1930s, his widow sold the property to those same "old black crows," and it became part of the campus. The Old Commons building—now St. Mary's Chapel—was constructed on the property line, and Houston's ghost is said to patrol the line to this day. Many people have heard the sound of boots walking—sometimes stomping—both inside and outside the chapel. So far, however, nobody has heard the voice of any angry old man yelling, "You old black crows!"

253

UNIVERSITY OF PORTLAND

5000 N. Willamette Boulevard, Portland, Oregon 97203

www.up.edu

PHYLLIS ISN'T TALKING
by Joanne M. Austin

IT WAS A RAINY NIGHT in New Jersey, and I was standing under a side porch at the Old Bernardsville Library with two friends, waiting to meet a ghost named Phyllis. Paranormal investigators Paula McGraw and Nelson Jecas had kindly invited us to an informal ghost investigation they had arranged at the building, and we weren't really sure what would be involved. Lennaire had been invited because he's sensitive to ghosts, and Kelley and I were along for the ride. A woman came along and joined us under the porch, followed by a bunch of giggly middle school girls, and then Paula and Nelson arrived with more people, making our group about twenty.

The Old Bernardsville Library is no longer the town library. Its contents were moved to a newer facility in the 1990s. The night we were there, the historic space was empty and waiting for new tenants of the living kind. That we had access to the site was really a special arrangement: It's not open to the public, at least currently.

We all congregated in the hallway, just outside of a room with a high ceiling and a huge fireplace, where Paula told the ghostly story to us. The library was originally the Vealtown Tavern, built in the 1700s. During the Revolutionary War it was owned by Capt. John Parker and frequented by soldiers in Washington's Continental Army, who were camped at Jockey Hollow, a few miles away in Morristown.

This is where history diverges into ghostly folklore, as nobody can prove that either of the key players actually existed. A patron, Dr. Byram, fell in love with Phyllis Parker, the tavern owner's daughter, and the two were engaged. But the doctor was accused of espionage and hanged for treason. His body was put in a box, brought back to the tavern, and stashed in the downstairs room we were now looking into, supposedly so Mr. Parker could gently break news of the death to his daughter. Phyllis, however, found the box before he could do so, and the unpleasant surprise led to a nervous breakdown. She never recovered, eventually dying a recluse at that location. She's been rumored to haunt the building ever since, and has been seen and heard crying by different people over time. The library even issued her a library card.

When Paula finished, she asked Lennaire to walk into the room and talk about what he was feeling. He did, but immediately walked back out and said he didn't feel good in the room—he had the same experience anyplace where bodies or coffins were kept.

Kelley, Lennaire, and I then headed up to the second floor, where we looked down at the spot where the infamous box once sat in front of the fireplace. We walked over to some windows that looked out on what is now Morristown Road (or Route 202), and Lennaire got the impression of a woman standing at one of them, gazing out. Perhaps this was Phyllis, watching as the world went by in the street below.

I was annoyed at myself for not bringing a camera, but I did bring a digital recorder. Kelley and I went to various locations in the building to see if we could pick up any electronic voice phenomena, even though we knew it was too noisy with all the activity of the investigators around us.

A SOUR SMELL

We started off in the downstairs corner of a bright front room with a high ceiling and two unlit fireplaces, and then moved to the other front room downstairs. We recorded a few more questions, and it was at this point that I caught a whiff of something sharp and acidic that was not quite citrus. Kelley smelled it, too, and immediately associated it with something unpleasant. We couldn't pinpoint what it was, so we left and checked out the "box" room again. The smell hit us there, too.

Back upstairs, we tried recording again by the window where Lennaire sensed a woman, then moved to the back of the room, where we got hit with the same acrid scent. Thinking she could sweet-talk Phyllis by bringing up something girly like perfume, Kelley said, "We'd love to know how you smelled. Can you share that with us?" No flowery or pleasant scent manifested, but the off-smell gradually faded.

Downstairs, the tour was winding down and once the large group had dispersed, we discussed our findings with our hosts. Lennaire said he had a brief glimpse of a party upstairs involving a group of men and two women and explained that this seemed more like a residual memory than a manifested haunting. In the large, bright room downstairs Lennaire sensed a man sitting in front of the fireplace with a little girl on his lap; the room gave off the happy sensation of a small child who is completely content with her world. Maybe it was a younger, happier Phyllis. He also felt the presence of another spirit—a man. Whether this was Phyllis's father or her lover, Lennaire wasn't sure.

Kelley and I talked about the smell, which reminded us more and more of a fragrance unsuccessfully covering the odor of decay. Knowing the story behind the haunting, we easily imagined we smelled the rotting contents of a box from long ago, badly masked by a citrus scent.

We said our good-byes and headed back through the rain to our car. The next day I played back the brief recordings that Kelley and I had made, finding nothing but a lot of background noise made by living people. If Phyllis or any other ghost was recorded, it was impossible to tell.

Several small businesses now occupy the building that housed the original Old Bernardsville Library, Two Morristown Road, Bernardsville, New Jersey 07924.

THE HAUNTS OF HARRIET HASKELL
by Troy Taylor

MONTICELLO COLLEGE, THE FIRST "FEMALE seminary in the West," was founded in 1838 by Capt. Benjamin Godfrey, a pioneer financier near Alton, Illinois. At the time, most girls' schools were finishing schools that emphasized music, needlework, and other "womanly arts." At Monticello, however, ladies studied mathematics, English, history, religion, philosophy, and foreign languages.

As the college grew, it attracted students from all over the country. During the Civil War, the campus became bitterly divided, as girls from both Union and Confederate families attended. That changed with the arrival of Harriet Newell Haskell in 1867. As the new principal of Monticello, Miss Haskell quickly mended the rift, and students took to her right away, perhaps because of her wit and her sharp sense of humor.

Miss Haskell's tenure at Monticello Seminary lasted forty years, and it was the school's zenith by both educational and economic standards. She had a knack for securing donations for the school and was respected by parents and board members alike. When she died, former students from across the country sent flowers and cards or came from great distances to attend her funeral.

257

Eventually, time and coeducational colleges caught up with the school. The last class graduated from Monticello in 1971, after which the campus became the home of Lewis and Clark Community College. Much of the campus has since been renovated, and what used to be dorm rooms are now offices. The old school chapel is now a library.

POSTMORTEM ACTIVITY

In 1971, on the day Monticello Seminary officially became a college, one of the largest and oldest trees on campus crashed to the ground. No storm, high winds, or act of nature caused the tree to fall. Some say that it was Harriet Haskell, upset over what had become of her beloved Monticello, who knocked it down.

Whether or not Harriet's ghost is real, the legend is firmly embedded in the college's culture. Believers speak quietly about the ghost, while nonbelievers refuse to acknowledge the stories at all. The college

has no official stand on the haunting, but nevertheless considers it a part of the school.

The stories about Harriet Haskell's ghost actually began shortly after her 1907 death. At the time, Monticello girls scared new students with tales of Miss Haskell's ghost wandering the hallways at night. Others told of seeing her face reflecting back at them from mirrors and of seeing apparitions in darkened corridors. Such ghostly tales may simply have been legends designed to frighten new arrivals at the school, although there are a handful of eerie events that can't be readily explained. Most notably, the lights and fountains of one of the oldest structures on campus have been observed turning on and off of their own accord, and the steam-operated elevator in the old administration building has been known to travel between floors at night.

THE LIBRARY

The campus's is the library, which was once the Monticello chapel, is among the most haunted sites at the college. Some say this was Miss Haskell's favorite spot on campus, so it's not surprising that her spirit is encountered here with some regularity. The distinct smell of lilac perfume, Miss Haskell's trademark scent, has also been reported in the library and many believe this phantom smell signals her presence.

A librarian working alone one night claimed she felt someone touch her on the shoulder, and when she turned to see who it was, found nobody there. She returned to her work and again felt a hand tap her arm. The woman later stated that while she doesn't believe in ghosts, there was something in the library with her that night.

A different librarian presents another account of a Harriet Haskell sighting. She was straightening magazines in a recessed corner nook one night and looked up to see a tall woman in a long, old-fashioned dress standing near the main desk. Before she could ask the woman if she needed assistance, the woman vanished.

One Halloween night, a student who was skeptical about the supernatural did a radio broadcast from the library. He set up his equipment to air a reading of some of Harriet Haskell's writings. Around midnight, the student signed off the air and had just shut down the transmitter when he felt a cool hand touch him on the shoulder. He turned quickly; and when he found no one there, he figured that one of his buddies was playing a trick on him. He pulled off his earphones, grabbed a flashlight, and searched the library. He found no one.

The student returned to his equipment, sat down, and put his headphones back on. His hands shook as he turned the dial for some music, and little by little, he began to relax. When he felt the familiar hand on his shoulder again, he tore the headphones from his head and, leaving all of his equipment behind, ran out of the library.

PHANTOM CRIES

One afternoon in the early 1990s, the college maintenance staff received a call from campus security notifying them that a female student was trapped inside one of the new elevators that had become stuck between floors. The young woman had grown agitated and was crying for help when two maintenance workers arrived on the scene and set to work on the elevator. The woman continued to call out to the workers, asking them to hurry; and after several minutes, she began to cry. A short time later, the problem fixed, the workers brought the elevator down to free the trapped woman. The doors opened, and they waited for her to step off. When no one came out, they looked inside—the elevator was empty. The maintenance men, and the security guards who made the initial call, said they had been talking with the woman inside of the elevator . . . even though they discovered no one was there.

259

MONTICELLO COLLEGE IS NOW LEWIS AND
CLARK COMMUNITY COLLEGE
5800 Godfrey Road, Godfrey, Illinois 62035, www.lc.edu

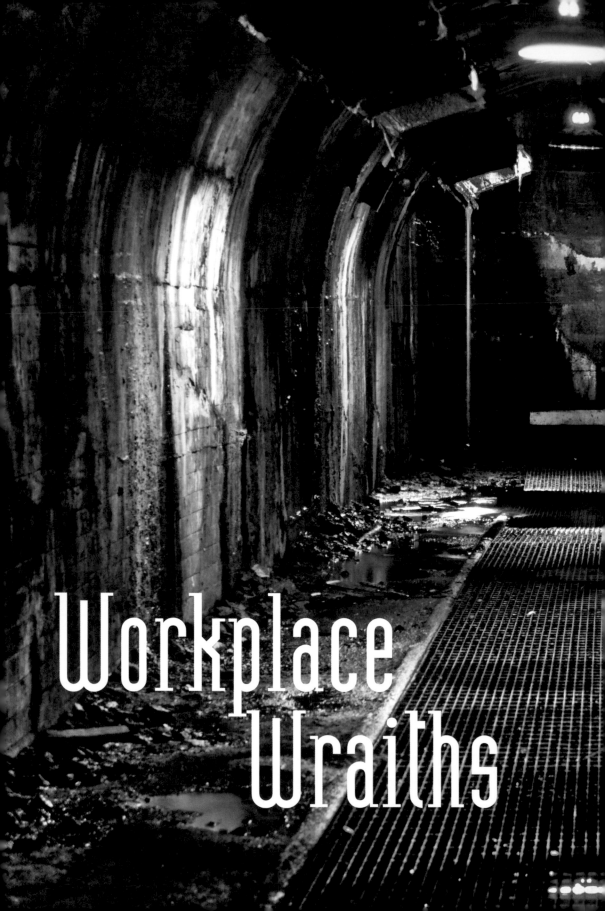

Workplace Wraiths

"I'm not going back in there alone."
—A fireman after a hair-raising experience at Station 42

HAVE YOU EVER HAD a coworker who's always at work before you arrive and never seems to leave until after you do? Some coworkers really *don't* have a life. They don't file a W-2 or punch a time clock, yet they pop up at all hours—most frequently when it's late and the workplace has quieted, or during a trip to a particularly dark and menacing storage area. Sometimes they might even appear when you're ringing up a sale or trying to be mindful of workplace safety.

This chapter of *Weird Encounters* offers stories featuring extrasensory employees in office, retail, legal, manufacturing, and uh, *service* jobs. There's a brothel in Nevada that houses a plethora of ghosts, including a particularly leggy apparition. In other service-oriented occupations, there's a haunted firehouse in Pennsylvania and a former Army Reserves base in Oregon where a sergeant's spirit lingers a half century postmortem.

There are ghosts in the music-making process, too. At a recording studio in Washington State, a deceased music aficionado continues to air his opinions, and in West Virginia a ghost with outmoded fashion preferences haunts a local radio station. A phantom dubbed Mr. Smith uses otherworldly intimidation techniques at a New Jersey hardware store, and a spectral secretary still performs her essential duties at a district attorney's office in New Mexico. And just in case you thought *your* job was hell, we'd like to acquaint you with a particularly frightening phantom at an Alabama slag furnace.

Whatever your profession, the workplace wraiths in this chapter are sure to raise the hairs on the back of your neck—and when it comes to paranormal payouts, that's the best raise you can get.

THIS GHOST STORY HAS LEGS
by Janice Oberding

A FEW HALLOWEENS AGO I was invited to speak on a local radio talk show about my experiences as a ghost investigator. During a commercial break, a caller explained that she owned one of the oldest brothels in Nevada and that some of the girls were getting the jitters over what they thought was ghostly activity. Would I come and investigate? The next week my husband and I headed east from California to "the ranch," a pink two-story building at the intersection of two busy streets in Elko. When we arrived, several young women, the manager, and the owner greeted us at the door. We put our equipment in the kitchen and asked if there had been any sightings in there. No sooner had we asked the question than the electricity went out, causing one of the girls to scream.

It was just a faulty circuit breaker, the manager told us. "But there's lots of action in the pole room." She noticed our expressions and smiled. "I meant the ghostly kind. . . ."

RANCH REVENANTS

We decided on the pole room—with its mirrors and comfy furniture—for our hair-raising discussion. Like most women who work in this industry, these ladies had all taken professional names, which I changed yet again to protect their identities.

We interviewed Angel first. She nervously twirled her long red hair around her fingers while she spoke:

> It was spring break. I'd been here about a week the first time I saw him. He came into my room and headed right for my closet. I thought he was a customer who was lost, so I said, "Hey! You're in the wrong room."
>
> He stopped and stared at me with this angry expression. Then he walked right through the closet door. Right through it! I've seen ghosts before. We always had ghosts when I was a kid, so I know what he was. My heart started pounding—I wouldn't have been afraid except there wasn't anything friendly about him.

A tall brunette named Karlee plopped down on one of the sofas and examined her freshly manicured fingernails. "There's this girl, maybe thirty or so, she walks up the stairs sometimes. She gets to the top and just disappears. I saw her a couple days ago. Someone said a girl was murdered here once a long time ago; maybe that's her."

Angel shook her head. "No. I know about that ghost on the stairs, and what I heard was that people only see the bottom half of her walking on the stairs."

"Well I know what I saw. Is she the one they said was stabbed?" Karlee asked.

Before Angel could answer, Stella joined us. A former manager at the ranch, she knew its history very well.

We had an old cook who died of a heart attack in the room that's now the office. There's something strange going on in that office, I can tell you. Plenty of times I've locked the door and gone home, only to come in and find all the chairs rearranged in a circle. No one had that key but me. No living person could have gotten in there. I think it's probably him just playing jokes on us. The girls blame him when the lights and the heaters go off for no reason.

If you want to know about something weird, it's the woman whose legs walk up the stairs. First time I saw that, it really gave me the creeps. It was about five in the morning, and everyone was sleeping. I was just about ready to head up to bed myself when I saw this woman's legs appear at the bottom of the stairs. Nothing else, just legs—and they start walking up the stairs. I was so surprised I just stood there and stared. There were baby-doll pumps from the forties or fifties on the feet. I still get goose bumps thinking about that.

A girl was murdered here in the forties. Her boyfriend shot her in the room next to your room, Karlee.

Karlee shivered, then Stella chuckled. "This place has more ghosts than you can shake a stick at. A couple of years ago there were these two girls who swore up and down that an angel appeared on the wall of the manager's bedroom one night. They didn't want to stay after that."

Cherie, a petite blonde, spoke for the first time: "That old cook has never bothered anyone, unless he's the one who ruined my birthday pictures." She handed me a stack of photos that showed her and other women smiling happily at the camera. "Is that a ghost?" she asked, pointing to a strange streak of light that appeared in every one of the photographs.

I shook my head. "It looks to be a reflection," I told her.

"That's what I thought. But they wanted me to ask you just the same." She placed the photos beside her on the chair. "If you ask me, the worst ghost here is that one in Angel's room. I used to stay in there, till I couldn't take him anymore. Always staring at me and sometimes he cries so loud. . . . He came up to me one morning just as I was falling to sleep and shook the bed so hard I thought it was an earthquake. 'Help me, please!' he cried. I jumped out of bed and ran into the empty room. I told the manager about him, but she just laughed and said I'd been watching too many scary movies. I know he bothers you too, Angel."

Angel nodded. "Soon as I can, I'm getting another room."

A Heist Gone Wrong

Our video cameras ran all night long in the locked manager's room. While going through the video, we noticed two shadows that crossed in front of the lens. We weren't able to duplicate the shadows, nor could we explain them.

I later searched through old records and newspapers for the identity of the man who seemed to haunt the brothel and found one possibility. One night in 1962, a man decided to rob the brothel. While he held employees and patrons at gunpoint, a woman sneaked out and alerted the police. When the robber attempted to make his getaway through the side door, seven police officers were waiting. A shootout ensued, and the man was killed where he stood. Since that time the building has been remodeled and the side door converted to the front door. Interestingly, the closet in Angel's room is located very near the original side door.

It's hard to envy these women. Sharing quarters with a pair of legs, a deceased cook, and a burglar bogeyman makes this inherently risky profession downright frightful. If—for whatever reason—you decide to visit this particular bordello, be prepared for some additional thrills.

NO ADDRESS, fOR OBVIOUS REASONS.

HARDWARE HAUNTS
by T. Zeus

I ONCE WORKED IN A hardware store located in an old building in central New Jersey, which I'll call "Smith's." About four years into my tenure, the owners started talking about selling it, which set off a ghostly chain of events I'll never forget.

I experienced the first frightful phenomenon while talking to a coworker in the warehouse. Right behind him, I saw a box rise off the rack and hover about twelve feet in the air for several seconds before crashing to the floor. My coworker spun around to see forty pounds of dry concrete mix all over the floor, very close to his feet. Someone seemed to want our attention, and boy, did he get it!

From then on, every time there was talk of closing the store, we would witness strange phenomena of this kind. We started to kid around that "Old Man Smith" was acting up.

One morning while making coffee with one of the warehouse workers, I heard my office chair rocking back and forth. We ran into my office, but the chair was still. After stepping out of the room, we heard the chair rocking again. We laughed and told Mr. Smith to cut it out, which he did.

METAPHYSICAL MISCHIEF

I left the company in the late 1980s but returned again to work there in 1993. As I was introduced to the employees, a young salesman greeted me with, "Hi, I'm Joe. Has anything weird ever happened to you here?" He then brought up all kinds of wacky events similar to what I experienced years before. According to one story, when someone from the main office fired an employee, Mr. Smith fired back: While the main office worker was about ten rungs up a ladder in the warehouse, something punched him between the shoulder blades, almost knocking him off. After that incident, he refused to work there again.

The chaos continued. For instance, while a worker loaded stock onto an electric forklift, it rolled toward him—even with the engine turned off and the emergency brake turned on. During the office Christmas party in 1994, a friend stopped by to catch up. After the party, I helped clean up, locked the doors, and returned to my office, where my friend and I continued to talk for another hour. When I opened the door to leave my office, however, we were greeted by a colossal mess! Office supplies had been thrown all over, mixed in with everything I had cleaned up earlier. The entrance door was just four feet from my office—surely we would have heard someone come in and throw things around—and only the general manager and I had keys. My friend and I bolted!

A month or so later, I arrived at work early and, as I passed by a display, saw a man looking at some merchandise. Wearing a black coat and Indiana Jones–style hat, he stood taller than six foot five. Surprised that someone had come in so early and during such bad weather, I said, "I'm sorry, sir. I didn't see you come in." However, when I turned completely around to face the man, he had disappeared.

268

Mr. Smith's "Death March"

As spring came, it appeared the owner was finally going to sell the building, and Mr. Smith kept up the activity. Tubes of caulk started shooting out of a rack across the floor right before our eyes on one occasion. On another, the general manager called me to his office and said, "You need to stay till six P.M. today and every day from now on. I refuse to be in this building by myself ever again!"

Mr. Smith had a final trick up his sleeve before the building sale was finalized in May 1995. I was in the showroom with two customers and Mary, the bookkeeper, when deafening static began to crackle through the store's speakers. I yelled at Mary to turn off the radio, but the static only got louder. "Mary, could you please turn it off!" I yelled a second time, but when I looked over in her direction, I was shocked to find her standing with the unplugged extension cord in her hand. At this precise moment, a horrendous, moaning rendition of the "Death March" came though the speakers. The customers asked if the store was haunted, to which I replied, "I think so!"

A month later, the store was sold. We never found out who was behind the ominous pranks, but remembering it all still makes the hairs on my neck stand on end!

269

ANONYMOUS LOCATION.

BOWLER-HATTED BOGEY AT WBTH
by Thomas Golliher

I LANDED MY FIRST FULL-TIME radio gig in 1976 in Williamson, West Virginia, at WBTH. The station predated World War II and was the only station on the dial that didn't require a significant antenna. I dove into my new public service role enthusiastically, spending hours at the station without the slightest suspicion that an eerie presence lurked nearby.

One Saturday afternoon, I was alone in a room behind the studio catching up on some commercial production. Soundproof glass divided all the rooms, allowing me to see through to the lobby. Turning around to face it, I was shocked to find an older gentleman in a bowler hat looking right at me. Now, a bowler hat in the summer of 1976—about fifty years past the hat's heyday—seemed an odd fashion statement. I looked down briefly at the script in my hand, and then up again. He was gone.

270   I dashed out of the recording booth and into the lobby. I searched the entire station, but no one was there. I made sure the front door was locked, and then checked the alley door. There was no way anyone could have entered without a key.

A few days later I asked the station's chief engineer if he had ever seen a strange gentleman in the studio lobby. Before I could get a word in, he started describing the man in the bowler hat to a T. He didn't know the man's name, but the engineer had definitely seen him. Then he told me the radio station's building had been one of Williamson's funeral parlors until the early 1930s. Perhaps this eerie fellow once lay in a casket wearing his beloved bowler just beneath the room where I gave my nightly radio spiels.

Months passed, and though I never saw the spooky gentleman again, I continued to feel his ghostly presence in that building late at night. Feeling strangely comforted, I bid him good night after every midnight signoff.

WBTH STUDIO

51 E. Second Avenue, Williamson, West Virginia 25661

271

THE SEARS HALL SPIRIT
by Jefferson Davis

SGT. JEROME SEARS DIED IN the Korean War while defending a small party of retreating comrades. For his actions he was posthumously awarded the Distinguished Service Cross, and in keeping with military custom, the army dedicated a building in his memory. Sears Hall, until recently an active U.S. Army Reserve Center, now sits at the same site on which Sears played as a child.

Increasing evidence suggests that a spirit may roam Sears Hall. In the drill hall, a supply sergeant heard locks rattling on lockers and ferocious banging on a garage door, but nobody was present. On the west end of the second floor of the building, employees wondered who kept stacking chairs in the evening after they all had left for the day. But the most compelling account of paranormal activity was witnessed by Major Smith.

SURELY, YOU JEST

In 1996, Major Smith worked in the training and plans offices on the second floor of the west wing at Sears Hall. He was approached by Tom, a longtime employee, who reported that he frequently heard the sound of rubber-soled boots walking down the empty hallway and doors slamming, while working many evenings at the facility. Furthermore he insisted that the originator of antics was none other than the spirit of Jerome Sears. Major Smith dismissed Tom's story, forgetting about it entirely until a few months later, when he found himself the object of the same paranormal prank Tom had described.

At about five thirty P.M., the entire facility had shut down for the night. The major was in his office when he heard someone in boots walk down the hallway and enter the adjoining training office. When, after several minutes of silence, he became curious and walked next door, he found the office empty. Five minutes later, he heard the footsteps coming back down the hallway toward him. He called out, "The training office is empty, but I'm here."

The footsteps halted. There was no reply.

A few minutes later, four office doors slammed in quick succession. He stepped out of his office and looked down the hallway but saw no one. At this point, the major decided to play along with whomever was obviously trying to spook him. He guessed that Tom was hiding in a nearby office.

Down on the first floor, the major looked out of the east windows to the parking lot below. It was empty. Had Tom hidden his car?

A SPECTRAL SILHOUETTE

Eager to finish his work and head home, Major Smith returned to his office a few minutes later. He again heard the footsteps come down the hallway. A quick peek out the office door revealed nobody in the hallway, so the major searched the entire second floor. It would have been impossible for anyone to hide in the offices, which were furnished starkly with small desks and office tables. He heard more footsteps and slamming doors and realized that this was no ordinary prank. As he watched his office lights and computer monitor flicker, he felt a ghostly presence pervade the building.

After checking the hallway once more, the major paused to watch the sun set out the window. As his gaze passed over the window of the door to the office across the hall, however, he caught the reflected image of a human silhouette. It was shadowy and backlit, and while Major Smith could not distinguish any features, he could tell that it was a man with a short haircut. To ensure that it wasn't his own silhouette, he moved his head back and forth, but the reflection remained motionless. After tracing the reflection back to a chair located in front of the west window, the major touched the back of it and experienced

something strange. The hair on the back of his arm rose up as if in contact with static electricity, but in stages: first the back of his hand, then his wrist, then his forearm. When he pulled away from the chair, the hair on his arm laid down again. Now truly frightened, Major Smith cleared his throat and said, "Jerome, I'm getting reading to leave. You take care of the building."

Major Smith doesn't believe the apparition intended harm, or that it necessarily was even aware of him. He feels strongly the figure existed in the same space as he did, but not in the same time. Did the dedication of this building, so close to his childhood home and playground, lure Jerome's spirit to the site? And with its recent decommission and impending conversion, would he continue to haunt its corridors? Now under lock and key, the building awaits its new tenants. . . .

FORMER SEARS HALL

U.S. ARMY RESERVE TRAINING CENTER

2731 S.W. Multnomah Boulevard, Portland, Oregon 97219

PARANORMAL PIG IRON AT THE SLOSS FURNACES
by Scott A. Thompson

THE FIRES BURN DAY AND night, with temperatures climbing to incredible heights. Those unfortunate enough to be here are worked till near death, and frequently beyond. The stench of burning steel and brimstone mixes with blood and sweat, and everywhere tired haunted faces covered in soot stare deep into the glowering structures. At the slightest sign of slack, a man appears, whip in hand, screaming to get back to work. No pity, no breaks, no holidays. There is only the heat—and the furnace, which demands incessant feeding.

This could easily be a firsthand account of hell, but the inferno depicted here is manmade and very much on Earth—in Alabama, to be precise. For almost one hundred years the Sloss Furnaces in Birmingham produced pig iron for building. From the time it opened its doors in 1882 until it closed in 1971, the furnaces had to be kept burning 24-7, requiring around-the-clock labor. And who had the illustrious responsibility of supervising the graveyard shift? That would be James "Slag" Wormwood.

274

UNFATHOMABLE CRUELTY

By all accounts Wormwood was tailor-made for his post, lording over his workers like Satan himself. He denied them breaks and forced them into dangerous tasks to increase productivity. All told, forty-seven men lost their lives, and many others were critically injured and robbed of their livelihoods.

Relief came to the Sloss workers one night in 1906, when Slag, standing on top of "Big Alice," the largest blast furnace in the plant, reportedly lost his balance after becoming dizzy from methane emissions. His body incinerated on contact with the molten metal. As Slag had never once set foot on the high walkway, many believed that he had been murdered, but none of the workers were ever brought to trial.

Soon afterward, Sloss discontinued the graveyard shift due to "strange" phenomena and accidents that hampered steel production. Each year Slag's legend grew, and many workers began complaining of an unnatural force that roamed the halls of the facility. Then, one evening in 1926, a night watchman met Slag. The guard, who was alone, was pushed from behind and heard a gruff voice shout, "Get back to work!"

One of the most startling supernatural events ever reported occurred at the plant in 1947. Amid reports of strange noises, voices, and steam jets that emptied themselves, three supervisors were touring the facility. When their guide turned to point out something that needed an upgrade, however, he was startled to find the supervisors gone. After a panicked search, all three were found unconscious inside a locked boiler room on the southeastern side of the plant. Although none of them could explain how they'd gotten there, they all agreed who had put them there. His skin was badly burned and he shouted, "Push some steel!" They'd come face-to-face with Slag, the Sloss Furnaces' phantom menace.

Slag didn't stop there. In perhaps the most investigated and most chilling ghostly encounter, a night watchman by the name of Samuel Blumenthal met his end. On the night before the facility closed in 1971, the watchman was taking a last look around when he came upon something he later described as, simply, "evil." The phantasm tried to push Samuel up the stairs and, when he resisted, beat him savagely. At the hospital, doctors were startled to find burns covering his entire body. There he succumbed to his injuries.

275

GHOSTS APLENTY

With so many deaths at the facility, one would expect ghosts aplenty at the old Sloss Furnaces, and one would be absolutely right. There have been well over a hundred documented reports of curious incidents ranging from whispers and phantom footsteps to steam valves that spontaneously release themselves. There are also occasional reports of assault by some potent, ineffable force. The violent attacks seem to happen in September and October, usually during the graveyard hours.

The only blast furnaces of their kind left standing, the Sloss Furnaces are open year-round from Tuesday through Saturday, and admission is free. Tours given during October contain some added spookies for hard-core thrill seekers. Visitors who pay the old pig iron plant a visit, however, should make sure to stay focused on the task at hand. Slag doesn't like slackers.

SLOSS FURNACES

NATIONAL HISTORIC LANDMARK

20 Thirty-second Street North, Birmingham, AL 35222

www.slossfurnaces.com

LEGALLY DEAD:
A HAUNTED D.A.'S OFFICE
by Gloria McCary

THE COUNTY-OWNED BUILDING THAT FORMERLY housed the D.A.'s office is on the southern end of what was the Plaza Meyer of the ancient settlement of Socorro, New Mexico. It's a long, relatively narrow, nondescript adobe building but is recognizable in photos of Socorro taken in the 1880s. I went to work in this building as a deputy district attorney in March 2001.

About two months into my employment, the first incident occurred. Our investigator, Juanita, was walking back from the restroom to the front of the building when she heard my voice calling her name. When she walked into my office, she was surprised to find it empty. Seated in a nearby cubicle, my secretary, Virginia, said, "I heard it too, but Gloria's been in court all morning."

A few months later, I was standing in the secretarial area speaking with Bella, the chief deputy D.A.'s secretary. Behind me I could hear Susan, another secretary, typing busily at her computer. I turned around to say something to Susan and found that not only was her workstation empty, but her computer was turned off. I turned back to Bella and said, "I swear I heard Susan working on her computer."

Bella laughed and said, "Susan's out sick today, but her computer has been typing all morning, even though no one's turned it on." We began discussing the invisible typist, and Bella, who often worked late into the night, said, "I always keep my radio on when I'm in here alone. That way I can't hear the weird noises. I've never seen anything, though. I just hear the noises."

A year or so later, Bruce, the chief deputy district attorney, was in the men's room when the top paper towel of the stack on the toilet tank suddenly rose straight up into the air, turned ninety degrees, floated a couple of inches toward him, and dropped to the floor. About six months after Bruce's experience, I was preparing for a vehicular homicide trial with another lawyer named Nikki when we distinctly heard Virginia come back from lunch and resume work, rolling her chair back and forth on its carpet-saver pad as she shuffled papers and moved files. Neither Nikki nor I could remember if an important witness in the trial had been subpoenaed. "Virginia will know," I said, jumping up from the desk and opening the door.

In fact, Virginia was still at lunch.

UNEARTHING THE PAST

Though no one has actually seen a ghost in the office, most of us have heard mysterious shuffling, typing, and other strange noises over the years. The cause of this ghoulish racket is unknown, but examining the site's history provides a few possibilities.

The area around Socorro was originally settled by Native Americans, followed in 1598 by Spanish colonists. The natives of nearby Teypana provided the struggling European settlers with food and water and the colonists later renamed the pueblo Socorro to commemorate the natives' succor, or help. However, relations between the native pueblos of New Mexico and their Spanish rulers became strained, resulting in the Pueblo Revolt of 1680. Many colonists were killed.

It is unknown when the current law office structure was built, but the building has served the famous lawman Elfego Baca, was a tuberculosis hospital and even a combination brothel-saloon during Socorro's wild and woolly days in the mid- and late nineteenth century. With such a long and varied history, the premises could have been the setting for any number of demises. There were certainly deaths during the building's years as a tuberculosis clinic, and probably more when it was a saloon and brothel and full of cattlemen and miners who were dry after a dusty day's work. In February 1862, wounded soldiers from the Civil War battle of Valverde were transported to Socorro for medical treatment.

They were housed near the central plaza, though it's unknown which buildings were used as field hospitals.

The most obvious explanation for the law office hauntings, however, can be traced to a fairly recent tragedy. A decade or so prior to my tenure there, a secretary had been disturbed by serious health problems, which impelled her to retire from the office and later commit suicide. Bruce believes that the unhappy woman has returned to her former workplace indefinitely, carrying out the duties she was unable to complete in life.

COURTHOUSE CREEPS

The D.A.'s office has since moved across the street to a more modern, 1930s-era building, which sits next door to the courthouse and the county jail. This "new" building apparently has its own resident ghost. Patricia, the head secretary, was taking her turn at the telephone and main desk when she saw a small boy walk into the building. Thinking he was the child of a witness being interviewed by one of the lawyers, she came out from behind the reception desk to speak with him. Before she was able to greet him, however, he had disappeared.

The county courthouse across the street was built as a Works Progress Administration project during the 1930s, but it's on the site of the old territorial courthouse and jail for Socorro County, where executions were carried out. Courthouse employees say mysterious noises and footsteps are common in that building. Perhaps it is the uneasy soul of an executed prisoner who is eager to share *his* side of the story.

THE FORMER DISTRICT ATTORNEY'S OFFICES

110 Church Street, Socorro, New Mexico 87801

GHOST IN THE STUDIO
by Jonathan Zwickel

FROM THE OUTSIDE, THE HOUSE doesn't look haunted. Robert Lang's whitewashed concrete and brick villa seems more suited for the Spanish coast than the Seattle suburb of Richmond Beach. Lang's home is also one of the Northwest's premier recording studios, and the framed gold records by Nirvana, Dave Matthews Band, Death Cab for Cutie, Damian Marley, and Candlebox hanging on the walls are proof. The legend of Robert Lang Studios goes beyond historic recording sessions and into the realm of the supernatural, however, with more metaphysical memorabilia: a photo of a ghostlike apparition, stories of inexplicable mechanical failure, and corroborating testimony.

Lang is a smallish excitable man with a spray of gray stubble on his chin, intense eyes, and a wry smile. On one bright autumn day, he and engineer Justin Armstrong were hosting Hills of Elysium, a Gothy Seattle rock band, recording their debut album. The band exited the "live room" on the bottom floor so that Lang could point out exactly where he dug up an arcane bag of money and where a photographer snapped an eerie photo.

The live room is the only place in the labyrinthine, four-story building with a palpably mysterious air. It's an oddly angled chamber built of slabs of marble and granite from floor to twenty-foot ceiling. Lang cut and laid the stone himself and also installed the electric candelabras that flicker a dim orange against the craggy walls. Except for the drum kit in the corner and the electric guitars leaning against the wall, the room could pass for a well-decorated mausoleum. The heavy stone construction, softened by rugs on the floor and baffles on the ceiling, offers terrific, resounding acoustics. Standing in the middle of the room—the exact spot where the ghost hovers in the infamous photo—I asked Lang if he knew the identity of the spook. "There's no doubt about it," he said quickly. "It's Dubby."

DUBBY'S POSTHUMOUS BEQUEST

In 1975, this place was just a suburban hillside, and Lang was in his mid-twenties.

It was a freewheeling time, and at a house party in the Capitol Hill neighborhood of Seattle he met Walter Westley Leonard—a.k.a. Dubby. The two bonded over their love of music and Harley-Davidsons, hanging together at Lang's house, and recording various local bands.

In September 1979, Lang said, Dubby told him about a stash of money he had squirreled away for the purpose of moving the Richmond Beach studio into bigger digs and establishing a second studio on Orcas Island off the Washington coast. The money might've been illicit: Dubby's father had run bootlegged liquor across the border during Prohibition, and an allowance check arrived from Dubby's mother at the beginning of every year. At this point in their friendship, Dubby was unfocused, and Lang wanted to help get him back on track. After a particularly bad hangover one morning, Lang took Dubby out to breakfast. "We came back and he got in his RX-7, and I remember he put one of those aquarium thermometers on his forehead," Lang said. "He goes, 'Bobby, what am I reading?' and I say, 'You're reading f***ed up, dude. Don't go.' He said, 'I gotta go; I'll see you later,' and he took off."

Two days later, Dubby was dead. It was the quintessential rock star departure: After too much drink, he passed out and choked on his own vomit. A few weeks after the funeral, Lang started digging the foundation for his studio. Weeks turned into months. And then, one night, he made a fateful discovery: "It was pouring down rain and I had this little orange trouble light hanging on the sewer line," Lang recalled. "I'm digging on the north side of the plot, and all of a sudden appears this big plastic canister, just the edge of it. I'll never forget this: I looked at it, and time just stopped." The canister was filled with hundred-dollar bills. Lang refuses to divulge the grand total, except to say, "It was a lot of money." Honoring his dear friend's wishes, he invested the cash into the studio.

VIBES AND A VISAGE
In the intervening years, there have been numerous occurrences that cannot readily be explained. Musicians and technicians have reported weird chills, unusual noises, and mysteriously opening doors. "Probably the coolest thing that happened," said Lang, "was with the band Afghan Whigs."

While the band was overdubbing songs for their *Black Love* album in the fall of 1995, they heard strange noises. A tape machine broke down without warning, and repeated calls to the manufacturer stumped technicians. Two nights in a row, engineer Steve Culp woke up Lang with phone calls, asking him to come to the studio and assuage the band. The second time, Lang said, he arrived to find singer Greg Dulli looking fearful. A friend of Dulli's—a medium—had been in the house and declared supernatural forces at work.

For the skeptics, Lang offers a photo taken in 2005 by the drummer for Drown Mary of the band's bassist playing in the live room, oblivious to the blurry visage that hovers above him. The visage in the photo resembles the agonized figure in Edvard Munch's painting *The Scream.*

Remembering the strange goings-on inside Robert Lang Studios, Whigs bassist John Curley disclosed a measured perspective on the supernatural: "Knowledge at its fringes is weird, whether it's science or philosophy or whatever. My worldview includes room for superstition. It's hard to not try to think of a real-world explanation for stuff, and many times there turns out to be one. But in case you're wrong, you have to be respectful. If there is a ghost there, you don't wanna make it mad."

281

ROBERT LANG STUDIOS is located in a private home.

SPIRITED BROTHERHOOD
OF STATION 42

by Jeffrey Wargo

THE FIRE-FIGHTING BROTHERHOOD BEGAN IN 1735 when Benjamin Franklin founded the first volunteer fire department in Philadelphia. Two centuries later, in 1929, the nearby small borough of Riegelsville chartered volunteer Community Fire Company #1, christened Station 42. Many of the "Fighting 42nd" have since put themselves in harm's way to protect both citizens and property.

Before his untimely death in the early 1990s, Howie Pursell served the Fighting 42nd for almost twenty years. Described as a "gentle giant of a man" with a great sense of humor, Pursell may haunt the firehouse, playing preternatural pranks on his former comrades.

EERIE FORCES AT WORK

282 Though years have passed since Howie's death, evidence suggests that he still performs routine procedures around the firehouse, as a shaken squadron

member discovered one hot summer night. He had just arrived for duty as the Fighting 42nd trucks pulled out of the engine room on a call; and as they blazed out of sight with sirens roaring, a silence settled over the empty firehouse. The lone firefighter went into the communications area near the engine room to await their return. There in the darkened building he was startled to hear the overhead doors closing and someone walking across the metal drainage grates at the front of the truck bay. Looking out, he saw no one. A few moments later he heard the distinct scraping sounds made when cardboard is placed under the trucks at the end of a run to catch dripping engine fluids. Again, no one was in sight. When the squad returned to the engine house that night, they found their late arrival leaning in a chair against the outside of the building. When asked why he was there, he reportedly said, "I'm not going back in there alone."

At other times firemen and auxiliary women were also startled by inexplicable noises in the building. The most commonly reported disturbance is remarkably similar to the lone firefighter's account: the sound of someone walking over the metal grates that line the front of the engine room. Some firemen have heard the scraping noise coming from under the very truck in which they were sitting, when no one was about and the cardboard hadn't moved!

Several firemen report also hearing disembodied footsteps walk about the empty bathroom stalls. Others allege hearing those same heavy steps coming down the staircase from the second floor. The fire chief recalled an occasion when, after a late-night fire call, the men were gathered in the communications room debriefing. He was standing in the doorway with his son when, in the midst of the conversation, footsteps began to echo in the stairway on the east side of the building. Steadily the footsteps turned and came up the hallway, as if someone was walking toward the room in which everyone was gathered. Leaning back and looking down the hall to where the sound originated, the fire chief and his son saw nothing. "It must be Howie," the chief said.

It's possible that Howie still performs truck inspections, too. At least it would seem that way to those who have heard hatches opening and closing on the fire engine and rescue vehicle when no one else is in the engine house. And then there are the doors. . . . Hefty bay doors on the engine house have been known to go up and down without anyone pushing the buttons to move them.

283

HOWIE: UP CLOSE AND PERSONAL

Personal accounts of close encounters with Howie's spirit, however, provide the most compelling evidence of his continued service to the Fighting 42nd. One day someone who knew Howie very well was at the front of the engine room changing a lightbulb when, suddenly, Howie's voice came over the Plectron speaker saying, "Get out!" Though Howie was always known as a jokester in life, this guy definitely was not laughing. On another occasion, two women from the auxiliary were in the station's kitchen preparing vegetables when footsteps moving toward them startled them. Looking up, they saw Howie's ghostly apparition. As they stood transfixed, he backed up quickly, moving out into the hallway again.

I too have witnessed Howie's pranks firsthand. In March 2006, I was invited by the brotherhood of Station 42 to become their first chaplain. A week later I joined the fire company, and the following week went out on my first call—a brush fire. After setting up a portable pond from which the other companies' trucks could draw water, I was standing with the deputy chief when a member of another station, looking distracted, said to the deputy chief, "Something wrong with your tanker?" He had been facing the tanker truck as we talked and saw the wiper blades move across the windshield. Surprised, the deputy chief checked them but found they were turned off. A short time later, the wipers moved again. Perhaps Howie had hitched a ride on the fire engine to cheer on his former squadron brothers.

To this day, some firemen refuse to be in the engine house alone at night, and some townspeople question how anyone could be in there by themselves. However, one fireman expressed the sentiment of many of his brothers in this way: "It doesn't feel like [Howie] is here to hurt us. It feels like he is still one of our brothers; like he's watchin' our backs."

285

COMMUNITY FIRE COMPANY NO. I

Station #42, 333 Delaware Road, Riegelsville, PA 18077

Institutional
Apparitions

"Okay, if there is a ghost in here, let's see you break this balloon." —Museum employee to a resident revenant

MANY PEOPLE WHO INVESTIGATE the paranormal ask why ghosts would bother to remain behind in unhappy places, such as prisons or hospitals. They may assume that a ghost has a choice about where it ends up, but perhaps that's not so. In death, as in life, you might not end up where you'd like to be.

In this chapter, we'll take you on a tour of four famous prisons around the country, each with the full complement of ghostly sights, smells, sounds, and sensations, and each with a star resident: a snitch in West Virginia, a murderer in New Jersey, a Union soldier in Missouri, and a coal miner/union rabble rouser in Pennsylvania. And that's just the tip of the iceberg. We'll also take you to a notoriously haunted former sanatorium in Kentucky that's available for tours and paranormal investigations, and then to a handful of other places to enjoy from the solitary confinement of your easy chair, including a modern hospital in Mississippi that shares one of its more life-celebrating wings with the ghosts of two nurses and a man in black (not Johnny Cash).

If you get a chance to visit any of these locales, please ask the ghosts if they're there by choice. We're dying to know!

WAVERLY HILLS SANATORIUM
by Scott A. Thompson

BEFORE THE DISCOVERY OF MANY medicines, the infirm were often quarantined to minimize the spread of disease. Some illnesses were so deadly that special facilities were built in which the dying could be shut away and cared for in their final days. In those places, where death was slow and painful, and hope dwindled, the psychic memories remain embedded in the brick, staining the tiles and scarring the hallways.

In the early 1900s, Louisville, Kentucky, had many victims of the "white plague," or "consumption," now called tuberculosis. Those infected with this highly contagious disease (for which there was no cure at the time) were sent to a hospital on Waverly Hill, a two-story facility built in 1910 with only forty beds. It quickly became apparent, however, that this modest structure could not accommodate well over one hundred patients begging for admission to the hospital. The state donated land and nearly $11 million for the construction of a new facility; and in 1926, the Waverly Hills Sanatorium opened its doors.

289

The facility was dedicated to developing innovative techniques to help treat tuberculosis patients. Unfortunately the treatments had a poor success rate, and

more than ten thousand people suffered their last breaths within the walls of the sanatorium, many of them children. Corpses were disposed of by way of a rail-driven tunnel that emerged on the far side of the building. It prevented patients from seeing the large number of bodies leaving the building and how frequently the hearses came; something doctors felt lowered the patients' spirit and impeded recovery. This "body chute" was originally used as an employee entrance and for delivering groceries.

By 1943, an effective treatment was discovered in the form of an antibiotic called streptomycin, which is still in use today. Within twenty years, cases of tuberculosis dwindled until there was no longer a need for the treatment at Waverly Hills, and the hospital was shut down in 1961. Less than a year later, the hospital was reopened as the Woodhaven Geriatrics Sanitarium.

SINISTER SANITARIUM

Whereas the doctors of Waverly Hills were sincere, if not successful, in their attempts to heal, anecdotal accounts paint a different picture of the employees of Woodhaven. Patient abuse was rampant; conditions were squalid. Over the next twenty years, upkeep of the sanitarium continued to deteriorate until the Woodhaven facility was shut down by the state in 1982.

Because of the many deaths in the sanatorium, many restless anonymous souls still lurk on the premises. There are a few specters, however, that stand out. Apparition sightings range from phantom children running about in the third-floor solarium, a boy bouncing a ball who disappears before visitors' eyes, to even an old woman bleeding from the wrists screaming, "Help me!" and running from the front door before vanishing. Other phenomena include rooms that appear lit even though there is no power in the building, doors that close by themselves, phantom voices, and even the scent of food cooking.

Even stranger is the frequency at which strange occurrences are documented at the sanatorium. During a location hunt for the television program *The World's Scariest Places*, one paranormal investigative team noticed that their electromagnetic field (EMF) meter continuously reacted, despite the lack of power in the building. Although there were no wires in place to run electricity, the meter continued to jump and eventually melted the circuit board inside. It was then they noticed a sharp temperature drop of nearly twenty degrees in the room. There were several witnesses, including the building's owner, and they were glad to get out of the building.

PHANTASMS IN 502

The sanatorium changed hands many times over the last two decades, and the current owners, Charles and Tina Mattingly, are restoring the place. Several ghost-hunting conventions have convened there, with all the proceeds going to fixing the damage that years of neglect and vandalism have done.

As for the hauntings, they continue. The Waverly Hills Sanatorium is known worldwide as one of the most active paranormal spots, with ghost hunters coming from hundreds, even thousands, of miles away to get a glimpse inside. Recently, in fact, the owners have procured permits to give tours of the place year round, with all proceeds going toward renovation.

There are several sites on the second and third floors where visitors feel presences, cold spots, and other phenomena, but it is room 502, an old nurse's station, in which a nurse hung herself after discovering she was pregnant. Another nurse who worked in 502 climbed to the room and leaped to her death. Most who investigate the building agree that this room is the second most active at the site. If one wants to feel the real icy hand of death and presences that cannot be denied, however, a trip down the long corridor known as the "body chute" is necessary.

291

WAVERLY HILLS SANATORIUM

4400 Paralee Lane, Louisville, Kentucky 40272

www.therealwaverlyhills.com

MOUNDSVILLE PENITENTIARY
by Jeff Belanger

THE BIG HOUSE, THE SLAMMER, the hoosegow—only the worst of humanity end up in a penitentiary. Prisons are a necessary evil in modern society, but these stone and steel fortresses hold more than just prisoners and guards. By many accounts, they also contain the tortured souls of inmates who lived—and died— within the guarded walls.

West Virginia seceded from Virginia in 1863, creating an immediate need for new government buildings and institutions, including a prison. The ten-acre site in Moundsville, West Virginia, was selected because it was close—but not *too* close—to the state's then capital of Wheeling. Stone by stone, it took more than ten years for prisoners to build Moundsville Penitentiary (also called the West Virginia State Penitentiary), and in the decades following its completion in 1876, ninety-four men were executed on the grounds—eighty-five by hanging and nine by electric chair—until West Virginia eliminated the death penalty altogether in 1963.

But these weren't the only deaths. As in many prisons, some inmates died of old age and others succumbed to various diseases, but thirty-six were homicide victims. Before the prison closed in 1995, 998 people had passed away there.

The most infamous was inmate number 44670, known on the "outside" as R. D. Wall. "R. D. Wall was considered a rat or a snitch," said Tom Stiles, the internal coordinator and tour guide for West Virginia Penitentiary. "He worked for the institution as an inmate down underneath the old administration building." On October 8, 1929, Wall was heading down to the maintenance area when three prisoners carrying dull shivs (or knives) jumped him. "They hacked him up pretty good," Stiles said. "He's one of the spirits here. . . . Some have claimed they see a headless image that they think is Wall." As early as the 1930s, guards reported seeing a prisoner walking the walls above the maintenance area. Fearing an escape attempt, they'd chase after the vision only to find no one in the vicinity.

R. D. Wall is a prominent ghostly figure at the prison, especially around the lower maintenance area, but he's not alone. The recreation area, known as the "Sugar Shack," where inmates went to get "sugar" from other prisoners, is also bustling with paranormal activity. Gambling, fighting, and raping all left a vicious mark on the Sugar Shack.

Pat Kleinedler, the tour coordinator at the penitentiary, can also attest to the prison's haunted reputation. She encountered an unknown entity while conducting a routine check during the prison's haunted house event one night: "When I turned to go down this other hallway I felt this cool breeze, and I definitely felt like someone was right there, but nobody was. I ran back to the lobby and I said, 'I need a person to go with me and I need a flashlight.' When we went back up the hall there was nothing there." While leading night tours and ghost hunt events, she has also observed numerous visitors suddenly overcome with feelings of pressure and sadness while walking about the prison.

The ghostly legends at Moundsville have attracted paranormal enthusiasts and investigators from all over. Brendan Skeen founded the West Virginia Ghost Hunters, and he and his team have investigated Moundsville on multiple occasions. "During one of our investigations there was an unidentified loud crash in the machine shop. We looked around. It sounded like something fell over, but there was nothing lying on the floor that could have made a noise like that. We never could figure that out."

On another occasion, Skeen and his group were investigating the maximum-security section of the prison during an overnight when they heard a strange noise coming from the upper two tiers of cells, which were locked to prevent access. The noises came at regular intervals, so the group attributed some kind

293

of intelligence to the sounds. They established communication by announcing that two noises indicated a *yes* answer and one indicated a *no*. "One of our investigators was really shaken up after that," Skeen said.

A Haunting Revelation

According to Kleinedler, Moundsville held up to three prisoners in each five-by-seven-foot cell at one time. "There's no way that three people can be in a five-by-seven area under good circumstances, let alone bad circumstances," she said. The tensions of living in such cramped quarters contributed to prison riots—inmates killing each other as they fought for breathing room, and guards gunning down those who attempted escape.

When Tom Stiles began working at the prison in 2000, he was an admitted skeptic. Though the ghost tours and hunts piqued his curiosity, he didn't become a believer until two horrifying experiences in 2007 changed his perspective on the spirit world.

294   Late one evening, Stiles was setting up props for the haunted fun house when he felt something grab him on the arm. "It wanted to stop me as I was walking

through there," he said. The experience shook him a great deal, but it wasn't his last encounter with the preternatural. During a storm that summer, Stiles was on site for some overnight investigations with a film crew. After setting up cameras throughout the building, the team borrowed a computer monitor from Stiles's office to observe live camera footage in a stairway. At three A.M., disappointed at the lack of supernatural activity, the team decided to wrap things up—and that's when it got creepy. According to Stiles,

> I came down here with one of the gentlemen to unhook my monitor and put it back in my office. When I got down here, I left him and went to unlock my office. That's when I heard him say, "Man, is there a lot of activity on this screen out here." So I turned around and went back out to see. There was something like a light bar moving around . . . like it was walking back and forth, pacing at the top of the stairs, which lead down into the basement of the penitentiary.
>
> So we watched for a couple of minutes and then went outside. You could actually see it with your naked eye. . . . It moved over against the building, and just went right down the stairs, and at the bottom of the stairs it turned into a . . . I won't say it was a human form . . . but it turned from a light bar to a cloudy mass of some sort. It just stood there and made its way inside the building. They actually have eighteen minutes of it on film.

Ghosts are not only a big draw for Moundsville, they're also a somewhat regular occurrence, considering the number of overnight visitors who walk the empty halls and cells, armed with cameras and audio recorders ready to capture evidence. Violence is what brought many to the prison in Moundsville; violence is how many inmates survived day to day; and violence is what took more than a few lives within these walls. That emotion, torment, and energy are still echoing around the penitentiary like screams from long ago.

MOUNDSVILLE PENITENTIARY

818 Jefferson Avenue, Moundsville, West Virginia 26041

www.wvpentours.com

1859 JAIL AT INDEPENDENCE
by James Strait

IN 1981, MIKE GILLESPIE WAS a college student who worked as a docent in the 1859 Jail Museum in Independence, Missouri. It was a low-key job that let Mike guide visitors through the museum—which counted outlaw Frank James and Confederate guerrilla William Quantrill among its infamous inmates—and still have time to do schoolwork.

Mike had worked at the museum for only a few weeks when he heard footsteps on the upstairs floorboards. Thinking visitors may have slipped in without his noticing, he left the front office and climbed the stairs, finding only the portrait of Beoni Hudspeth hanging on the wall. Hudspeth was an Independence resident who left for the California Gold Rush in 1849 and was subsequently murdered. The portrait's painted eyes had a creepy habit of following people as they walked up the steps.

296

Mike initially attributed the footsteps to creaking floorboards, but he soon began to note a pattern of unexplainable phenomena. An alarm system would go off after having been correctly set, requiring him to re-enter the building and walk the dark hallway past the original six jail cells. He hated this, because he always felt compelled to look into one specific jail cell.

Museum visitors regularly commented that the building left them with an uneasy feeling. One afternoon, Mike fell into a conversation with a psychic who had just completed a twenty-minute tour of the jail. The psychic, visibly shaken by his brief experience in the museum, explained that he had sensed much malevolence and death in the building. The pair then embarked on a room-by-room tour of the facility, beginning upstairs. Mike described the footsteps he'd heard, and the psychic explained that the original marshal's wife had been pregnant and that the pacing in the upstairs room was that of the expectant father. As the two started downstairs, the psychic noticed Hudspeth's portrait and reached out to touch it. He was immediately repelled by the power fed back to him through the picture and said Hudspeth's spirit was a permanent resident in the building.

They moved on to the downstairs rear portion of the jail. The psychic was drawn to one unit in particular—the same cell that Mike repeatedly felt compelled to look into when walking past. Although deeply unsettled by the energy emanating from the cell, the psychic extended his arm through the slatted iron door. The hair on his forearm immediately rose. According to the psychic, someone had been killed in the cell and the angry presence wanted out. The vengeful spirit didn't want anybody else in there, either.

The psychic moved on to the marshal's office and remarked that the room had an overwhelming sense of death. Mike knew that the marshal had indeed been killed in that office, and he was impressed when the psychic pointed to a spot, saying the deceased had fallen there.

Museum records indicate that a man by the name of Jim Knowles had been incarcerated at the 1859 Jail during the Civil War for his connection with the Union militia, which had been harassing or stealing from the families of Confederate soldiers. When the Confederates took possession of the jail during the battle at Independence, they administered their own form of justice by shooting Knowles in his cell. Which one he occupied isn't known.

POPPING REALITY

Signs of an incarcerated spirit emerged again when a high school student visited the museum one afternoon. She and Mike struck up a conversation while standing in the jail's gift shop in the front of the building, and when she asked Mike if the jail housed any ghosts, he said, "Naw." At that moment, an

297

inflated balloon on display in the shop popped. The student insisted that Mike had popped it to scare her, but he maintained his innocence.

Later that day Mike inflated a balloon and said, "Okay, if there *is* a ghost in here, let's see you break this balloon." The balloon popped. Mike chuckled over the coincidence, picked up another balloon, and announced, "Okay, I don't believe this. If the ghost of Jim Knowles or William Quantrill or Frank James is here, let's see you break *this* balloon." This time as Mike was tying off the end of the balloon, it popped in his hand.

Mike stopped working at the 1859 Jail in 1982, turning his responsibilities over to a college student with whom he shared his ghostly encounters. The new caretaker soon got in touch with a local radio station and arranged for a Halloween séance with an experienced psychic. A twelve-year-old female cousin of the new caretaker, who happened to be sensitive, stood off to the side of the table during the séance and, at one point, ran hysterically into another room. As it turned out, she had looked into the same jail cell that had caused the first psychic's arm hair to stand on end and spotted a man wearing a long dark coat with metal buttons.

So who was the phantasm? Jim Knowles is the most likely candidate, and although it isn't known which unit he occupied, the cell where Mike, the psychic, and the young cousin all sensed a ghostly presence is an obvious possibility.

If you're a ghost hunter, thrill seeker, or die-hard skeptic, the 1859 Jail may be the venue to reinforce the connection between our material world and the world of footsteps, vaporous shadows, and mysterious energies. Go prepared with a handful of balloons and some bare forearms, as they may be your most useful investigative tools.

THE 1859 JAIL, MARSHAL'S HOME AND MUSEUM

217 N. Main Street, Independence, Missouri 64050

INTERRED APPARITIONS AT OLD CARBON COUNTY

by Linda J. Adams

AFTER SEEING MY YOUNGEST SON off on a camping trip, my boyfriend and I stopped in the town of Jim Thorpe, Pennsylvania, to find the Old Carbon County Jail, hear its stories, and photograph it to the hilt. The road to the jail was winding and steep, but we finally caught site of the foreboding structure, which dates to 1871, perched atop a hill.

During the tour, we learned an eerie story behind a curious handprint found on the wall of Cell 17. It belongs to Alexander Campbell of the Molly Maguires, a secret society of primarily Irish-Catholic miners who protested the dire working conditions in the mines of northeastern Pennsylvania. The society's attempts to unionize may not have been on the up-and-up, and seven members were convicted of murder. Four, including Campbell, were hung at the jail on June 21, 1877. Before his execution, Campbell allegedly rubbed his hand on the dirt floor of Cell 17 and slapped it onto his cell wall, proclaiming that the resulting handprint would forever announce his innocence to the world. And despite repeated attempts to remove the print by cleaning, painting, and even replacing the concrete, it remains to this day.

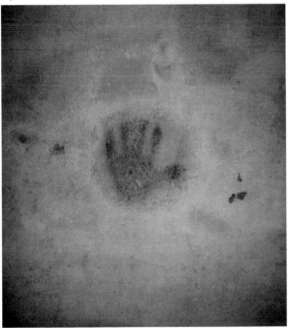

When the tour guide ushered our group away, we snuck down into the dungeon, where the basest prisoners had been confined. Even though the bottom of the stairway was well lit, the inside of the dungeon was filled with almost impenetrable darkness. As I peered into the gloom, however, I saw something unbelievable: a bright, white round light—I dare call it an orb—about the size of a baseball, sailing through the air. It moved in an arc-shaped path from left to right and then disappeared. I initially thought my digital camera had caused it and tried to recreate the orb by moving my camera around while standing in the same spot—alas, without success.

We crept gingerly into the dungeon, which was bone-chillingly cold, and I took a number of photos as we moved about the darkened space, peering into every jail cell. While standing in the corridor facing the dungeon's back wall, another strange entity caught my eye: A dark shadow moved across the door of a cell located midway down the corridor. Like the moving orb, it traveled from left to right, but it was long and horizontal, with no definitive lines.

I took photos of the cell door and its interior, and then moved to the left of the corridor to take photos of the cells on that side. That's when I encountered yet another surprise: While looking through the digital viewfinder at an open cell, I watched as a dark, human-shaped form moved along the back wall. Thoroughly spooked, my boyfriend and I decided to call it a day and left the old jail.

PARANORMAL PAINS

Over the next few days, evidence mounted to suggest that we had much more than a case of the creeps. As soon as we walked out of the jail, I felt as though I had twisted my right ankle, but the pain left as soon as I sat down. In bed that night, I saw a shadow on the ceiling of our room, gliding around in the dark. The next morning, I awoke feeling a sore, burning sensation in my ribs. The pain was accompanied by a strong feeling of foreboding and a sense that my soul was somewhere dangerous and unfamiliar—a different dimension.

The pain and bad feelings went away after about three hours, but something evil from the jail seemed to accompany us. The pain in my ribs returned again at dinner that night, leaving suddenly three hours later. This pain returned off and on during the next few days while we stayed in Cape May, New Jersey.

I also had a vivid dream that first night in Cape May, in which a young man resembling my older son committed suicide with a handgun, and on our way out of the vacation spot, another driver almost crashed into our car. It was a terrifying near miss, but from that point on I had no more pain, no more feelings of displacement, and no more bad dreams. It was as though a bad spirit had vacated my body.

On the evening of our engagement, my boyfriend and I returned to Jim Thorpe and went on a walking ghost tour. The last stop was the jail, where I took six exterior photos. Curiously, as we got closer to the haunted fortress, the soreness in my ribs returned, only to dissipate after we walked away.

Back at the tour's starting point, I asked our guide to take a photo of my fiancé and me. She obliged, and I immediately checked to make sure the photo had come out nicely. It had. However, the following day I discovered that the last seven shots taken—six of the jail and one of my fiancé and me—were gone. Had the interred apparitions intervened once again?

I still can't bring myself to look at the photos I took of Old Carbon County Jail's haunted interior, but I plan to return one day. If you dare to enter this sinister site, be wary: You might not come back out alone.

THE OLD CARBON COUNTY JAIL MUSEUM

128 W. Broadway, Jim Thorpe, Pennsylvania 18229

Delivering a Few Ghosts
by Alan Brown

The sprawling complex that has become Jeff Anderson Regional Medical Center in Meridian, Mississippi, began humbly in 1910 as a two-story brick and wood building named for its chief surgeon, Dr. R. I. Turner. When Turner died in 1927, Dr. Jeff Anderson purchased the building and began converting it into a major hospital for Lauderdale County. After he died in 1951, a board of trustees assumed control of the daily operations of the hospital, and today, Jeff Anderson Regional Medical Center is a state-of-the-art facility. Of course, a hospital is only as good as the doctors and nurses who work there. According to the medical personnel who work in the labor and delivery unit, two former nurses have taken the word "dedication" to an entirely new level.

Phantom Nurses

Michele Hollingsworth, who has worked at the hospital as an obstetrics technician since 1999, has experienced some paranormal activity. Her first encounter took place in 2000, after she begun working the night shift. "I was sitting at the desk when out of the corner of my eye, I noticed a heavy set black lady standing there wearing one of our little hospital hats, our long-sleeve blue gown, and our scrubs. I turned to look at her because I thought she was one of the ladies I worked with. I was going to say something to her, but when I turned my head again, no one was there."

It happened several more times that night, and when Michele described the apparition to her coworkers, "They said that the person I described was actually a nurse who used to work in Labor and Delivery. One night, the nurse had gotten off work and gone home. A few hours later, she had some sort of attack. By the time they got her here, she had aspirated and died in the ER."

In February 2008, a travel nurse named Shirley also witnessed the phantom. Shirley, who had heard Michele talk about her ghostly experience, came in at about one a.m. and said, "I saw your 'friend.' I was sitting here at the desk, and a heavy set black lady walked up to the desk about two feet from me and looked to her right at another nurse, Teresa, who was at the computer doing something. . . ."

At first Shirley thought the lady was looking for someone she knew. Shirley wrote a sentence on a chart and then turned to the woman to see if she could be of some assistance, but the woman was gone. The other nurse, Teresa, didn't see her that night, but told Shirley that she had seen the lady before. Five people were at the desk that night, and three of the five saw her.

Apparently another nurse who has passed away is still working her shift. One night in 2000, Michele left Labor Room 3 carrying a patient's tray. On her way to the OB Hall she passed by room 178, glanced in, and saw an elderly white lady with brown hair and glasses looking out the window toward the parking garage. She walked back and looked into the room, but the woman wasn't there. Michele then went into the room and looked everywhere for her. Whoever she was, she was gone.

As Michelle left the room she noticed a picture on the wall. "Something told me to take a look at the picture. I realized that the [brown-haired] lady was director of nurses for the OB Hall from 1946 until her death in 1987. "

The ghosts of former nurses are not the only spirits haunting Labor and Delivery. In February 2008, a nursery nurse insisted that she heard what sounded like an older baby crying from an empty labor room and the ghost of an older child has also made an appearance in Labor and Delivery. One night, Michele was watching television in Labor Room 1 when she felt cold in the room. "Then I began hearing a young child whimpering, as if she was hurt." The next morning, Michele learned that Labor Rooms 1 and 2 in the new department used to be the old intensive care unit rooms. Many years ago, a little girl between the ages of five and seven was taken to what is now Labor Room 1 and placed on life support. She died a few hours later.

The most mysterious ghost haunting Labor and Delivery is the spirit of a "man in black." In 2007, an OB tech and a nurse were taking a patient down the hallway for a c-section. As they guided the stretcher into the room, the tech asked the nurse, "Who was that man walking down the hallway? The one dressed in black." The nurse hadn't seen anything, but the patient said, "Yeah, he was walking down the hall right in front of us, going toward those end double doors."

Even though none of the surveillance cameras captured the image of anyone dressed in black walking down the hall, the OB tech is still convinced that she saw a ghost that night. What a male ghost is doing haunting Labor and Delivery is a mystery to her.

303

JEFF ANDERSON REGIONAL MEDICAL CENTER
2124 Fourteenth Street, Meridian, Mississippi 39301
www.jarmc.org. Access to any part of the medical center, including Labor and Delivery, is restricted to authorized personnel.

DOING GHOST TIME AT BURLINGTON COUNTY PRISON
by Joanne M. Austin

IT WAS ONE OF THOSE mid-March weekdays when the sky was spitting raindrops, and I realized that I was once again visiting something haunted on a miserable day—in this case, the Burlington County Prison Museum in Mount Holly, New Jersey. Coincidentally, at least two different stories that had been submitted to *Weird N.J.* in previous years about this particular prison had stressed that rainy weather enhanced the building's creepiness. Perfect . . . though I was possibly more creeped out by the proximity of the newer prison behind it than the precipitation.

I got my bearings by walking around the front of the old prison, which is gray and imposing. Smack dab in the middle is a heavy wooden door with a round hole in it. It looked as though it could hold back a lesser battering ram, and I found it was locked. Doubting that the voices I heard behind it belonged to long-dead prisoners, I gave the museum curator, Marisa Bozarth, a quick call, and she told me to meet her at the door to the warden's office, just a few steps away.

After a quick introduction, Marisa led me upstairs to an office where we sat and discussed the prison's history. Architect Robert Mills had designed the facility as a rehabilitation center rather than a penitentiary and envisioned each prisoner with his or her own cell, complete with a small window and a fireplace. A workshop in the basement was intended to help the inmates cultivate skills they could use to become productive members of society upon release.

Ultimately human nature intervened, and the one-prisoner-to-a-cell idea soon died. From 1811 until 1965, the prison held all criminals regardless of the crimes committed, but prisoners were separated by what they did, by gender, and even by age, as juveniles were held there as well. Burlington County Prison even boasted among its residents the infamous Albert DiSalvo, who was briefly incarcerated in his pre–Boston Strangler days. So much for Mills's notions of rehabilitation.

UNDYING ANGUISH
There were nine executions at the prison between 1832 and 1906, all by hanging. The first two were conducted off-site, the other seven in the prison courtyard.

Each of the executed had committed first-degree murder, and one in particular may still haunt the "dungeon," located on the third floor.

Yes, the third floor. This maximum-security enclosure, located in the middle of a line of cells, is a smaller room with a window but no fireplace. It's where the most contemptible prisoners were sent to await execution. In their final days, they were chained to the floor in the middle of the cell and under constant surveillance by guards.

The dungeon is where Joel Clough spent his last days in 1833. According to a story by Kate Philbrick in *Weird N.J.*, a woman had jilted the twenty-nine-year-old Clough, so he stabbed her to death. He had escaped from the prison, but was recaptured and sent to the dungeon. According to Marisa Bozarth, he was hanged about a mile away, but his body was buried in the courtyard.

The night after Clough's execution, guards "started hearing the chain rattle on the floor, smelled cigarette smoke coming from [the cell], and heard noises, like moaning when there was nobody being held in there." Both guards and prisoners feared even passing by the dungeon because they believed it was haunted by Clough's spirit.

Today you can only stand on the other side of the bars and look in at a stark, white mannequin that sits chained to the floor.

BOILER-ROOM BOGEY

Clough's story is the most famous of the haunts at the museum, but there are others. Marisa recounts that, during renovations in the 1980s, workers reported lights going on and off, hearing odd noises, and feeling as though they were being watched or followed. They'd also put away tools before heading out to lunch, only to come back and find a tool sitting in the middle of the floor—where they *knew* they hadn't left it.

Visitors and volunteers recount similar ghostly experiences. In the spring of 2007, four individuals—on four separate occasions—saw a strange man in the basement of the building. According to Marisa, each witness said he looked like a worker who belonged there, but nobody knew who the man was, and he hasn't been seen since.

Who could this lone worker be, and why would he haunt that particular part of the prison? Although two murders have occurred in the basement, including one in the hallway where the man was seen, his description doesn't match up with anyone involved in those events.

SHADOW OF A DOUBT

Marisa has seen shadows twice in the building. The first time, she and a volunteer were in the basement cleaning up when something on the stairwell caught their attention. "We both spun [around]," Marisa said, "and I looked at the stairwell and said, 'Did you see that?' and he said, 'No, but something touched me.' He swears that something poked him in the back." She had seen what looked like a blob move up the steps; and, at a loss for an explanation, the two left the building in a hurry.

The other time Marisa saw a shadow, she was alone in the gift shop closing up when she saw something out of the corner of her eye. "I turned my head and it looked like a shadow walked out of the warden's office and walked toward the back door," she said.

The shadow moved at a normal walking pace and had human arms, legs, and a nose. Marisa went to a window behind the counter and looked outside for the shadow, wondering how it could have walked through the locked door. She hasn't seen anything like it since.

COURTYARD GHOSTS

A volunteer named Anthony shared an experience he had while in the picnic area of the prison courtyard with a group of volunteers. "The one guy I was talking to kept seeing something out in the window of the warden's office. It kept poking its head back and forth."

Apparently when the volunteers went up to the third-floor office to check things out, they found nobody there. One of the volunteers was a bit sensitive to the paranormal, and according to Anthony, "She just stopped there and started crying all of a sudden." The warden's office is also where Anthony felt "wobbly" or off-kilter, similar to what The Atlantic Paranormal Society (TAPS) had experienced during their investigation.

307

The week before I visited, the show *Ghost Hunters* aired a segment on the museum, and Marisa said that the resulting influx of visitors was like nothing she'd ever seen. People drove for hours from neighboring states, and we marveled at the continued popularity of the paranormal.

BURLINGTON COUNTY PRISON MUSEUM
128 High Street, Mount Holly, New Jersey 08060

INDEX

INDEX OF SITES BY LOCATION

ACKNOWLEDGMENTS

To START, I'D LIKE TO THANK the usual gang of suspects for their help with this book. Mark Moran and Mark Sceurman, for another hauntingly wonderful opportunity to work with ghosts and the people who see them; Ryan Doan, for being a wonderful illustrator (and writer) to work with; and Richard Moran and Susan Roselli for their behind-the-scenes support.

The authors who contributed to this book, regardless of whether or not their stories appear in the end product, are kindred spirits of the live sort. From working with them, I continue to learn and grow in all that I do and they have my eternal thanks.

A special thanks to those I interviewed or who invited me to experience ghosts as they (or others) do, including John Quinn, Tracy Potter, Mike McCarthy, Steven Bursey, Marisa Bozarth, Paula McGraw, Nelson Jecas, Catherine Holderby, Paul Viggiano, K. C. Daniel, Kim Kowalczyk, Laura Helbig, and Steven LaChance. And to those of you who run the publicity machine through radio shows and podcasts that cater to the paranormal, it's been a blast talking with you.

I couldn't go without recognizing those who advise and support me in other areas of my life, such as my family, especially Robert and Susanne Austin and James Fay; and friends, including Abby Stillman-Grayson, Kelley Green, Heather Blakely, and Anita Marie Moscoco.

Thanks also to the staff at Sterling Publishing for assembling another excellent book.

The people who seriously research and debate the existence of ghosts take a lot of knocks from the "mainstream" scientific community and skeptics. Through my research and talking directly with you, I've learned much about your methodologies and the time and effort you put into what you do, and you've definitely earned my respect for your efforts.

Lastly, I know this book wouldn't exist without at least the possibility of ghosts. And from what I can see, the ghostly life is not always a picnic; so if you do exist, my paranormal peeps, you have my gratitude, too.

—Joanne M. Austin

313

DEDICATION AND ACKNOWLEDGMENTS

To my wife, Margarita. You are the beautiful face that welcomes me home when I journey too far into my world of monsters and the unknown. Then, being the supportive angel you are, you dress my wounds and send me off on further exploits. I couldn't love you more and this book is dedicated to you. I truly adore you. You are my greatest adventure.

To Mom and Dad. The greatest friends I ever encountered. For teaching me how to truly see people and, in that, the worth of everyone's story. For your unrelenting support and faith in my craft and path. Dad, the ocean and humor is our playground and the catalyst to our iron-clad bond. My greatest pride is that I am so like you. Mom, you are the brightest star in this universe and the source of the good in my heart.

Lori, your talent is powerful and transforming. You change the life and faces of the booger-heads that look up to you. You are the best sister a guy could ask for. Sorry about locking you in the shed.

To Frank and Eu. For teaching me all the bad words and sharing both your laughter and daughter with me. Frank, you really make me work turning such a good man into such hideous creatures. You both are truly family to me.

To Papa, Grandma Liz, Renee—I love you SO much.

To the Nightstalkers: Ray, Dave, Lou, Cono, and Mike—I love you all. Jeff, for not stealing all the covers (just kidding). Land cannot separate our bond, brother.

To all my dear family and friends—thank you so much for your support.

FIRST AND FOREMOST, none of this would have been possible without the foresight and talent of Mark Moran and Mark Sceurman. You saw the possibilities in me and gave me a chance to prove myself. You are the Romulus and Remus of "Weird" and it is an honor to work and play in the empire you have built. Thank you for giving me all that you have and know that I will always be indebted to you for opening the door to my career. Thanks also, for listening to my Quick Chek stories.

Joanne, you hold the wheel to this Weird car as we zip down the unknown highway. You know all the right turns as I hang out the window snapping photos. Without you and your immense talent I would be sitting on the porch with all my gear wondering where my ride was. You are beyond a pleasure to work with and I was lucky enough to do it twice.

To our various authors, most who I have met only through words. Thank you for entertaining me so. Your words gave the swirling things in my head something to hold onto.

To the many photographers whose brilliant work did and did not make it into this book. Thank you so much for sharing your eye with us and riding shotgun on this wonderful trip.

To my reference models, some new and some old friends, you were a blast to work with.

To the rest of the Weird N.J. staff—you folks are the best.

Thanks to the creative staff at Sterling who will be laying out this book and making it possible.

—**Ryan Doan**

AUTHOR BIOGRAPHIES

JEFF BELANGER is a writer and journalist who launched Ghostvillage.com in 1999, which has grown into the Web's largest supernatural community. He is the author of several books, including *The World's Most Haunted Places, Our Haunted Lives, The Ghost Files,* and *Weird Massachusetts.* He's been a guest on more than a hundred radio and television programs and is a regular lecturer on the subject of the supernatural. He currently haunts Massachusetts with his wife and his daughter (who isn't afraid of ghosts).

FIONA BROOME is a psychic and a ghost researcher, investigating hauntings in the U.S., the U.K., and Ireland. She's writing a series of ghost-related books highlighting haunted places that anyone can visit. Fiona's popular ghost Web site is HollowHill.com.

ALAN BROWN has been a professor of English at the University of West Alabama since 1986. He has written several books of ghost stories, including *The Face in the Window and other Alabama Ghostlore, Shadows and Cypress, Haunted Places in the American South, Stories from the Haunted South,* and *Southern Ghost Hunters.* His latest book, *Haunted Georgia* (Stackpole Books), was published in February 2008.

CHARLIE CARLSON, a.k.a. Florida's Master of the Weird, is the author of fifteen books, including *Weird Florida.* He is a frequent guest on talk radio and has appeared in several television documentaries, including playing a professor on the SciFi Channel in *Curse of the Blair Witch.* In addition to writing and producing two independent films, *Hunt for the Devil* and Henry Blackhart Is Dead, he resides slightly south of Daytona Beach within his own certified wildlife sanctuary.

RICK CARROLL, creator of *Hawaii's Best Spooky Tales, Vols. 1–7,* and *Madame Pele: True Encounters with Hawaii's Fire Goddess,* is a survivor of inexplicable encounters in Hawaii's spirit realm. A former daily journalist with the *San Francisco Chronicle,* Carroll is the author of twenty books on Hawaii and the Pacific, including *Huahine: Island of the Lost Canoe.* His new book, IZ: *Voice of the People* (Bess Press, 2006), is the biography of Israel Kamakawiwo'ole, the late, legendary Hawaiian singer.

JEFF DAVIS has traveled to many faraway places where he has encountered the paranormal and strange, but he always returns to the Pacific Northwest, where he has written five books on ghosts, including *A Haunted Tour Guide to the Pacific Northwest* (Norseman Ventures, 2003). He is also co-author of *Weird Washington* and *Weird Oregon.* Visit his Web site, Ghostsandcritters.com, to learn more.

Antonio R. Garcez's maternal grandfather was a Mescalero Apache from southern New Mexico, his paternal grandmother was an Otomi Indian. He has been featured on such television shows as *America's Scariest Places*, and lectures throughout the country at universities and conferences. His Web site is Ghostbooks.biz.

Linda Godfrey is a Wisconsin author and artist specializing in the eccentric. She is the author of *Weird Michigan* and co-author of Weird Wisconsin. She has also written *Strange Wisconsin: More Badger State Weirdness* (Trails Books, 2007) and several books on werewolves and other strange creatures, such as *The Beast of Bray Road* (Prairie Oak Press, 2003). She's been featured on national radio and TV shows, including History Channel's Monster Quest episode "American Werewolf" based on her book *Hunting the American Werewolf*. She is cohost of the weekly show UncannyRadio.com.

Boyd E. Harris peddles ice cream by day and horror by night in his twenty-four-hour assault plan to dish out the chills. He is the president of KaleidoScoops Inc., a retail ice cream chain that has outlets in twenty-one states, and he owns Cutting Block Press, a small press publisher that specializes in horror fiction anthologies. Harris resides in Austin, Texas, with his neurotic boxer, Phoebe.

L'Aura Hladik started ghost hunting in 1993 and founded the New Jersey Ghost Hunters Society (Njghs.net), the largest paranormal investigating organization in the state, in 1998. She has appeared on various cable and network television shows such as *Family Talk* and *The Montel Williams Show*.

Scott A. Johnson is the author of novels *An American Haunting, Deadlands,* and *Cane River: A Ghost Story*. He is also the pen behind *The Mayor's Guide: The Stately Ghosts of Augusta* and *Cold Spots: The Ghosts of San Antonio*. A lifelong interest in ghosts and studying the paranormal landed him a position at Dread Central, writing the column Cold Spots about some of the most haunted places in the United States. Visit him online at Americanhorrorwriter.net, or read Cold Spots twice a month at Dreadcentral.com.

Matt Lake is a science and technology writer and longtime contributor to the Weird book series, including *Weird Pennsylvania, Weird Maryland,* and *Weird England*. He has had only one ghostly encounter—one that landed him in the emergency room and then in intensive care. He is anxious not to have any others.

Greg Myers served as a co-administrator, lead investigator, and EVP specialist of Missouri Paranormal Research, then founded Paranormal Task Force, Inc. in October 2006, which is a not-for-profit incorporation devoted to paranormal and historic related issues. Greg and Paranormal Task Force, Inc. can be found at Catchmyghost.com and were featured in the 2007 documentary *Children of the Grave*.

JANICE OBERDING is the author of *The Haunting of Las Vegas* and five other books on the paranormal. She teaches classes on ghost hunting, historical research, and self-publishing at local community colleges. Janice lectures at various venues and has appeared and consulted on numerous television shows on the paranormal. Her Web site is HauntedNevada.com.

WALTER O'BRIEN spent most of his adolescence huddled away in dark rooms listening to radio signals from around the world. After nearly three decades of traveling the world with heavy metal bands as personal manager, he retired to become a writer and journalist. He is now a full-time staff writer for the *Courier News* in central New Jersey, where he tries to keep his tenuous grip on reality.

ELLEN ROBSON is the author of *Haunted Highway—The Spirits of Route 66* (Golden West, 1999) and *Haunted Arizona—The Ghosts of the Grand Canyon State* (Golden West, 2002). She is at work on her third book of haunted sites, which will cover the entire United States. Her Web site is Spirits66.com. She lives in Tempe, Arizona, with her husband.

318 **DUSTY SMITH** is the president of the Daytona Beach Paranormal Research Group, Inc., which has investigated cases all over the southeastern United States since 1997. She's also president of The International Association of Cemetery Preservationists, Inc. She owns and is chief tour guide for Haunts of the World's Most Famous Beach Ghost Tours and has authored more than forty titles on the paranormal and cemetery preservation, including her latest book, *Haunted Daytona Beach* (The History Press, 2007).

JAMES STRAIT has lived almost six decades slightly out of phase with the rest of his fellow planetary residents, discovering, investigating, and writing about the Show Me State's strangeness for the book *Weird Missouri*. This transplanted Missouri boy is also a retired professional aviator with a career involving almost every aspect of aeronautical pursuits. The author lives with his artistic wife in historic Bucks County, Pennsylvania.

TROY TAYLOR is the author of more than fifty books on ghosts, hauntings, and the unexplained in America. He is the founder of the American Ghost Society and the owner of the Illinois Hauntings Tour Co. Born and raised in Illinois, he currently resides in the central part of the state in a decidedly non-haunted house.

LARRY D. THACKER is a seventh-generation native of the Cumberland Gap region and lives in Middlesborough, Kentucky, where he serves as an elected city councilman. A prolific writer and artist, he writes columns for the *Middlesboro Daily News* and *Premiere Overlook*, is a reader-bloggist for the *Seattle Post-Intelligencer*, and authored *Mountain Mysteries: The Mystic Traditions of Appalachia* (Overmountain Press, 2007). Visit his Web site at Roadkillzen.net.

MARY TROTTER KION is an author and poet. She has written a mystery romance novel, two history books, and some six hundred historical articles on the Internet. She lives, not quite alone, in Kennewick, Washington. The site of the haunted house she lives in is, of course, private property, but she is glad to speak by phone with anyone interested in visiting. She may be reached at (509) 582-4553.

JEFFREY A. WARGO, author of *Ghosts in the 'Ville: True Experiences of the Unexplained in Riegelsville, PA*, and *More Ghosts in the 'Ville: Continued Tales of the Unexplained in Riegelsville, PA*, lives in this small Delaware River borough with his wife and their two dogs. An ordained minister in the United Church of Christ, in his spare time, Wargo continues to collect ghostly tales from the sites and businesses in his community and is the webmaster of Ghostsintheville.com.

SARA WEBB QUEST has seen real ghosts in her native Cape Cod, Massachusetts—the first while gazing at the old Hall Family burial ground. Since then, Sara has researched the paranormal, such as during visits to haunted Cape Cod inns. She cowrote *The Other Side of the World* with Sally Odgers. Her articles have been published in *Prime Time*, *Woman's World*, and *Parenting*. Sara remains in Cape Cod, Massachusetts, with her husband, daughter, and cat. Her writing Web site is Authorsden.com/sarawebbquest.

JAMES A. WILLIS has been chasing after ghosts and visiting crybaby bridges for more than twenty years. He is also the founder and director of The Ghosts of Ohio (Ghostsofohio.org), a paranormal research organization. Willis's previous brushes with weirdness include being a contributing author to *Weird U.S.* and co-authoring *Weird Ohio* and *Weird Indiana*. He currently resides in Columbus, Ohio, with his Queen-loving parrot and the world's whiniest cat.

JANE WOLFINBARGER grew up in South Carolina with its rich tradition of ghosts and ghost stories. She moved west as an adult and now lives in Wyoming with her family, where she still keeps her eyes and ears open for the supernatural. Jane especially likes writing fantasy and has a number of stories on her Web site at Shewolfy728.wordpress.com.

JAMES WYSONG has worked as a flight attendant with two major international carriers during the past seventeen years. Under the pen name of A. Frank Steward, he has authored *The Air Traveler's Survival Guide* (Impact Publications, 2001), *The Plane Truth* (Impact Publications, 2003), and *Air Travel Tales from the Crew* (Impact Publications, 2005); he also has a weekly column for MSNBC.com and Tripso.com. He lives on the East Coast with his wife, Antonia (a pilot), and sons Oliver and Matthew.